Prison Ministry In Covid America

The New Normal for Effective
Spiritual and Social Justice
For Today's Incarcerated

Written by:
Michael F. Maraschiello, Ph.D.

Cadmus Publishing
www.cadmuspublishing.com

Library of Congress Cataloging-in-Publication Data

Maraschiello, Michael F., author.
Prison Ministry In Covid America: The New Normal for Effective Spiritual and Social Justice for Today's Incarcerated/ Michael F. Maraschiello, Ph. D., First edition.

ISBN 978-1-63751-063-6 (electronic library copy)   Subjects: 1. Prison Ministry. 2. Social Justice. 3. Social Justice—Religious aspects. 4. Prison Culture—Restorative Justice aspects 5. Mentorship / Sponsorship – Counseling. 6. Veterans (Incarcerated) – aspects. I. Title.

Unless otherwise noted, all scripture taken from the Holy Bible, King James Version®, KJV® Copyright © 1970, 2001, by Thomas Nelson, Inc.® Used by permission. All rights reserved worldwide. KING JAMES VERSION ® and KJV ® are registered trademarks of Thomas Nelson, Inc. Use of either trademark for the offering of goods or services requires the prior written consent of Thomas Nelson US, Inc. (www.ThomasNelson.com)

Copyright © 2021 by M. F. Maraschiello, PhD

All rights reserved. No part of this book may be used or reproduced in any manner whatsoever without written permission except in the case of brief quotations embodied in critical articles and reviews, and short excerpts for educational purposes. As per the Copyright Act of 1976.

Library of Congress Control Number: 2021921612

Cover design by Terry Phillips
Photo taken by M. F. Maraschiello, PhD

To order or request information, please call 615-781-9204
Or dr.m.maraschiello@gmail.com

Printed in the United States of America

MICHAEL MARASCHIELLO

Prison Ministry In Covid America

MICHAEL MARASCHIELLO

Table of Contents

Prologue	i
Acknowledgments	iv
Introduction	v

THE CALL TO MINISTRY

Jesus, St. Paul, and the "Least Ones" (Matthew 25:34-46)	1
Chapter 1: Setting up a Prison Ministry that's real	2
Chapter 2: Finding Volunteers to "talk and walk" (Not just feeding the animals at the zoo)	24
Chapter 3: Breaking down the Fear of Prisons	46
Chapter 4: Building up Prisoners for Success	78

EFFECTIVE MINISTRY MENTORSHIP / SPONSORSHIP

Doing all things through Christ – the Best Teacher (Phil 4:13; II Tim 3:16	117
Chapter 5: Leadership	119
Chapter 6: The 4 Levels of Prison Ministry (The Four Types of Volunteers)	160
Chapter 7: Making the Commitment to Change a Life In Covid America	188
Chapter 8: Parole and Re-Entry: Dragging the Sponsoree Out of Prison/Jail	213
Chapter 9: Incarcerated Veterans and Their Needs: A National Failure	236
Epilogue: The "Pay Off" (Victory) with Christ-centered Dividends for Spiritual, Social, and Restorative Justice	255
Notes	**275**
Appendix	**283**

Prison Ministry In Covid America

PROLOGUE

The growing interest in social and criminal justice reform in today's culture, both religious and secular involvement, still centers around the core of providing meaningful care and alternative solutions to those in society who have gone astray – errants (for which this author chooses to use this label sparingly on its citizens for obvious reasons of inappropriateness and misleading connotations) – for one reason or another and need our help. The nature, need, and dynamics of social justice -- especially needed more than ever with prisoners being "cut off" from outside organizations and churches coming in to the prisons due to COVID-19 concerns -- are not only representative of an advanced nation's character in its overall treatment of its people (of all races, religions, credos, etc.) but also a thermometer. A measure of the inherent heart beat of a nations communities, religious institutions, and family or other relationships that feel for our fellow man and fellow woman that we all – whether we committed a crime or not – have just as much a right to enjoy life, be free, and have access to opportunities just as the next person has to be successful in life. As Fyodor M. Dostoyevsky said in his book *Crime and Punishment*,

"A society is known by the way it treats its prisoners." [1]

In short, it is the "Golden Rule" [of Life]: "Treat others as you would like them to treat you" which represents the Utopian System or its people on how they look out for one another properly, especially when some need some assistance in life for one reason or another. Where as the opposite is the "dog eating dog" brutality of *man's* belief which Dostoyevsky points out are the failures of criminal [in]justice in which there is no relief for human suffering as he points out in his book.

My major objective here is, then, to present a semi-comprehensive and efficient book which would serve as a "pocket carry" learning package in the area of prison ministry and sponsorship to relive this condition of human suffering which prisoners are inherently enchained. This is both a criminal and social justice issue; however, we will focus primarily on the social justice and spiritual aspects because this book is about the human struggle as people are *social* beings rather than criminal beings. Being "criminal" is a man-made application subject to interpretation [by man] which is another subject all together. For this book, the focus has been on the fundamentals in theory and applications to promote a learning experience through detailed and timely information from experience and tried and true methods that are pragmatically helpful to both religious and secular groups and individuals enthusiastic about helping establish a productive social relationship to affect a prisoner's rehabilitation and beyond.

    The language in this book is clear, non-technical, straightforward, in most parts; and the delivery of topics is systematic and easy to follow, with emphasis on learning schemes of exposition, synthesis, application, and evaluation to be an effective mentor and/ or sponsor whether in a program or just on your own. Although this book is written primarily for the religious "volunteer" who seeks a disciple-like relationship with their incarcerated subject(s), it would still satisfy the requirements for non-religious persons (i.e. those of any other or non-faith) to benefit from this book in learning effective ways to help their incarcerated family member, friend, or those in organizations particularly in connection with prison ministry-like objectives or the objectives of criminal and social justice reform. Prison idioms and vernaculars will be used sparingly as "ice breakers." If you don't know what they mean, I encourage you to take the time or do some investigation . Learning all there is to know about prison [culture] will help you better understand and communicate effectively with those whom you intend to help. This makes for flexibility where diverse uses for this book would be a useful reference for sponsors, mentors, friends, family, corrections officers, chaplains, church pastors, community organizers, politicians, counselors, etc. learning the pathway to best help a prisoner(s) for rehabilitation and to prepare them for successful release and beyond.

    It was intended that the core is for organizations to model, form, or re-structure how they provide assistance to prisoners so that their ministry is effective. Topics are organized into two parts with a total of nine chapters. The first part comes under the title "The Call To ministry," which is an essential backdrop to the whole area of prison ministry, primarily *Christian* ministry. It includes four chapters: Chapter 1: Setting up a Prison Ministry That's Real; Chapter 2: Finding Volunteers to "Talk and Walk" (Not just feeding the animals at the zoo); Chapter 3: Breaking Down the Fear of Prisons; and Chapter 4: Building up Prisoners for Success." The second part is dedicated to the "Effective Ministry Mentorship / Sponsorship." It includes four chapters: Chapter 5: Leadership Chapter 6: The 4 Levels of Prison Ministry (The Four Volunteers); Chapter 7: Making the Commitment to Change a Life in COVID America; Chapter 8: Parole and Re-Entry: Dragging the Sponsoree Out of Prison / Jail; and Chapter 9: Incarcerated Veterans and Their Needs: A National Failure. Epilogue: The "Pay off" (Victory) with Christ-centered dividends for Social, Spiritual, and Restoration Justice. These chapters represent the "nuts and bolts" that put everything together that ministry representatives, mentors, sponsors, family, friends, etc. should be doing to be *effective* with providing and applying practical necessary assistance empowering (enabling) meaningful changes and or positive outcomes as the keys to a successful life which should be the goal of every prisoner.

And the big question is:

> "How long can the "COVID Card" be played as an excuse to keep volunteers from doing their job of helping prisoners – and society – by denying them access because the jails and prisons alone are a failure at rehabilitating people solely on the use of "time" and "separation," which have been proven for centuries not to foster spiritual, mental, physical, and emotional well-being in prisoners to ready them for release?"

This book, my first, I believe I've done my job; however, may not be "error free." Readers are invited to critique it for errors, and any suggestions for improvement are welcome to improve the quality of the text for the next edition.

ACKNOWLEDGMENTS

This book, my first, has its origins in the last quarter century sitting in "church" at prison chapels and gyms. There, I listened to many preachers & speakers who talked about *mentorship* and *sponsorship,* and what they promised to do for inmates. Observing both the genuine god-fearing ones and comparing them to the charismatics who gave "drive-by" *hash tag* messages of quasi-conditional friendship and salvation, I learned many incredible spiritual lessons to discern the "wheat from the chaff." My special thanks go to Rev. Willie A. Darrow, Jr. and Rev. Ted Welsh who inspired me to undertake this project, having been the focal arch-type sponsors for the type of work needed today. In addition, gratitude goes to Mr. David & Laura McCarthy who visited & energized me with their human compassion reflective of the ideal attributes of disciples as described by Jesus and St. Paul. They strengthened my belief that – to me, a prisoner – society still sees *value* in me – the marginalized -- to do God's work amidst a society that shuns its incarcerated to a second class with labels that no-longer apply. To Mrs. Marilyn Wagner, my Godmother, for over twenty years she encouraged me to see life with promise again, giving me hope and a future. Without her kindness, I would not have transformed myself to obtain my Doctorate of Christian Education (DCE), nor endeavor to write this book. Also, to all those who purchased books for me and kept me from utter poverty while I was in prison, especially MAJ(ret.) Daniel J. Lachut, LTC(ret.) Orest M. Logusz, Jo Ann Maraschiello, Susan Worst, and Jeff Samoska who believed in me and helped me prove getting a Ph.D. while in prison can be done. Lastly, to the Riverbend Prison Education Department and Library who, without their professionalism, I could not compose this book. So many I have to value having done the same and my apologies for not mentioning them all. Nothing; however, could be done without God whom I give all the glory to in my life and for making this book possible. And last, but not least, to my parents, who forgave me for my faults and showed me *unconditional* love [of others] is *serving* God.

Michael Maraschiello

INTRODUCTION

M. F. Maraschiello

"Show me, I'll probably not remember it. Tell me, I'll probably forget. But involve me, and I'll understand." (Chief Warrant Officer Four Shirkus, U. S. Army (ret.), 1979.)

This wise phrase, above, from a military combat veteran of World War II who was one of my father's close friends in his army unit, has resonated in my life as a teaching tool for maturity not just for myself, but for others as well. Effective prison ministry cannot take place unless a *transfer* of Jesus' character attributes are first displayed by the volunteer -- mentor or sponsor, then identified, accepted, understood, and implemented in the life of the prisoner who is to be the recipient of a "spiritual overhaul" for a change in life-style that sets them on the path of success – a realization in a life-altering transformation based in Christ.

Theoretically, *Christian* mentors and sponsors are to promulgate Christ's basic principles for living a god-fearing life, and give back to God a spiritually-empowered outlook and zest for glorifying God, others, and making the right decisions which benefit the kingdom of heaven. A transition from living in context with the *world* as a guide must be made to one of the realm of Christ's world in which He is the standard for what is pleasing to God as Holy Scripture has revealed for us to reflect upon and apply in our daily lives.

This book arises out of the need for *meaningful* effective prison ministry that had been building up to, during, and because of the COVID (*Coronavirus*) virus pandemic. It offers hope to the "least ones" (offenders, felons, prisoners, inmates, those in jail or prison, confinement centers, etc.) whom today's postmodern Millennial culture define as "marginalized" because they are a segment of the population in American culture and society that is shunned, ostracized, abused, stereotyped, discriminated against, and considered – for the most part – spiritually lost or hopelessly undeserving. This book describes some of the "fake news" surrounding those incarcerated, and how genuine disciples of Christ can step outside the box as modern-day "pimpernels" who relieve people from injustice, oppression, and tyranny, and give others hope to develop new or better prison ministries in their church or parachurch organization to foster deeper spiritual standing within church leadership to manifest ways that reach prisoners – on their level – to foster change in the prisoner's behavior, goals for successful parole or release plans, and re-entry and post-incarceration strengths for life with their family which the [former] prisoner can continue to spiritually thrive rather than survive in the world. This takes a joint effort on the part of the church and mentor / sponsor to provide the resources (i.e. time, money, programs, research, etc.) that invest in the prisoner to drag them out of the "CJ System" (Criminal Justice) which seeks more *retributive* punishment than it does *restorative* justice to build [up] the prisoner by helping them correct themselves in comparison to the CJ System which focuses mainly on warehousing. Obviously, Jesus never intended to ignore prisoners, otherwise he would not have been so specific about visiting the "Least ones." (Matthew 25: 34-46) Jesus recognized ALL people have value, and as with the Good Samaritan (Luke 10: 29-37) needing assistance to be brought back to health, so too must prisoners be brought back [in]to health spiritually, morally, and – yes – even sometimes materially. That takes brothers and sisters willing to "step up" and act as disciples. Not just "talk the talk" but rather 'walk the walk" by taking a prisoner under one's wing and providing what is necessary for them to see the same kind of love and compassion Jesus and St. Paul talked about. Needs met which instill in a person's heart a real sense of the faith because promises are kept by the way the mentor and sponsor extend their hand – as Jesus and St. Paul taught -- to raise up marginalized people who need a little help and guidance to sustain themselves on the right path. Many churches or organizations; however, don't like change, especially when it involves money and resources going out and not coming in, per se. Yet, Jesus never asked for anything in return other than to say, "Go in peace and do likewise." (Luke 10:37) Especially with the two commandments he emphasized: ("Love the Lord thy God with all thy heart, and with all thy soul, and with all thy mind..." and "Love thy neighbor as thy self." (Matthew 22: 37-40))

Further, some churches are reluctant to invest in prison ministries because they often feel their church would become filled with criminal elements (e.g. identity thieves, con-artists, rapists, and the like) drawing resources away from other church projects or groups more "popular" to church leaders or boards who focus on attendance records and donations going for things other than the *lowest* priority of all church ministries which is the prison ministry. This is due to the numerous excuses, of which the worst is a church stating it simply can't "afford" to pay for prison ministers or pay for what they arbitrarily *think* prisoners need. Jesus – at a minimum – encouraged visiting prisoners. Why? Because as brothers and sisters in one "Family of (Christ) God" we are to look out for each other. This would be called "***Social Justice***" in Jesus' day which applies today to help alleviate oppressive and unjust conditions for prisoners and whomever else in the community was in need of uplifting their condition whether it be physically, spiritually, or economically. Jesus sent out his "A-team" of apostles to not only spread his message of love, peace, and forgiveness, but also to perform miracles and to give people the promise they too can have everlasting life within a community that cares about them and their circumstances. "Networking" and getting in touch with volunteers or others who can contribute or raise funds reflects a sincere church [body] of zealous Christians wanting to build up prisoners, especially ones who will be coming out of prison and returning to that church, their family, and community. "Cutting off" prisoners -- who once belonged to a church -- shows that church was *religious* about its church leadership concerns which is "hollow", according to Christ's definition of what the church body is supposed to be doing for it's "least ones" in need. No clearer can this be seen than at funerals and when a member of a church goes in the hospital. The church throws a reception for the dead person's family, comforts and mourns for the bereaved, and sends out *hospice* teams to visit and comfort the sick. The same with other "safe" church activities like: field trips, soccer games, picnics, music programs, and choir practice. But prison[er]s? Hardly anyone wants to visit the "leper colony" of law-breakers – the "hardcore" sinners who carry the stigmas. It requires navigating the bureaucratic quagmire of: pre-screening paperwork, proof of COVID testing, PPE (Personal Protective

Equipment (e.g. masking) precautions, electronic technology, and generates other fears dealing with *COVID* with all sorts of negative stereotypes to match, especially believing the "fake news" that all prisoners are: "con artists" (grifters), liars, thieves, homosexuals, child sex perverts, untrustworthy, illiterate, racists, and drug addicts who seek sexual relationships with female volunteers and to get male volunteers to bring in contraband drugs and cell phones. The list is endless, and Satan knocks off many volunteers considering the prison ministry with these "scare tactics" who avoid prison ministry like the plague without ever going to a jail or prison and experience for one's self the truth to many of these *myths* regarding prisoners.

Ergo, prisoners – human beings and children of God to Christ – get ignored by *weak* church leadership who don't stand up [for Christ], but rather allow fear and ignorant-trending societal intimidation to direct their decision-making that allows this *marginalized* segment of society – prisoners -- to go without even the least priority. Many prisoners are incarcerated because of bad lawyering or pled guilty to avoid a crime they saw no way out of getting justice, but now wear the label of "felon" and are treated as if it were the *Mark of Cain.* (Genesis 4: 15) Some churches decide to "pass by" helping them stay spiritually healthy – like in the story of the Good Samaritan – in favor of pleasing religious bigoted leadership, and doing the popular social media "feedback thing", in the face even of the *cancel culture* trying to squeeze out the Christian faith and people who just want to do good for their fellow man no matter what religion, race, or creed. That is, they to avoid condemnation for showing support to prisoners and instead are involved in the *safe* activities such as: soccer games, choirs, Bible studies, bake sales, clothing drives, and the like. This is reminiscent of the clichéd "Dog and Pony Show" or presentations, ministries, or events just "looking busy" to make their church appear involved in many holy and popular activities. Some churches *facade* Christian values when, in fact, they are really hypocritical, and fail to "see the light" and employ Christ's compassion and love needed most – meaningfully -- in the lives of struggling, the marginalized –the at-risk, which includes the segment of society known as the incarcerated.

In my discourse of the material in this book, I extend some simple methods and recommendations for churches and /or civic and other organizations including individuals who can become better *effective* volunteers (mentors and sponsors) of prisoners. Above all, a volunteer must **show** prisoners they care, not just talk about caring. "If a man needs an egg, you don't give him a scorpion." (Luke 11:12) The *effective* prison ministry volunteer helps propel prisoners out of their current spiritual, social, and even financial situation to one of discipleship, helps plan out the prisoner's plan for changes in their life with meaningful involvement, and supports *competent* resourceful sponsors to help create a drive inside of the prisoner to stay on the right path for them to thrive back in society not just survive.

People need to realize there is light at the end of the tunnel dealing with these "new norms" from COVID in prison ministry, especially the "Coviddiels" – the generation affected by COVID. Many wonderful success stories I've witnessed involving prisoners and ex-offenders who have outstanding support groups to help keep them from falling down again because of dedicated effective volunteers' hard work. I hope this book can help churches, parachurches, families, and groups considering on starting a prison ministry or improving one to do so. Also to help both prisoner and those wishing to do the same as an effective mentor or sponsor. Many of the situations in this book are from *first-hand* and *second-hand* knowledge. I've seen these methods and recommendation work effectively in the lives of prisoners and eager new sponsors who have helped several prisoners make parole and/or provide them with jobs, a place to stay, and a future when released from prison. That's the goal and a major sign of a successful prison ministry -- one that sets a prisoner "on fire" for life in both his faith and personal life, in which Christ is clearly in charge as the sponsor or mentor *walks with* him or her with Christ's motivating light as their shared guide.

Finally, in the appendices, Appendix 1 offers a sample of a mission statement and volunteer's portfolio they can create for success. (I urge your church and/or ministry/ organization to create a checklist of objectives, and write a mission statement to help ensure you have touched all the right buttons.) Appendix 2 has results and answers to the inmate survey regarding literacy (preparation for parole/ release.)

Appendix 3 explores a typical parole packet to help inmates create one for effective use at the parole board. (I urge you to create your own checklist for each inmate you intend to sponsor.) In Appendix 4 has some sample letters to the parole board people can write or e-mail supporting an inmate's release. And in Appendix 5, are some Re-entry tips, ideas, and facts.

"Prisoners are always in a struggle for their lives, which is why they need to be rescued and lifted up." - *M.F.M.*

Transformational Revelation All Sponsors and Mentors Need to Make Sacred for Accountability to Take Hold

On Empowerment (Teaching <u>All</u> People (Nations))

"And Jesus came and spake unto them, saying, All power is given unto me in heaven and in earth. Go ye therefore, and teach all nations, baptizing them in the name of the Father, and of the Son, and of the Holy Ghost: Teaching them to observe all things whatsoever I have commanded you: and, lo, I am with you always, even unto the end of the world. Amen" -- Matthew 28: 18-20

"Without counsel plans go wry, but with multitude of counselors they are established." – Prov. 15:22

On Discipleship (Becoming a Good Shepherd.)
On Kenosis (The Kenotic Life [of Christ])

"Therefore doth my Father love me, because I lay down my life, that I might take it again." – John 10:17

"Empty one's self and be a servant like Christ." – Phil. 2:6-11

On Guiding Others (Enlightening the World)

"I am come a light into the world, that whosoever believeth on me should not abide in darkness." - John 12:46

"The kin of any poor relative should try and relieve him." – Lev. 25-28, 35-38, 47-55

On Sharing Christ's Promise (Sowing the Word)

""And he ordained twelve, that they should be with him, and that he might send them forth to preach…" - Mark 4:14

"*Real* messages <u>really</u> take hold." - *M.F.M.*

Michael Maraschiello

THE CALL TO MINISTRY

Jesus, St. Paul, and the "Least Ones"

"Then shall the King say unto them on his right hand, Come, ye blessed of my Father, inherit the kingdom prepared for you from the foundation of the world: For I was an hungred, and ye gave me meat: I was thirsty, and ye gave me drink: I was a stranger, and ye took me in: Naked, and ye clothed me: I was sick, and ye visited me: I was in prison, and ye came unto me.

Then shall the righteous answer him, saying, Lord, when saw we thee an hungred, and fed *thee*? Or thirsty, and gave *thee* drink? When saw we thee a stranger, and too *thee* in? Or in prison, and came unto thee?

And the King shall answer and say unto them, Verily I say unto you, Inasmuch as ye have done *it* unto one of the least of these my brethren, ye have done it to me.

Then shall he say also unto them on the left hand, Depart from me, ye cursed, into everlasting fire, prepared for the devil and his angels: For I was an hungred, and ye gave me no meat: I was thirsty, and ye gave me no drink: I was a stranger, and ye took me not in: naked, and ye clothed me not: sick, and in prison, and ye visited me not.

Then shall they also answer him, saying, Lord, when saw we thee an hungred, or athirst, or a stranger, or naked, or sick, or in prison, and did not minster unto thee?

Then shall he answer them, saying, Verily I say unto you, Inasmuch as ye did *it* not to one of the least of these, ye did *it* not to me. And these shall go away into everlasting punishment: but the righteous into life eternal."

- Matt. 25:34-46

Takeaway: People in-need recognize *Doers*, not "promisers." God only knows how many "phonies" dashed prisoners' hopes.

Chapter 1

Setting up a Prison Ministry that's Real

First a look at Reconciliation - it's not just with God

The act of "reconciliation" -- in a broad sense -- is the process with which a friendship or relationship is restored to harmony. For an inmate, that can be with a victim, family, friends, or – as applied to restorative justice – restored to harmony with the community -- society.

In the world of religion and Theology, this presumes that the inmate(s) in trouble with the law are in conflict not just with society in a broken relationship that needs fixing, but also with the relationship with the Creator. Society can't forgive, per se, but people can forgive other people. In his book *"Facing Unresolved Conflicts: Theotherapy – God's Healing,"* Dr. Mario E. Rivera states:

> "Unless you can forgive that person, you are in bondage and you are keeping the other party in bondage. An unforgiving heart is a heart in chains." [1]

So, not only do individuals have to open their hearts to inmates, but societies, communities, and groups as well, including all institutions to start thinking of ways to effectively reconnect inmates with them which includes forgiveness and guidance.

Take the Holy Qur'an for example in *Islam*. Clearly we see even in the Qur'an the message of receiving guidance from Allah (God) and through his servant, Moses, rings out and emphasis to guide the people. Leadership, therefore, is not a monopoly just for *Christian* leaders, but Muslim leaders too who are charged to step up to sponsor and mentor inmates who are in need of guidance as part of God's people as it says in SŪRAH 20: 82:

> *"But, without doubt, I am (also)He that forgives again and again, to those who repent, believe, and do right – who, in fine, are ready to receive true guidance."* [2]

Prisoners in need of guidance should receive help from all religions, not just from Christian and Muslim faiths, but other faiths and organizations and or group even if non-religious.

In his book, *Changing Lenses: Restorative Justice for Our Times*, Howard Zehr describes what is called "Covenant Justice, The Biblical Alternative." Zehr writes that the Criminal Justice System (CJS) has to get away from the "Eye for eye, tooth for tooth" mentality of *Biblical* Justice (Leviticus 24:20; Exodus 21:24). [3] Clearly, this is different today for most New Testament (NT) Christians, as this old style of thinking in the Torah was for a purpose then; however, with the arrival of Jesus on the scene as the New Covenant, according to Zehr:

> *"Clearly the New Testament must be our primary standard."* [4]

No more clearly presented in Zehr's book is his identification that even in the days of Christ, people (i.e. prisoners) had a right to basic living conditions which rings true even for inmates today. Zehr says:

> *"Contrary to common assumptions, shalom usually refers to material or physical conditions or circumstances. God's intent is for humanity to live in physical wellbeing, At a minimum, this means a situation where things are all right. At some points, however, it seems to point to more, to prosperity and abundance. At any rate, the visions of the future, articulated so graphically by the prophets, include health and material prosperity and an absence of physical threats such as illness, poverty, and war."* [5]

Zehr further points out in *Shalom* that in Old Testament (OT) days, according to Yoder:

> *"Shalom defines how God intends things to be. God intends people to live in a condition of "all rightness" in the material world; in interpersonal, social, and political relationships; and in personal character. There can be no shalom when things are not as they ought to be, and the absence of shalom is at the heart of the criticisms the Old Testament prophets leveled at God's people. The vision of shalom also shapes hopes and promises for the future."* [6]

In short, Zehr uses the definition in *Yoder* explaining that shalom – the condition of living in peace without enmity to reflect as well why it is important for restorative justice over retributive justice the OT condoned until Jesus' arrival. In Yoder's words, "Jesus came so that things might ne as they ought to be both among people and between people and god and even in nature. [7]

Thus, reconciliation is an important theme in the NT, but the state of "all rightness" that God intends continues to have the material and physical dimensions that it had in the OT. [8] This is why, today, prisoners need to be guided and prepared with meaningful assistance in all dimensions of "shalom," so they too have the opportunity promised by God for a successful re-entry back into society and the Family of God which all people should enjoy.

Wherefore, here is where we begin the work of setting up and tailoring a prison ministry that is effective with meaningful service and results.

Establishing ministry objectives

As stated before, this book is designed for the straight-up no-bones-about-it prison ministry mentor or sponsor or any volunteer, friend, or family member. Simple, without lots of technical and religious minutia or mumbo-jumbo, but right to telling you what works to make an effective ministry and/or be giving meaningful assistance to a prisoner hopefully who see Christ reflected in you, and becomes better in life to overcome incarceration and never return.

Terminology

Throughout this book, terms will be rendered for the various ways prisoners are described. Not all prison vernaculars, slang, or jargon will be used; however the main ones, below, describe correctly what a prison minister, sponsor, family member, social and/or criminal justice reform advocate, etc. should know as a part of one's edification dealing with the aspects of making a connection / relationship with prisoners.

Prisoners. For the purposes of this book, the term *prisoner* is interchangeable with the words:

- inmate
- offender
- errant
- convict

These words essentially all mean the same – an incarcerated person, a prisoner – one sent to prison or jail. Errant will not be used, as explained in the preface because it is not politically correct (PC). It may, however, be seen or read in many *federal* publications. The terms "ex-con," "ex-felon," and "ex-offender" refer to those prisoners no-longer incarcerated in prison or jail who are living in the "free-world" now.

This book is not intended to be an esoterically-abridged manual for penology or criminology students, but rather an aid for understanding how to be better effective prison ministers, sponsors, or mentors by connecting (getting involved) with prisoners to help assist them change their lives for preparation to be successful upon re-entry.

Sponsors are those that not only mentor, but facilitate the next step or "level" by being more resourceful, usually providing financial and/or other support as we'll see in the chapters to come. In comparison, *mentors* tend to be only those volunteers who provide limited "spiritual" support or other *verbal* encouragement. As we'll see in Part Two, the differences are unique, with sponsors doing more for inmates like "big brothers" or "big sisters," getting personally in gear to help the inmate transition to the free-world by being a "life coach" or "accountability partner / coach" assisting their sponsoree with more meaningful abundant care that even the "Good Samaritan" ("Who is my neighbor? (Luke 10: 29-37)) would be in competition with.

NOTE: It is often forgotten about the part where the Good Samaritan paid money out of his own pocket for the innkeeper to house and feed the man in need.)

So, if you want to learn the vernaculars or "prison lingo" then get involved today and become an engaged volunteer.

Meaningful Objectives met define a Successful Prison Ministry

Sayings to remember:

- "Golden Rule" Treat others as you would like them to treat you."
- Frame your ministry around Jesus' love and fulfilling prisoners needs, not yours."
- "The harvest truly is plenteous, but the labourers are few." Matt. 29

On Categorizing Prisoners and Those Who Help Them

In the book, *Reflective with Scripture on Community Organizing* by Jeffrey K. Krehbiel, he says:

> "Nevertheless, it's hard to read the gospels and see humility as Jesus' most important attribute." [9]

He uses the scene in the Bible where the woman pleading to the judge to give her justice for her issue which she believes important; however, to the judge insignificant from his lofty view. This "pride vs. perseverance" example in Luke 18: 1-8 shows two weapons at use: one persistence, and the other public exposure of the court. Below is what the result is:

> **Faith + Justice Seeker = Power [from God] to affect Change**

Faith, like the widow, who keeps on battling the judge until she get what she wants, can move one person, then another, and another. Frederick Douglas famously said, "Power concedes nothing without a demand. It never did and it never will." The widow is wholly without power. A woman alone in a male-ordered culture, she had few individual rights of her own. In the Hebrew Scripture, the widow is singled out as a <u>category</u> of persons who deserve particular care within the community of faith.

Sound familiar? Widows, orphans, cripples, the sick, the hungry -- prisoners all in need of particular [societal] care because they don't have any ***power*** due to their category or situation?

That's why it takes righteous people *with* power to revitalize and empower prisoners who need particular assistance for justice to be obtained by equipping prisoners before they leave prison so they can thrive, not just survive, when released. In building up their lives to become free citizens again, prisoners become not "ex-cons" or "ex-felons," but rather viable productive enriched citizens no-longer making the mistakes of immaturity or criminal means for solving problems, but rather living right as God intended them to. (Jn. 8: 11) [10]

Ministries need to begin doing the right things

In the book, *Pastor to Pastor: Tackling the Problems of Ministry*, by Erwin Lutzer, he says, "Perhaps God is trying to teach us that we cannot depend on human agencies to turn this nation back to Him ... we must repent of our <u>comfortable</u> relationship with the world." [11] The first thing Lutzer says pastors are to do to change others is *lead* our congregation(s) by example in witnessing, community involvement, and teaching. He adds to "teach our people how to defend their faith in our pluralistic world." Lutzer continues to explain (paraphrasing) that there's a shift or schism of theology today, with many people holding to Biblical conservation, or moving towards cultural liberalism:

> "*Many evangelicals have left the Reformation doctrine of total depravity, the bondage of the human will, and man's need for sovereign grace. A general commitment to Christ substitutes for repentance, and emotional feelings replace worship.*"

"Today, a spirit of accommodation permeates the evangelical pulpits of our land. Sometimes obvious, sometimes subtle, but always dangerous, much preaching today is shaped by the culture of our times. The Bible is bent to accommodate culture rather than to change it. [12] A New Reformation is needed to shape the criminal and social justice "thinking" of society in the way it perceives those sent to prison for their mistakes. So, instead of punishment, <u>*assistance*</u> is the NEW norm over *corrections* which has been a failure for decades. *Corrections'* goals have morphed into being synonymous with warehousing now, which implies absolutely no change in the *condition* of the prisoner when they come into the system and when they leave. Relatively speaking then, for example, a can of tuna fish put on a store shelf remains a can of tuna fish when it leaves the shelf. No change. The same is for most prisoners. They come into the system broken, then leave in the same condition or worse, especially for the elderly inmates physically broken down, without skills, and too old to get a job. Worse, sent out with no drivers license, no computer skills, no financial support only to be dumped on the public assistance rolls to sap more taxpayer funds, and end up bitter because they've run out of time in their lives having lost everything and no time to get it back.

So what about a New Reformation in America needed today?

The difference between the sixteenth-century Reformation and this new reformation are obvious. Gone is the idea that a knowledge of God is one's highest goal; a knowledge of ourselves and our need for self-respect is now the <u>first</u> item on the theological agenda. God is not so much a judge who has been offended as He is a servant who is waiting to affirm our dignity. [13] We come to Him on the basis of our self-worth rather than the blood of Christ.

This reformation, then, is basically a call to a new preoccupation with ourselves rather than with God. This is the problem of today's Millennial American culture of the world.

Unfortunately, as man is lifted up, god is dethroned. [14] Sin, traditionally thought to be against God, is now defined as against man:

> *"Any act or thought that robs myself or another human being of his or her self-esteem."* – Robert Schuller, **Self-Esteem – The New Reformation** (Dallas: Word, 1982), 14. [15]

Our country is therefore encompassed by a man-centered theology, that is not biblical, and the reason why so many fall victim to crime doing things "our way" instead of God's way in obedience to Him (His laws). The same with bad ineffective prison ministry. Those who want to mentor or sponsor a prisoner with *man's* "self-image" influences pay God the ultimate slap in the face because they are not only leading another person away

from God's plan, but pushing the prisoner closer to the world and the counter-culture of sin the prisoner needs to avoid because that's what got them to prison in the first place.

That is why it is absolutely critical for a prisoner to have an *effective* mentor or sponsor to be a guide with the right path plan of Christ's example. And if the mentor or sponsor's are not willing to do what is necessary for the needs of the prisoner, or at least something(s) meaningful, collectively, the prisoner is only partially assisted and unable to become fully-equipped for a successful transition back into free society. Only this time, he or she has the means to get back some of what she or he has lost and is less bitter.

THE REASON FOR SETTING UP PRISON MINISTRIES: THE NEW DEMOGRAPHIC CATEGORY: OLDER PRISONERS

This is the new demographic in American criminal and social justice: Incarcerated people coming out of prison without meaningful skills and un-prepared for transition back into society. I've talked to many young prisoners over three decades who left prison or jail without discipline, only to go back to cultural or regional environments knowing only what they learned to live by when they came into the system. They came back with no new job skills or discipline other than some basic mobile device skills and longer sentences as they were deemed "repeat offenders" now and given more time. In a book written by John L. Allen, Jr. titled: *"The Future Church: How Ten Trends are Revolutionizing the Catholic Church,"* Allen reports from statistical research that most older prisoners who have had many years in prison tend to be physically limited to work, have little or no computer skills, and no real means of financial or family support, except for public and charitable assistance. [16] In a similar study I myself conducted recently with inmates, I too found similar findings giving all ministry leaders, volunteers, and social justice advocates a call to "wake up" and take note. [17]

Large Church faiths, like the Catholic Church, have taken notice of the demographic population of rising elderly social welfare roles and the Millennials' dilemma of having to pay more taxes and the expected future taxes for social welfare of the elderly in America.

Allen adds:

> "Leaders within the Church who work on public policy questions – bishops, theologians, social action directors, lobbyists, and activists of all sorts – will find that "elder equity" is perhaps the dominant domestic policy issue of the future. Assuring that societies make adequate provisions for their elderly, and that available resources are distributed fairly across lines of race, class, and gender, will be a towering challenge. [18]

The risks of a rising number of elderly people living without adequate support systems, and without even minimal resources to provide for basic safety and comfort, was illustrated in shocking fashion in France in 2003, when a summer heat wave caused a stunning total of 11,000 deaths. Most victims were elderly people living alone, who couldn't afford air-conditioning and who had no one to check in on them to be sure they weren't in danger. Given that 16 percent of the population of France is already over 65, these dangers will only grow. The same pattern is unfolding almost everywhere, with greatest intensity in the rapidly aging countries of the developed world.

Even this year, the COVID-19 pandemic proved devastating, killing more elderly in nursing homes in America, percentage wise, than any other at-risk group.

This is why all Christian churches need to start becoming actively involved before their churches fall behind. Millennials not invited to be a part of the solution will then view the churches "anti-Millennial," and not only lose generations for their church(es) to sustain themselves, but the culture will suffer as well because people of all ages are not seen in that church as looking out for the interests of all, but rather sub-groups or categories with priorities that do not benefit the entire congregation.

Inevitably, the impact will fall disproportionately upon women, the poor, and those who are non-white. As Boston College theologian

Lisa Sowle Cahill notes, retirement incomes for women average only 55 percent of those of men, and for older African American or Hispanic women, poverty is the rule rather than the exception. Such affronts to human decency will command both a mortal and a practical response from the Catholic Church." [19]

That is why there needs to be a moratorium on the way state and federal governments are handling prison incarceration practices by applying a "band aid" with warehousing, rather than and pedagogical approach of teaching people who made mistakes how to live and work as productive citizens. It make no sense to lock a person up for ten years only to come out the same way they came in or worse because the skills they may have learned ten years ago are now obsolete. Then dumped back on the streets, no drivers license, no education, and no job skills only to fall back on whatever they knew in the first place because that's what human beings do – what works for them based on what they know. And when they re-offend, the taxpayer once again is forced to "flip the bill" for incarceration, rather than 'redirection work programs' where the prisoner can be supervised and still maintain a job but is still paying his or her debt to society by going on the weekends to a supervised program as an alternative to incarceration. This can even apply to some deemed "violent offenders" because many who commit assaults or spousal killings do not necessarily reflect a pattern or "habit" of criminal behavior, but rather lack some social skill(s) of dealing with stress and situations of aggression which could be solved in appropriate social and psychological treatments. These are available without sending the offender to prison costing the tax payers more burden, especially as the population of elderly is increasing for the younger generations to have to pick up the tab.

That is why all churches, civic organizations, private citizens, etc. should petition their political representatives for action to give the current and future generations the relief of knowing that they are not going to be paying a burden later that can be resolved now.

Allen further adds:

> "At the same time, the [Catholic] Church will need to be attentive to a corollary possibility, which is that as a rapidly growing of percentage of social resources is diverted to the elderly, mostly through entitlement programs, young adults and families may feel victimized. Some social theorists worry about a crisis of "intergenerational solidarity." [20]

As Allen explains, this is with young workers squeezed to support a ballooning population of elderly retirees, eating up more and more of their income through payroll taxes and other measures. Compounding the resentment such a situation could create is the likelihood that soaring budgets for pensions and elder care will make new investment in programs of interest to young people, such as child care or parental leave programs, more difficult. This is a special risk if older people simply vote their class interests. The night mare scenario is that in such a world, the young could end up hating the old. [21]

These alarming trends must be virulently addressed with programs needed to offset such potential dangers of discrimination of particularly older prisoners leaving prison and going directly into becoming tax burdens and other costs for younger people who will be saddled into paying for all the elder care especially social services and medical support of re-entry prisoners.

Thus, without intervening protection for both the Millennial generation inheriting the funding responsibility for the elderly by reducing the number of incarcerated and prisoners leaving prison at older ages or being sent to prison at older ages and coming out without any time left on their life to contribute to their own financial independence or skills, the living conditions in America could become so impossible to maintain a level above poverty, that Millennial families could find themselves in economic collapse or dire straits because if the trend is not reversed, young people could find themselves working exclusively to fund programs for older people of which prisoners are included in that category.[22]

DISCIPLESHIP AND DISCIPLINE:
Connecting with others to Connect a New View

So, how do we CONNECT with others? To get people involved in helping our fellow men and women with a new way of thinking? In getting involved in groups or ministries to foster growing concerns for social change[ing] and re-alignment of our priorities to make this category of people and their sponsors or mentors a part of the "solution team" helping guide people to be better citizens, not deteriorate in incarceration centers?

In a book I came across entitled *The Daniel Dilemma*, by Chris Hodges, M.M., he makes the significant point that you have to "connect with people before you can correct them." [23] This is the *shift* needed for society as a whole to reach out with its body of mentors, teachers, sponsors, counselors, civic leaders, religious faiths, etc. to give rise to viewing help for prisoners as good for helping society by returning prisoners well-equipped and re-oriented for productiveness in society, rather than a drain or "threat" as some see prisoners. The same with society seeing those who want to help prisoners as being "community life-architects" who help re-shape and re-form men and women labeled by the courts as *criminals*, removed and isolated from the general public [society] and made to be separated from growing and living with the mainstream.

<u>Understanding people before correcting them is what the connection does so the prisoner can be assessed where they are, where they were, and have a plan for where they need to go.</u> This implies that a prisoner's condition [state] is temporary, and only in relation for a time based on what a person has come to know and utilize as a philosophy for living.

This, therefore, leads to the goal of prison ministries to be performing unconditional involvement assistance not just for Christian ministries with the Word of God, but invaluable life-changing faith that is demonstrated by acts of discipleship witnessing that is meaningful not "hocus pocus lip service" without merit. When Jesus gave "His word," he meant it. For a *volunteer* to invoke Christ's name and make a promise and not keep it, this invites one of the Trickster's best tools for destroying confidence, and that is doubt. Legitimate sponsors and mentors demonstrating the fellowship of Christ in His discipleship role-training He did with his apostles to spread Christ's love and the Word of God must reflect Christ and not the world. For a prisoner, reflecting the world -- with a weak faith and actions -- is seen to have already caused separation from God, and a sponsor or mentor making false promises and committing acts which don't reflect Christ's love [of action], can do more harm than good to a prisoner who has already been weakened by situations which have caused pain and sorrow the prisoner no-longer wants to experience with an in-effective sponsor or mentor who's not the "real deal."

This where *real* prison ministry begins.

The makings of a Sponsor or Mentor Who Change Lives

Prison sponsors and mentors need to be what Jesus called his apostles which is to be a "disciple."

But first, the word "apostle," as defined in the *Holman Bible Dictionary*, is an English word which comes from the Greek term *apostolos,* which means a messenger, envoy, or ambassador. [24] It is related to the verb, "to send," it refers to one who is "sent" on behalf of another.

In the *New Testament*, the term 'apostle" is used primarily to designate that group of leaders within the early church(es) who were historical witnesses of the resurrected Lord and proclaimers of God's saving mercies enacted through the death and resurrection of Jesus. Jesus originally gave the title to His closest circle of friends, the twelve. (Luke 6:13) He especially indicated their status as emissaries He had set apart to announce (as He had done) the good news of the kingdom. (Matt. 10: 1-23; Luke 8: 1,9: 1-6).

The term "apostle" did not, however, have limitless applications in the *New Testament* period. It extended to gospel

witnesses other than the twelve but not to all proclaimers of the gospel. [25]

In short, the term "apostle," most immediately brought to mind its central function: to preach the gospel.

Other terms for apostle in the Pauline **missionary party** were called, for example, "brother," "fellow worker," or "bond servant." (Rom. 16:3; Phil. 2:25; Col. 4: 7-14; 1 Thess. 3:1)

Second, the term "disciple" comes from the Latin root. It means: "learner" or "pupil." In the Greek world the word "disciple" normally referred to an adherent of a particular teacher or religious / philosophical school. [26] It was the **task** of the disciple to learn, study, and pass along the sayings and teachings of the master. In rabbinic Judaism the term "disciple" referred to one who was **committed** to the interpretations of Scripture and religious tradition given him by the master or rabbi. Through a **process of learning** which would include a set meeting time and such pedagogical methods as question and answer, instruction, repetition, and memorization, the disciple would come increasingly devoted to the master and the master's teachings. **In time**, the disciple would, likewise, **pass on** the traditions to others. [27]

Do you see a pattern here?

Discipleship / Mentorship/ Sponsorship:

- Missionary Party (Idea)
- Task (Essential Plan)
- Commitment (Personal)
- Process of Learning (Action)
- In Time (Building a Connection)
- Change (Passed on Knowledge)

In the *New Testament,* 233 of the 261 instances of the word "disciple" occur in the Gospels, the other 28 being in Acts. One can assume that Jesus used traditional rabbinic teaching techniques (question and answer, discussion, memorization) to instruct His disciples. In many respects Jesus differed from the rabbis. He called His disciples to "Follow me." (Luke 5:27) Jesus oftentimes demanded extreme levels of **personal** renunciation (loss of family, property, etc) (Matt. 4: 18-22; 10: 24-42; Luke 5: 27-28; 14: 25-27; 18: 28-30). He asked for lifelong allegiance (Luke 9: 57-62) as the ESSENTIAL means of doing the will of God (Matt. 12: 49-50; John 7: 16-18). [28]

Thus, the "twelve" (Apostles) were sent out as representatives of Jesus, commissioned to preach the coming of the kingdom, to cast out demons, and to heal disease. (Matt. 10: 1, 5-15; Mark 6: 7-13; Luke 9:1-6) Such tasks were not limited to the twelve (Luke 10: 1-24). Smaller groups like the "seventy" were formed (Luke 10: 1,17). The term "disciple" them morphed into referring to all those who believe in the risen Lord (Acts 6: 1-2, 7; 9: 1, 10, 19, 26, 38; 11: 26, 29).

In the final commissioning, it appears in Matthew's Gospel (28: 19-20) also suggests a use in the early church of the term "disciple" as a more generalized name for all those who come to Jesus in faith, having and believed the gospel. [29]

Discipline. The word "discipline," according to the *Holman Bible Dictionary*, comes from the Latin word "disco" which means to learn or get to know, a direct kind of acquaintance with something or someone. [30] God prescribed a way of life for His people. They had to be obedient. The process by which God's people learned obedience was the "discipline of the Lord." (Deut. 11: 2 NIV)

Discipline, therefore, refers to the process by which one learns a **WAY OF LIFE**. [31] A "disciple" was like an apprentice who was learning a trade or a craft from a master. Such learning required a relationship between the master who knew the way of life (discipline) and a learner (a disciple). Within this relationship, the master led a learner through a process (the discipline) until the learner could *imitate* or live like the master. [31]

In conclusion, through the connection of positive godly "disciples" (e.g. mentors and sponsors) using the encouraging powerful Word of God in a meaningful relationship with others to train and/ or educate them in living a new and better life, and effective transformation can take place that reaches both prisoners and other 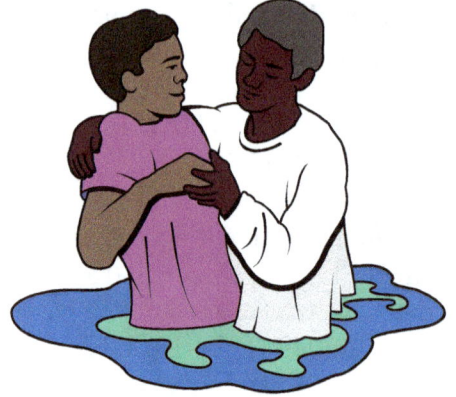 people to see that there are better ways of treating prisoners and those in society who just need a bit of guidance in their lives. Like the master and student relationship, a transfer of knowledge and experience shown by the master can influence a prisoner who gains a different life-building set of skills from the mentor or sponsor to make changes to improve his or herself to be made into a new person with whom society is more accepting [to] and expects of its citizens to be conforming to the norms of society and its laws. *Spiritual maturity* -- as well as human maturity -- can be achieved in a relationship of discipline that is obedient to God and to laws of the society through instruction which fosters change in the learner. Successful discipline in the newly transformed person then results in conforming behavior that is not just pleasing to one's self, but to the society and to God who should be first in a believer's life.

It should be noted, that the earliest setting for discipline was the family unit. (Deut. 6: 20-25). Today's society, with the counter-culture of "self first," progressivism, liberal-extremism, and hateful anti-Christian propaganda, has destroyed many families and the lives of people which many in prison are the result of a demographic of broken homes (i.e. homes with no father, no faith in God, no parenting, abuse, etc.), drug addiction, poverty, and otherwise no "family unit" which is a child's *first* contact for a <u>way</u> of life.

Hollywood, the media, peers, cults, etc. all spin "life" into fantasy which – for some – that's all they are exposed to and become products of that influence where family, fathers, parents, etc. are no-longer viewed as relevant to be consulted for advice as to living right in life.

This book is not about exploring reasons for why people end up breaking the law, nor is it meant to be a psychology or sociology book. But what skews a young person's mind eventually leads to skewed thinking patterns and skewed behavior not aligned with the rest of the society and therefore can lead to conflicts with the law – and God. And a child, broken, grows into a broken adult if there is no help or intervention along the way; they'll stay broken.

Bottom Line – Are You a Living Witness? Living the example to help others see Jesus in you to offer hope to others to break their chains holding them back in life?

So, "discipline," biblically understood, results in blessing. [32] Within the "discipline of the Lord," expressed in and through the lord Jesus Christ, one can live the kind of life which is pleasing to God and of benefit to others. (James Berryman)

How so? By being a **witness** to others, as Jesus did representing the Father. Teachers are "masters," and are inherently witnesses who project the right way of life. Teachers, mentors, sponsors, and parents do the same modeling all the time for their children or students. Early church believers were called "witnesses." [33] They were challenged by Christ Himself to be *His* witnesses throughout the world (Acts 1:8). As Jesus had indicated earlier, this witness is informed and empowered by the Holy Spirit (John 15: 26-27). Throughout the *New Testament*, believers are instructed that their witness is to be true and faithful, reflected both in speech and life-style (Acts 4:33; 14:3; Heb. 10: 15-17; 1 Thess. 2:10).

That's how you mentor and sponsor effectively: By a life-style *reflecting* Jesus which others will recognize you "walking the walk" as a real disciple – and apostle – who can teach (benefit) another human being to change his or her life for the better in a meaningful way. Jesus did it by <u>connecting</u> on their level and guiding them through the process by understanding their needs, their pains, and bringing the healing *word of God* to **action** – not just words – miraculously transforming people out of their bondage and free them of the yokes of ignorance or old life styles that the world placed on them for one reason or another.

Now, mentors and sponsors can show prisoners the healing love of Christ and the promises of hope living *His* way – the right way (through faith (1 John 5:4; 2 Thess. 3:9)) – rather than the way they (the prisoners) did or want to do things – the broken wrong way of sin, failure, pain, and calamity.

Author's Comment to Atheists.

From the two mission statements on the previous page, which one offers more to help people? The one including God's powerful resources through His Son, Jesus Christ and the world, or the one with just the *world*?

The whole point of having a mission statement is to keep both volunteer and the inmate(s) focused on making appropriate changes to meet the goals set for the inmate to work on. Evaluation, on-going communication, and measurable outcomes (e.g. assessments, checklists, short-term and long-term objectives to meet the goals, etc.) to monitor the progress of the inmate based on the principles fostering growth and transformation of the inmate into a better person.

Remember, there are no perfect solutions and the "time lines" are not set in stone, as jail and prison environments are often unpredictable with "lockdowns," visitation cancellations, no phone call periods, slow mail, no letter (only postcards), and available materials to foster good progress. Patience is something one must have in this volunteer type of work. As we used to say in the military, one has to "maintain a rigid state of flexibility." Another oxymoronic idiom is "hurry up and wait." Prison is just like any bureaucracy – you are at the mercy of a system that sometimes does correct things incorrectly, and incorrectly does some correct things. Meaning, patience is required.

So, with a good mission statement, everyone is kept focused on the objectives and goals. The mission statement and your evaluated plan of objectives and goals is what "drives" everyone in the right direction. (See Appendix 1 for sample mission statement and basic guidebook index portfolio for sponsor/mentor)

Prison Ministry Members are a Part of the Community Organizing Team

Religion and philosophy have tended to provide frameworks for the conduct of social welfare. These are often handled by community organizers also called welfare services or social work. [34]

Community organizers can be church or non-church group members in any purposeful capacity. Their basic concerns of social welfare – poverty, disability and disease, the dependent young and elderly – are at the core of charitable or dutiful responses to render assistance to those who struggle for a daily existence, including those incarcerated in prisons, jails, mental institutions, and holding facilities. The well-being of these categories of distressed people in need of assistance is of importance because it defines a society as to its moral obligation to have stronger "healthier" people look out for its "least citizens" that require assistance or emergency measures. The sick, the disabled, the at-risk – the vulnerable -- all affect a society who pay taxes or render resources to address these people, especially social services who place a high value on keeping families together in their local communities. [35]

Volunteers for hospitals, nursing homes, after-school soccer programs, school lunch programs, elderly share-a-ride programs, kid's little league or other activities, etc. all help people in the community who have obstacles or less means of living. And this help costs time and money – taxpayer's money and/or revenues from other sources.

Wherefore, organizations and/or ministries set-up to address these socially at-risk groups must have a priority if we are to rescue disadvantaged people from further distress, and from making the rest of the community ill, harmed, or fail if their condition of need is not slowed, reversed, or "healed" with effective involvement (i.e. mentorship and sponsorship) and the funds to fix them early before its too late.

Destination: Success

Michael Maraschiello

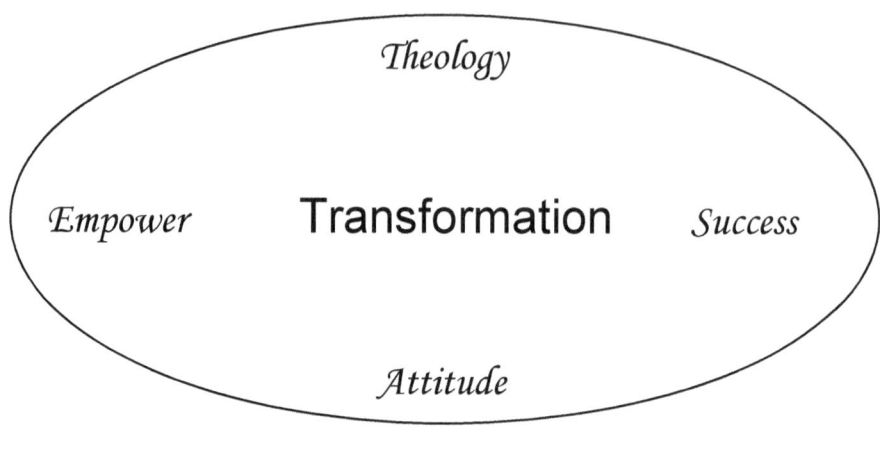

Chapter 2

Finding Volunteers to "talk and walk" (Not just feeding the animals at the zoo)

Simple and Basic Guidance - A recipe for success.

The hallmark of this book is what my godmother, Marilyn Wagner, and her husband, Jack, would tell me every time they visited me each weekend at the prison which told me I was **worth** God's time. More heart-warming, their time. And that was [paraphrasing] they told me the *best* Bible verse for prisoners was from Jeremiah (28 v. 11):

> "For I know well the plans I have for you, says the LORD, plans for your welfare, not to worry, and plans to give you a future full of hope." [1]

Folks, let's face facts with a "reality check" from *Realville*. Even from a prisoner's perspective, there's an expectation of what a prison ministry *should* bring to the prison[er]. Ministering to "convicts" is far from the minds of many "on the outside" looking in.

In fact, prison ministry is, sadly, at the bottom of most churches' priorities because of funding, participation, and time.

Why?

Because prison ministry is not popular, plain and simple. More troublesome, the excuses pile on with prison ministries being "fund takers" not "fund maker." Prison ministries all involve "people" who are on the lowest end of the societal realm of being disenfranchised, abused, discriminated against, uneducated, drug-addicted, and without skills, or "written off" by the courts, main-stream public, and worse even, by family many times.

Do these people sound like folks you want to get involved with? To go visit? Spend time with? Introduce to your family? Spend money and resources on?

Discussed later in chapter 5, we'll discuss the four (4) types of sponsors and what it takes to be a real minister, sponsor, or mentor for a prison. Right now, this chapter focuses on just the volunteer aspect of prison ministry because while some people's hearts may want to participate, their minds may not have the cognition to realize later they made a mistake and now have remorse believing they made a mistake getting involved with a bunch of prisoners who have tattered lives needing repair as will be explained later. One doesn't have to look far, especially one television or the  Internet, to hear snide bromides and slanderous "fake news" about stereotypical "inmates" doing all sorts of diabolical and deviant things portraying most all prisoners as deadbeats, losers, -- unworthy *useless* people who should just be "forgotten," not seen. It takes a certain type of person – a strong person – to love someone unconditionally, especially one branded by the law and discarded in their feeling society has held them down for so long.

So who are these people that want to help inmates by becoming prisoner ministers?

Where do real ministers come from that can make meaningful differences in the lives of prisoners as *effective* accountability partners, sponsors, and mentors?

Are they your brother, mother, sister, father, or friend?

Really, who is *called* to minster to prisoners?

Qualities. Just love -- unconditionally?

What *qualities* – not qualifications – does one have to have to be a prison minster? Your pastor's? Your own? Jesus'?

And who, really, wants to minister to murderers, sex offenders, drug addicts, burglars, child molesters, sex traffickers, and internet identity thieves?

"Are you nuts?," I remember a friend of mine tell me when I told him I was sponsoring a soldier – a "convict" -- at Ft. Leavenworth, Kansas, in 1992, when I was stationed there as a Captain going through the U.S. Army's Command and Staff Service School (CAS³) as a part of my officer's military Uniform Code of Military Justice (UCMJ) law training. I voluntarily went to the U.S. Disciplinary Barracks with other officers in my class to see where the soldiers were stockaded for their offenses committed while on active duty. We each had to take one soldier and mentor them and help them with whatever they needed.

"What was the point?" Someone asked me later.

I explained that as a part of my military training as a commander of troops the "lesson learned" from that experience was to understand what a punished soldier goes through because – as an officer – I had the *power* to send someone to prison – that prison. I was to learn how prison affects peoples lives and to use what that prisoner conveyed to me so I could share that knowledge with others before they made mistakes in order to help them correct their problems when counseling, and to understanding how important my decision was when I gave out rendering a punishment that I absolutely made sure my decision was just.

The reality was, I didn't just read about prison from a book, but rather I was now spending time there and becoming **involved** in another human being's live to see the perspective he had in order to become more knowledgeable for me to be a better officer. And the more I spent time there, the more I became emotional about making a difference because I saw myself free and with benefits to appreciate that soldier more who had nothing materially, but had his Bible with hopes, dreams, and a future he could live for expecting to be free one day. A vision all prisoners have.

Empathy and Compassion.

Plainly stated, empathy is the "vicarious experiencing of another's feelings." [2] That's what I experienced when I was visiting that prisoner at the U.S. Disciplinary Barracks in 1992. It's the same experience I had for my *special needs* disabled adults whom I was entrusted to care for in 1984 when I was a Special Needs Teacher (Evening Program Instructor) working for People, Inc. of East Aurora, New York. The condition or *state* of disability that prisoner was in was no different from that of the disabled person or "challenged" -- as Millennials say today -- because both groups are marginalized with difficulties in life needing assistance and/or repair.

That leads to the next definition which is "compassion," meaning a "deep feeling or understanding of someone else's misery."

Sound familiar?

Did Jesus have feelings for others? To take action?

Volunteer versus *Followteer*?

As will be discussed in Chapter 5, there are types of volunteers who become sponsors, mentors, advisors, drivers, sandwich makers, *retreat* bakers, money donators, vocal spectators, and a visible shakers who come in all shapes and sizes with different reasons or "agendas."

Seriously, are those that volunteer really doing it for others? Or are they doing it for themselves? What about for Jesus? Maybe a combination.

Regardless, *who* is the subject of the volunteer that is to be benefitted? Aren't they the one for who the volunteer is supposed to serve or affect?

Isn't the prisoner the reason for the volunteer's work or mission or ministry?

"Professional volunteers" stay in it for the "long haul," but the wanabe's never do because they can't muster up to the unconditional love part of genuine prison ministry which desires men and women to look past the cultural and legal aspects of labels, shaming, and prejudice to reach into the prisoner's mind and heart and make the commitment that you are not going to abandon them and leave them for dead.

This is one of the major "calls" to prison ministry and signs of an effective minister – one who makes a commitment and sticks with the prisoner till they are free even if they are on death row because there is <u>always</u> hope with Christ. ³

What level of commitment are you will put up?

The Meat.

"Don't talk the talk, but walk the walk," is an axiom widely used by inmates when church and other group volunteers visit the prison, often making false promises that zap the hopes and dreams of many who depend on even the smallest of prayers for someone to help them. This is the worst thing a person can do to a prison which destroys confidence and faith in that inmate who could very well be on the fence for suicide, going back to drug use, or even so much as to get a job when released because some outside 'free-world" person, whether sponsor, family, ember, or friend, made a promise to a prisoner who's invested everything in the hopes that that promise would come true. And to a prisoner who has nothing, everything is of huge importance because that's all they have.

Simply put, the message is that what a prisoner's eyes see is sizably differently proportionate to what importance the free-world person may attach to the promise. This is a big issue, because what the prisoner believes – that the free-world person understands their concerns – may not always line up with what the free-world person believes. Communication is key; however, involvement to find out what is the meat of the relationship between the prisoner and the free-world person – who could be a volunteer – must be understood so both inmate and volunteer can accept that relationship, modify it, or reject it. With talk, and no "action' or substance to back up a promise, the immediate emotional response of the inmate is their loss of faith in that free-world person because the old cliché' "actions speak louder than words" comes into play, often visibly, when things don't appear to be happening.

As we'll see in later chapters, *effective* sponsors who do **meaningful** things to help prisoners (e.g. pay for the inmate's birth certificate they can't afford so when they leave prison they can obtain a driver's license) makes a huge impact on their life. The inmate's morale, faith in the sponsor, faith in society, health, and faith in God all increase because the sponsor is "walking the walk" and helped give the prisoner what he or she needs, not what the sponsor thinks the prisoner wants. Sponsors, as we shall discuss later what they and their "sponsoree" should be do to "drag them out of prison," must take Christ's simple message to heart with an attitude of altruism and empower their inmate or inmates they have volunteered to help and foster a transformation of the prisoner's current life situation. By "re-routing" the inmate, so to speak, like a truck on a road to a destination (freedom), the volunteer sponsor or mentor can help orient or guide the inmate towards the goals we will discus later such as personal responsibility, drug-free life, job training, victim awareness, and a stronger personal relationship with Jesus Christ to forever be on the right path with a support group that is second to none.

That's how sponsors and mentors can "Get'er done," by becoming involved and making a difference, not just talk about it or worry about the cost when a *life* is in the balance. Prisoners are human beings with blood in their veins, who have value as Christ sees and we are to respect and assist as our neighbors in need.

Sadly, as some people see prison ministry, they go to the prison as if on a school field trip to the zoo to "feed the animals." Everyone wants to go to the zoo, throw some peanuts, make a few speeches, then the novelty is over, the animals no-longer amusing to look at, and everyone goes home. "High five," we had a fieldtrip to the zoo. Same with a trip to the prison, for some. Yet, it is sad because a polar bear at the zoo has a room 10 times larger, a pool, and if mistreated, the animal rights groups demand -- and get – immediate publicity for the polar bear to be treated "humanely," whereas, when human beings cry out in the courts for justice or appeal to the deaf ears of the governor of the state for mercy, there's no relief, there's no voice, there's no hope.

Who does the prisoner call when he or she is mistreated?
Think about it, *Realville*.
ALL a prisoner has is Jesus Christ. And maybe – just maybe, there is one – just one – person out there who can make a difference in just one prisoner's life to make that prisoner's life a little easier or give them hope to hang on and fight for their life.
Are YOU that volunteer?
Are you that one Jesus is calling?
Can you walk the walk Jesus said people will point you out for doing what is right? What your heart and conscience tells you is God's Word calling you day and night, twenty-four / seven to make a difference?

In the next chapter, we'll discuss the fears you must over so that you are given the courage to "step up' and be a disciple, not just some lump on a log in church on a pew filled with wishy-washy sheep. Rather, being a Christian, and proud of it, to be under some prisoners wings so they can soar and reach the heavens like God intended them to do in the first place. And volunteers – like the great apostles, also stepped forward to the challenge to muster resources and take the light into the darkness and fight for those Christ said were his children, brothers, sisters, and friends no matter their color, race, creed, or disability or situation. He showed unconditional love, and feared no evil to give hope to the hopeless and we'll see in the second part of this book.

More Character Traits of a True Christian Volunteer

Members of the church were called on to demonstrate the power of Christ's redemption in their own lives by exemplary conduct, embracing every area of life. (Rom. 12:1-13:7; Col. 3:12-4:1). Jesus led a kenotic lifestyle, as we are to imitate as in Philippians 2:6-11: "Empty of one's self to be a servant like Christ." Throughout the old testament, helping our neighbor was the call as exemplified that "the kin of any poor relative should try and relieve them." (Lev. 25-28, 35-38, 47-55)

Prison Ministry In Covid America

Service is Life

What Should Prison Ministers Do?
By M. F. Maraschiello June 2018

Christ taught that true greatness is measured by <u>moral</u> worth. In the estimation of heaven, greatness of character consists in living for the welfare of our fellow men and women, in doing works of love and mercy. Christ the king of glory, was a servant to fallen man. None, are more worthy of mercy and compassion as to bring the fallen prisoner back from the depths, change their hearts and souls, and reclaim and welcome them back into the kingdom. By relying on the Word of God, those that hear His voice have a chance at redemption. And it is by discipleship that His message can reach the "Least Ones" – the marginalized prisoner.

"Not to be ministered unto, but to minister."	Matt. 20:28
"By love serve one another."	Gal. 5:13
"Give to the needy… and not minister for show"	Matt. 6:1-4
"Love God first, show love second to thy neighbor.."	Matt. 22: 37-40
"Forgive others who sin and God will forgive you."	Matt. 6: 14-15
"Don't judge lest ye be judged."	Matt. 7:1-2
"Lost sheep hear me… safeguard the little ones."	Matt. 18:1
"The sheep and the goats… I was in prison and you visited me…provided for my needs"	Matt. 25: 35-40

The *true* prison minister will be known by his **character.** Christ's Holy church will be known by those from His churches commissioned with caring for their flocks *as the shepherds* of the people in the community.

Just as Christ came to heal the sick and provide needs for the hungry, the poor, children, and widows, prisoners too are among the needy and believe to see <u>hope</u> in prison minister(s) who visit them.

• Can you live up to the **standard** Jesus set by casting off "self?"

• Are you able to fight Satan and his angels who prejudice prisoners with negative stereotypes, shouts for no mercy, and demands for no forgiveness?

• Do you believe Christ has the POWER to help you help others?

Then, perhaps, the calling prisoners is for you. Only your heart is like, and ability to make a difference. restorative justice in mind

from Him to minister to you and God know what whether you have the With mercy, love, and – you can!

ON THEOLOGY

Peace, love, and harmony are inherent in all the Natural religions of the world. A Theologist's goal is to relate the faith to everyday life and interpretation of the Scriptures. All ministers, rabbis, and mullahs who are obedient to God teach these fundamentals to everyone.

THOUGHT QUESTION: "HOW MUCH DOES A PRISONER HAVE TO SUFFER BEFORE HIS OR HER DEBT TO SOCIETY IS PAID FOR?"

ON DISCIPLESHIP & TRAINING

[1], M.J. Alhabeeb, PhD (Wiley & Sons, Inc.) p411-412 (2015)

In his book, "Entrepreneurial Financing: Fundamentals of Financial Planning and Management for Small Business," Professor Alhabeeb says, "Training is necessary, not only for the new employees but also for the current employees, in order to keep up with the process of skills and technology, and to face the never ending market challenges." [4]

To be a disciple of Christ, Compare these secular terms and steps I paraphrased that Alhabeeb suggests are necessary for training people effectively:

A. <u>Types of Training</u>
   1. Apprenticeship – One who learns by watching. A "watch and learn" approach.
   2. Internship – A mix with a theoretical side of college education or cooperative schooling.
   3. Cross Training – Learning more than one skill.
   4. E-Training – Learning theory and practice in the electronic and digital fields mastering online interactive techniques.
B. <u>Methods of Training</u>
   1. Education – Traditional way of absorbing knowledge & learning skills.
   2. Lectures, Workshops, Conferences – Formal structured focus on specific area for short time.
   3. Field Rotation – Doing time in one job, then moving to another.
   4. Role Playing – Act out hypothetical scenarios to learn from.
   5. OJT – (On-The-Job) – Traditional training method placing person in the work atmosphere and have them perform their job.
C. <u>4 Steps for Any Training Program to Maximize Learning</u>

1. Exploring Phase – Find out what the person knows – where they are in their life (skills, how they learn best, personality, personal life, what motivates them).
2. Demonstration Phase – Introduce person to the details – what they need [to know] listening and watching the demonstration and going over questions and problems then solve them. (This is where the person needs to understand what's expected on them, and communication is critical to successful learning (change).
3. Performance Phase – After demonstration, it's time to see what the person has learned / changed, with some supervision and correction, if required.
4. Review Phase – This is the reviewer's final inputs for the person to receive any last constructive criticism for the person to be finally, with some measurement, set on his or her own as ready or qualified – certified – to act, do, or perform to a competent degree (level).

RELATING TO INMATES: "PEAS AND CARROTS"

Like the line repeated many times by Tom Hanks in the movie *Forrest Gump*, "We go together like peas and carrots," the message was clear: People can be from all sorts of different backgrounds or life experiences and may or may not ever understand each other but be together nevertheless by fate, luck, or divine intervention. "Breaking the ice" about a prisoner's past or even "record," can be a difficult subject for many to talk about, especially to a total stranger.

Two frequently asked questions most prisoners have when meeting volunteer mentors, sponsors, counselors, chaplains, etc. for the first time are:

"How can this person relate to me if they don't know who I am and where I come from?"

And,

"How are you going to tell me how to "live right" when your definition of everything is different from mine?"

What comes to mind with most people is the old adage:

"When you walk a mile in my shoes, come and tell me how it feels."

implying that for <u>understanding</u> to be realized about someone else's situation or life, one must have tried it or experienced it because *everybody* is different.

Without turning this book into a sociology treatise, people are formed into the person they are today as to how they walk, talk, think, respond, and live according to what they've learned and experienced in life and what they've come to believe or have made to be their philosophy in life to live by.

So, what's the point of this, then, for mentors and sponsors in prison ministry to take away?

Simple. The learning point is to consider HOW you are going to relate, communicate, and expect your *mentoree* or *sponsoree* to listen to you and respect you and what you say to benefit them if you've never experienced what they've lived (gone through) in life.

For example. How would you explain what a "good home" is or a "good mother/ father" is to a prisoner? For some prisoners – and I will use real inmate case examples but not use their real names – who were "junkies," "meth addicts," "crack heads," or "stoners" (those with substance abuse problems or drug dependency diseases of addiction), and grew up in homes devoid of adequate parenting because of a mother who was a "crack smoker" and alcoholic who was never at home, having an experience totally different from others who's mother were home. The prisoner you may be talking to may have very low self-esteem and low expectations or opinions of mothers and parenting compared to others. This one particular guy (prisoner) told me that a "good mother" to him was one that would just "stay off drugs." Another guy told me his mother "never cared" about him and just "stayed drunk" all the time. One guy told me his mom didn't even make dinner, just stayed out all night "screw 'in." One case was a guy from an affluent family who killed at old lady while driving DUI, said all his mother did was give him money but never showed him any love.

So, for mentorees or sponsorees, describing what a good *father* is, expect to hear often "one who comes around" or "one that isn't *high* and beats you" as typical answers from some who even had the opportunity to know their dad or "step-dad(s)." Another may say, "I don't know, I never knew my dad, just mom's boyfriends, but he didn't care about me."

"Home life" and "growing up" subjects for prisoners are very touchy. Many inmates have been abused, neglected, and traumatized to say the least in socially and economically deprived home environments. Relating is very important because knowing you care is high on an inmate's "expectation list" of your character attributes one needs to be considered effective.

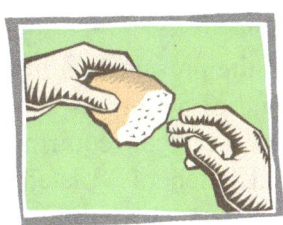

THE VOID CAN BE DEEP SO LISTEN.

To someone thinking of becoming a prison minster, sponsor, or mentor, who may have come from a home with a working mother or step-mother, that was a high school or college graduate, and/or a home with a working father or step-father who was a high school or college graduate that didn't do drugs or wasn't an alcoholic, physical abuser, or otherwise really bad "parent," conversing with an inmate – who often blames their parents for not raising them right – conversing with them and conveying what it means to change to "live right" can be a daunting challenge. The distrust brought on by upbringing of learning one's parents let them down can be a stigma of shame many feel and don't want to discuss or face. And for a volunteer mentor or sponsor – who has no formal counseling experience – this can be disastrous and turn the inmate inward rejecting any help you may be offering because you may really not be understanding what the inmate needs to hear from you or not hear from you. More so if there is a multicultural divide between you and the inmate based on race, religion, or other issue between you that may be a source of contention.

Just remember, a prisoner is in prison because their life is in 'distress" right now having broken a law(s) – and been "bagged and tagged." That – to some undisciplined young inmates – can be a joke, especially if they don't feel ashamed or the humiliation which is normally felt in most people of society who are law-abiding. Your job as a sponsor or mentor, as you'll see in the Part II of this book, is to not judge the person on what their past was, but rather to move them from the present to a future path that every day [present] is law-abiding and of acting responsible regardless of their past. This issue is absolutely critical requiring mentors and sponsors to be – above all – "good listeners." Listening and taking copious mental notes of a prisoner's current conditions and measure their past to see what voids can be filled in to complete the bridges missing so the inmate can stay on the path and not have to negotiate a broken road which led them to prison in the first place. It's this simple:

Most prisoners want to know what you are going to do.

And when they "feel you out" and see you care, their walls of distrust come down and fears melt because you are staying the course with them – all the way, not abandoning them as they have had people – including parents – do in the past. "Authority figures," including some loser teachers or "counselors," who just gave them the time of day in life and passed them up the chain until they were out of school with little knowledge of how the world really works and how to live and function viably with basic life skills accepted by society. And as the inmate hears and sees you sharing your successes – and failures – in life describing how you have overcome some of your hurdles – not theirs, they'll see you are trying to relate to them as best as possible and begin to believe your sincerity to help. Help they will want to know what you can do that is realistic and meaningful for them to now look at themselves to see what they can do to plan to reach some goals that they need to set to become productive responsible men and women and make the changes for release.

"PUPPY LOVE" DOESN'T WORK.

"Everyone in prison ministry says they want to help. But are they?

This leads us to the subject of broken promises – the *worst* thing you can do to an inmate due to being "let down" and lied to since arrest and incarceration by numerous "authority figures." From parents to police, lawyers, clergy, friends, counselors, prison guards – everyone seems to treat "convicts" with disdain and disrespect. And as a sponsor or mentor, failing to "come through" on a reasonable issue, or just providing "puppy dog" efforts, prisoners will smell out fake intentions in a heart beat and begin to reject or separate from those who don't have a genuine desire to seriously make a difference in helping mentor or sponsor a them.

Folks, let's talk *Realville* here for a minute. "Blowing smoke" at an inmate will diminish your credibility "rickety tick." Inmates can spot the "con job" when they see the "same-O same-O" such as:

- failing to show up for a scheduled mentorship appointment without calling the chaplain or writing a letter to reschedule
- failing to write a letter to the parole board
- failing to get you a Bible or order a book
- failing to respond to your letters
- failing to e-mail the halfway house to hold your room
- failing to pick you up the day you get out of prison
- not sending a Christmas or Birthday card
- Forgetting to spell your name correctly
- Promising to buy you some shoes but never do
- Not willing to write you a support letter for a job
- Getting the "silent treatment" (No response at all)

"Hash-tag" ministry or sponsorship and mentorship of inmates just doesn't cut it to have any meaningful effect for success for the inmate to develop (learn) or be able to be released and succeed in society. Just showing up and being a "time filler" or providing "drive-by" volunteerism- like token assistance and sitting with an inmate for 2 hours talking about minutia that doesn't accomplish any of Christ's goals or even secular goals to move a prisoner forward in life.

Simply put, having a "do nothing" absent or uncaring sponsor or mentor is like having no sponsor at all and is counter-productive to the needs of an inmate who has an expectation to be uplifted – especially by a "Christian prison ministry volunteer" -- given what Christ expects. Christ taught his disciples to do what they can, and that is all an inmate should expect from a legitimate prison ministry, not one that is conventicle in its establishment for purely ulterior motives related to "hash tag" religious service to be seen as do the *hoi polloi*.

Sadly, as many inmates have pointed out to me, and from my own eyes, many "Phony Holy Rollers" have come in to jump and sing and pontificate with promises of donating guitars, money, free this and free that, only to never be seen again at the prisons. Worse, some have even taken money from desperate prisoners searching for Christ, only to have their money and resources dwindle and the courses and/or books or halfway house reservations never materialize. (Pitiful – stealing from a prisoner who is already down on his or her luck. What a world! One guy lost $400 dollars for a halfway house bed reservation that was non-refundable.)

Puppy dog efforts, like visits with smiles and laughter, or letters and cards all about the weather, Jesus, Buda, Muhammad – whomever and whatever that "side skirt" what a prisoner really needs, isn't effective except for filling time. Many prisoners can quote the Torah, Bible, and Koran backwards and forwards. Prisoners know that not all sponsors are "superman" or "superwoman." After all, mentors and sponsors have lives of their own, families, jobs, etc. It's easy for an inmate – who has no one or nothing – to become narcissistic, understandably, because "the world" – in prison – focuses an inmate inward because he or she has had many things taken away from them.

So, sponsors and mentors must realize the scope of what is small to a free-world person may be a "gi-normous" deal to a prisoner who has nothing and is totally dependant on free-world people for survival and answers that have merit.

FACT: Tennessee prisoners coming into the prison system make 17¢ / hour for a prison wage. If them owe court costs and fines, ½ that is taken out. Sometimes for years. Typically then, that prisoner makes only $10.00 a month with which to buy soap, toothpaste, coffee, salt & pepper, etc. which is far below what he or she can possibly live on or even buy a TV or pair of sneakers. So, many – if they can't get outside free-world support – resort to human trafficking sex acts, selling drugs, robbing other inmates, stealing from the prison chow hall, etc. to "survive." If not for family, friends, sponsors and mentors, or some religious organizations helping out, many in prison would be forced to acts of desperation in an already de-humanizing environment of "dog-eat-dog" survival because the government does not provide for the basics – "as advertised" (what they claim their *corrections* budgets pay for to address the medical, food, and program needs of inmates as told to the public and legislature).

Don't be shocked, but I am telling you like it is after seeing it and living with it for over 25 years. Prisoners don't live in "country clubs." I've seen homosexual acts, rapes, gang-attempted murder, robbery, assault, kid-knapping, a hanging, theft, staff abuse of inmates, extortion of inmates, and other "crimes." One of the worst scenes of cruelty to an inmate I talk about, is when a male corrections sergeant gave an inmate a loss of 6 months good time for a *sausage biscuit* which denied the man his parole. The officer claimed to be Catholic – a Christian – yet deliberately targeted this obese 62-year old inmate sentenced for rape and wrote him up for the biscuit. A biscuit he got off his own tray at the chow hall he wanted to eat back at his cell. That man's father was 92 years old, waiting for him to get out.

Talk about a bitter experience! Loss of six (6) months for a sausage biscuit over a stupid rule that you can't take food out of the chow hall. Yet, no other officers write inmates up for it because it is so petty. Except this officer – who knew the "policies" and how to oppress "Cho Mos" (child molesters and rapists), even if they just pled guilty to avoid long sentences and kangaroo courts because their "public defender" lawyers were worthless. (I know of many instances of inmates being targeted after pleading guilty to "sex crimes" which most resulted in plea deals because of being threatened with long sentences even if they were innocent.)

Prison ministry, my friends, is not for "puppy-lovers" (people who just think you come in to prison like "Santa Claus" or a knight in shining armor going to save a prisoner from the bowels of sin and hell), but rather for the strong-hearted and sincere. Good intentions don't make you a good prison minister, sponsor or mentor. It's the

action that matters in the long run. What "benefits" you bring to the inmate, not what benefits you get out of it. Servant's and disciples "serve" and give away, not collect accolades and badges or boast of being "Chief prison minster." God knows WHO you are, and the inmates will smell you out too if you are acting self-righteous and not right of heart abound in Christ's love.

So, remember keep it real -- make a difference in a prisoner's life and uplift them to stand up on their feet again. Inmates want to believe mentors and sponsors are really going to help.

Can you do that?

That's why you have to realize WHO you are talking to and try to understand a prisoner's point of view because it isn't all puppy-love and bubble gum drops. The "broken system" doesn't and hasn't been working which is a void that needs to be filled by real people wanting to make a real difference. Inmates want to be successful on the streets so they don't have to come back.

Therefore, prison ministry heads -- when you meet-n-greet after a few times -- begin to identify the strengths and weaknesses of each of your volunteers and match them up with the needs of the inmates you may have. Find out what your ministry and its volunteers can and cannot do. Cooperate with other groups and churches if necessary to provide for your mentorees and sponsorees. Experienced sponsors and mentors are a great source of reliable information as to what works and what does not. That's the job: relate / connect, identify the needs, help set goals, fix what's broke, and show real Christian love by taking the position you care. Use common sense and research sources and prepare your ministers before they just assume going to help prisoners is a "piece of cake," because it's not. In part II, check out what ministry mentors and sponsors can do to be armed with not only the Armor of God, but also the love of Christ to give help to a man or woman depending on you to show them the way [out of prison.]

"Christ's values overrule personal values."

"Mind-building and visualization" (Seen) = Human
Things unseen but promised (Thought provoking) = Faith

MORE ON PRISON MINISTRY

In one of his early calls for prison reform, Pope Francis stressed looking to Jesus as our Strength is one of the most important first steps for a prisoner not to give up hope.
"... I want to share with you what I do have and what I love. It is Jesus Christ, the mercy of the Father. Jesus came to share the love that God has for us. For you, for each of you, and for me. It is a love that is powerful and real. It is a love that takes seriously the plight of those he loves. It is a love that heals, forgives, raises up, and shows concern. It is a love that draws near and restores dignity." [5]

Given his trip to Pennsylvania in 2017, the U.S. Bishops put it clearly: "Evangelization leads disciples to accept God's desire for us to go forth as missionary disciples wherever we are." [6]

The article focuses on evangelicals need to seek "spiritual resolutions" to many problems with missionary problems, especially dealing with an inactive or *passive* faith. Signs of an inactive Faith can be:
- Not going to church
- Not praying daily
- Not reading the Word of God
- Not participating in community assistance projects
- Not helping others in need

This is why it is important for missionaries or disciples who have accepted the call to stay on the road in the "driver's seat" for prisoners who have trouble just getting into "Jesus' car." When you live as a Missionary disciple, you are: encountering Jesus, accompanying others on a connecting journey, growing in the community of God and neighbors, and going forth making other missionary disciples.

Being a missionary disciple means having a "grown-up" faith. Many we encounter in prison do not have but a basic understanding of Christ, may not be baptized or be hearing the Word of God for the very first time seeing Christ by your actions.

At the end of the day, Christ calls us to bring *Him* to others. (Matthew 28:18-20) It's up to you to do that at all times, all places, and in all things, especially in prison. [7] The face – of Christ – people see may be yours.

Chapter 3

Breaking down the Fear of Prisons

ON DISAGREEMENT, TOLERANCE, NON-VIOLENCE

Today's culture of labels, especially in social media, one can be branded for anything at anytime, especially when people disagree or groups of people disagree even with a level of religious care for prisoners, the "outcasts" on the fringe of society.

"Tolerance implies disagreement," says David Platt, author of the book: *Counter Culture: Following Christ in an Anti-Christian Age*. [1] Pratt says:

> "As soon as someone today says that homosexual activity is wrong or sinful, he or she is immediately called "intolerant," "offensive," "bigoted," or "hateful," as we've seen, but we'll stick with "intolerant" for now. This supposed intolerance is often based upon that person's belief in the Bible. Simply because that belief is different from others' beliefs, it receives the "intolerance" label." (p.248)

Being labeled a *Christian*, today, can have any one of a dozen or so meanings attached to it either positive or negative; however, it is the context in which one is acting, perceived, or using the name in a figurative or adjective form where people can get mixed signals as to how to define or accept the label Christian. The same with being labeled a minister or sponsor; inmate, or ex-felon. People have many imaginative interpretations of what they perceive or define people with these words and their power to *shape* decision-making, especially when it comes to criminal and social justice reform programs or activities such as ministry work.

So what's the solution to re-defining labels and/or accepting or rejecting them? Easy:

"Look at lawbreakers not as "bad to be good" people,
but rather "sick to become healthy" or "incomplete
to become whole."

Platt says, "The solution is to patiently consider where each of us is coming from and why we have arrived at our respective conclusions. Based upon these considerations, use can then be free to contemplate how to treat one another with the greatest dignity in view of our differences." [2]

As we'll see later, being a prison minister, sponsor, or just wanting to help a person get back up on their own two feet and be a productive citizen again implies a level of care [stigma] attached to the one giving "aid and comfort to the enemy" as far right extremists pro-incarceration advocates would gladly label. Yet, as we are finding out today, this draconian way of thinking that has shaped the landscape of the criminal justice system over the last three decades since President Bill Clinton's administration's "Get Tough on Crime" bills which were passed in the 1990s, the pendulum has swung to the other side now for less incarceration. This is primarily due to increasing cries from groups such as *Families Against Mandatory Minimums* (FAMM), *Black Lives Matter* (BLM),

and others to include budgetary problems in states hit hard by the Covid pandemic, primarily in large urban city states whose need for funding priorities are being earmarked more for social justice rather than criminal justice now. The same for large cities expressing more outcry for police reform laws to *correct* lawbreakers rather than incarcerate them all under old laws now causing a backlash of racial and class disproportions that don't meet society's measure of fair treatment of its minority citizens' right to be treated justly and humanly nationwide.

That is why when deciding to be a prison minister or sponsor, one needs to be very honest in their intended mission (ministry) with the understanding that the *role* and the labels may not always be what some people or groups in society define them to be. Genuine prison ministers, as we shall see, have a very important duty to God, their ministry, and the individual they are serving (investing in) to "drag out" of the jail or prison, as my friend, Dean Hansford once said. The goal is for the re-entry of prisoners to be viable independent citizens in the community once again in spite of those that disapprove of such a role of the minster or sponsor and the inmate who may happen to be a sex offender, murderer, or crack/meth head. Being ready to accept the challenge of scorn and abuse of helping these "criminals" can be heart breaking, especially if trying to convince a group of people in a church or organization to invest funds for prison ministry objectives when people would rather see funds go to other projects or groups instead that are more to *their* -- man's – liking, not Christ's merciful and compassionate mindset.

As we'll see later in this book, not every prisoner is illiterate, a killer, mentally ill, or a "Cho Mo" (Child Molester). And if they were, they still need mercy and forgiveness as Christ demands they be shown such love as an example of how to be treated. That form of love fosters change and a future for these "least ones" provided them back in free society so they can live again as God intended them to.

FREEDOM TO WORSHIP, TO SPEAK, TO HELP PRISONERS

So, do you think you can stomach being a *politically-incorrect* Christian or secular sponsor or mentor?

To be called toxic, like the criminal you are wanting to help?

To be ridiculed, like Job in the Old Testament by your family? Friends? Co-workers? Employer? Or fellow church members scorning you from diverting church funds for "criminals" (prisoners)?

As we know, political correctness destroys free speech. One group over another cries "foul!" Or, as in today's society, "prejudiced" is no-longer viral enough, so "racist" or "hater" is substituted for more of a piercing blow. After all, who wants to be associated with a cause that helps sex offenders? Helps a white cop who shoots a Christian black man? A black woman who shoots her husband? A Muslim man who kills a Christian deacon? A gay pornographer? A neo-nazi skinhead who kills a Muslim? A Jew who rapes an atheist? An Asian woman on drugs who pimps her own daughter? Or anyone of any race color, creed, sexual orientation, city, state, barrio, vegan eater, animal rights lover, etc. of any one of a million diverse backgrounds or histories sent to prison or jail for a crime that's in one category or another?

Aren't all these people still *loved* by Jesus?

Do "bad apples" (sinners and criminals) ever go away?

Do you believe only *good* people attend churches, mosques, synagogues, or other places of worship and/or assembly?

Don't all human beings make mistakes?

Wouldn't you want a second, or a third, or a seventh chance after making a mistake?

That's why Christ's example must be FIRST for all, not just for a few in the world.

So, to get people re-path, the *divisive* thoughts and statements need to be replaced with *decisive* thoughts and statements converted into actions that move the current environment of complacency in helping society's "least ones" (i.e. those who suffer from illnesses out of their control and/or need social assistance to re-adjust their lives to be well again). Prisoners, the infirm, the mentally ill, those with disabilities, with illiteracy, the marginalized, widows, orphans, etc. are all in some need in one form or another in "plain view' of the public-at-large. The views, therefore, related to public polices or statements concerning race, affirmative action, feminism, gender bias, homosexuality, egalitarianism (equality rights), class diversification, multiculturalism, religious beliefs, etc. need to be re-examined for the priorities today with keeping focus on the transcending power of Christ's love for others to still be vibrant at the end of the day no matter what the tension is between differing beliefs people have.

Folks, let's face facts. CRIME – LIKE DISEASE – IS NO DISCRIMINATOR OF PERSONS. Neither are earthquakes, death, mental illness, ignorance, hunger, or sin – making mistakes. These things never go away. There is no "catch-all" phrase more thrown around than political correctness (PC) which just puts a negative label on anything another ideology has to be considered by one party. And if "fake news" is applied, and negative [spun] stereotyping attachments piled on make it worse, free speech is then eroded to 'anything goes' transcending liberal extremism to where one can't even stand up for one's own "philosophy" or core beliefs and values. "Free" – in America – no-longer means you can say anything or do anything you want without someone taking offense.

Why?

When does it end?

As Christians, we therefore should step up and take our faith to the streets and court houses just as Jesus went to the temple to denounce the errors of the Jewish temple priests who allowed the temple to be used as a "den of thieves" (Matt. 21: 13) rather than a sacred holy ground for worship. Just as the "PC Police" (often the media) demand satisfaction and blood from those the liberal counter culture deems "unclean," we have to stand up against the false views and perceptions ignorant people have that helping prisoners is a bad thing to do.

Common throughout this book, is the example of Christ helping the "least ones" we are to care for, specifically naming prisoners in that category. (Col. 4:6) Our "calling" to be prison ministers, sponsors, or accountability partners – brothers and sisters -- for prisoners didn't come with roaring cheers and rose pedal ticker-tape parades from a culture of friendly Utopian-like or an entirely mysterious epiphany. Rather – like most people, it came with a hesitation of caution knowing that consequences exist for wanting to "go against the grain" – the norm of society wanting to punish people, not shown them mercy. Mercy that we shall see, although noble, comes with a price as Jesus said would bring HATRED towards you just as it did Him. [3]

FACT: The Pew Research Center discovered that among adults they characterize as "consistently liberal," close to half (44%) have hidden, blocked, defriended, or stopped following someone on Facebook because they disagreed with the political content of that person's postings. Less than one-third of those who are "consistently conservative." (31%) censored people in the same manner. [4]

So why is all this about labels, political correctness, and the consequences of being a prison minister or sponsor so important?

Relevant to the success of the relationship a sponsor or mentor has with his mentoree or sponsoree is the understanding that in spite of opposition, the sponsor or mentor is going to endeavor to persevere regardless of the opposition, hurdles, and frustrations. More so, dealing with those 'free-world' people and/or groups that sabotage, disagree with, or are opposed to a mentor's or sponsor's efforts and actions that provide meaningful assistance to a prisoner.

Consider the article I had published in the *Tennessee Register* in 2015 to break the "fake news" about myths of prisoners and the excuses not to help those behind bars become well again as worthy citizens – and fellow human beings in God's eyes! (See: Figure 1.)

Bluntly, "helping prisoners" – the "lost drags on society" -- is not "cool," "chic," "hip," or politically correct or popular especially when there are victims involved most of the time. Notwithstanding the financial commitment it takes to fund helping prisoners, which is very unpopular with people and groups who have been propagandized into believing all the negative stereotyping about prisoners and what is invested is just wasted money.

This is the "Big Lie" Satan likes to use, as we'll discuss later in the book.

What do you think a voter in a church, mosque, synagogue, or secular civic group would want to spend money on first? Unless it's a specifically-funded group for providing [outreach] assistance to prisoners, the majority of people and groups do not think of prisoners first, second, or even third but mostly last. If at all, proposals to help prisoners fall in the "least of the least" (bottom) category to receive assistance. That's why we see all over the news for decades, state's failing their cities and communities by releasing many from prison without driver's licenses, financial assistance, or job skills to be self-sufficient / independent even to properly apply online for a job. And as programs for prisoners decline or are ineffective providing out-dated and un-usable information for prisoners to benefit from for job use, those needing re-education and a new start are again back to where they started from only to fall victim to a cycle of repeat offending. They know no alternatives in the prison system. That's why investment should be cried for by all communities to see that their loved ones get adequate meaningful job training, drivers licenses, and some means to make some money before they leave prison so they are not just dumped on the streets as most are who flatten their sentences.

Priority Funding for Religious and Social Groups.

How many churches chose to fund $10,000 church flower beds or street festivals of food and festivities rather than divert a small percent of that money to buy books, clothing, driver's licenses, or a month's rent for a few prisoners in their county, which --- for a 501(c)(3) – are "tax deductible" write-offs? How many civic groups claiming to be for re-entry prisoner's benefits won't lobby for prisoners to be furloughed to get jobs or be furloughed to work at a job outside the prison for a month or so before they leave? Why are some churches and civic groups claiming to be for **_all_** of "God's children," yet won't stand up to the insurance companies and take sex offenders at their halfway houses?

● Would Jesus turn away a sex offender? ●

Of course not.

That's why it's important – to make it abundantly clear that an awareness has to take place to raise the priority of caring for **_all_** prisoners to a higher level to heal these men and women with their social ailments just as first responders help the medically-in-need. So too must prisoners be given "priority treatment" for them to return to society – whole – as health care patients are returned home from hospitals.

This "view" – helping prisoners – is a NECESSARY GOOD IDEA, because when the prisoners are no-longer thinking to make criminal mistakes as a part of solving their situational problems, then they are not going to prison. Prison should be reserved for those who absolutely need to go there for social care to become healthy social citizens, not a "dumping ground" for the mentally ill and every conviction conceivable and sentence just to feed the Prison Industrial Complex of mass incarceration and mass numbers of incarceration centers to be built.

As you'll see in Part B, once you get past the fears and stereotypes of prisoners as flying "Chupacabras", demons, perverts, and going to rob you of your 401K life savings or identity, prisoners are just like other human beings with families, feelings, wants, needs, and warm hearts just begging for someone to give them a chance again with the respect they deserve to prove they are not "animals in the zoo" to be downcasted and left behind.

Figure 1. Article: "*Prison Visitors Extend Hope and Mercy to Those Behind Bars,*" M. F. Maraschiello, Tennessee Register (October, 2015).

2015 TENNESSEE REGISTER ARTICLE
BY MARASCHIELLO ON CHRISTIANS IN PRISON

16 TENNESSEE REGISTER — OCTOBER 9, 2015

Prison visitors extend hope and mercy to those behind bars

ANOTHER VIEW

MICHAEL F. MARASCHIELLO

Those of us in prison, the least ones as Christ called us, need your help. In fact, we need you.

Taking up our cross and following Christ has always been hard. Sure, you could make a little sacrifice and just donate $5 or $10 to a prison ministry program and clear your conscience. But is that really the unconditional love Jesus would be proud of? Is that the best you can do?

We all need to be people filled with the Holy Spirit who follow the example of Christ and be a doer like him, visiting the sick, the hungry, the poor, the prostitutes, the forgotten prisoners – society's least ones.

The Bible is loaded with examples of people reaching out to others with love, such as the Good Samaritan who went out of his way to help a wounded man who could not help himself. This is the example of the prison minister, an example of someone who is not afraid to assist a fellow human being in need.

Help for prisoners is not just bringing the word of God, but also bringing your physical presence to prisoners who have been lied to, given false hope, cheated and abused most of their time in prison, and many before coming to prison.

Maybe you've heard or seen the horror stories of prison life often depicted in movies and in television shows. There are plenty of myths out there about prisoners. Here are some common ones:

- All prisoners are out to swindle you, find out your credit card numbers, and take all your money. False.
- No matter what the prisoner says, it's always a lie. False.
- All prisoners are out to have a sexual relationship with their visitor. False.
- At a maximum security prison, all the prisoners at visitation are "maximum" – killers and rapists. False.
- When visiting prisoners, even minimum security, you have to sit in a room divided by Plexi-glass. False.

Do you see prisoners as garbage to be discarded? Or like sheep that went astray? Or like Jesus sees them, as brothers and sisters? As God sees us, as his children? All we can do in this world is take each day as it comes and use the assets, gifts and talents God has given us to make our lives and others' lives and society better so that our world can thrive.

Prison ministry can seem scary. Just like children taking their first steps at walking, those in prison ministry must learn to stand on their own two feet. They must have faith in their own ability. And to stand on one's own feet requires confidence and a strong belief not just in God, but in one's own realization that they sincerely want to help others – a prisoner. Especially a prisoner who sometimes is on the edge of losing hope and faith in themselves because of feeling let down by the system or forgotten by their family, or because they are dealing with a mental illness, a disability, or some other situation needing Christ's mercy shown from you.

No one is saying prisons are all filled with happy, changed prisoners singing "Kumbaya." In prison, a person must change from criminal ways of thinking to make it out alive. Sometimes it is like crawling through a sewer pipe that is miles long and takes years to get out of. Along the way, it is impossible not to get filthy, dirty, become disgusted, and lose faith.

I became a born-again Catholic in 1995 while in prison. I've tried to be a Christian example, showing God's love to other prisoners, many of whom are socially crippled or have never felt unconditional love that comes from simple caring. It can sometimes be unpleasant to be a Christian example in prison, and you can feel unsupported when you try to help other human beings.

But hope is alive with the help of Christ and our Christian brothers and sisters along the way, whether fellow prisoners or "free-world" Christians who want to make a difference in a prisoner's life.

To earn the privilege of a visit at "Visitation Gallery," to sit in lounge chairs with a non-threatening person, someone who is not a prison guard, is a miracle many in prison don't have the opportunity to experience. I know. I am from out-of-state and have no family in Tennessee to visit me.

That is why visiting prisoners is so important. The visits give prisoners like me the chance to talk and interact with a loving, kind and real "free-world" Christian person. It can also help the visitors experience real compassion. Even though you may not know it, I feel it and see it. That love gives us hope as human beings.

A shepherd goes out of his or her way to find a lost sheep. He does not forget about the lost sheep because the sheep has value. Jesus sees all of us as valuable, and not to be discarded, as the world would like all prisoners – the bad people – to be.

The best experience at visitation is the humility which makes us human and is at the core of being a Catholic. You are giving me hope, and I am helping you stay strong as a disciple – a shepherd whom your church has placed its trust in to carry out watching over the flock, all of the flock, even the sinner and fallen Christian like me as I pick my life back up to one day stand firm on my own, whether it be in here or in the free world. The end result is the same: Victory and salvation by helping guide the least sheep back into the flock.

I hope these words will encourage more support from people who really want to make a difference in another's life, especially a prisoner who fell down and needs your help getting back up. You may be the one who will no longer see prisoners in prison as garbage in a trash can, but the one who will save a life and help give them another chance like the Good Samaritan.

Michael F. Maraschiello is an honorably discharged Gulf War disabled veteran with a Bronze Star and Air Medal as a helicopter pilot who was convicted of murdering his estranged wife and is serving a life sentence at Riverbend Maximum Security Institution in Nashville. He receives regular visits from members of the prison ministry at Holy Family Church in Brentwood.

Columns and letters to the editor represent the views of authors alone. No viewpoint expressed necessarily reflects any position of the publisher, of any *Tennessee Register* staff member, or of the Diocese of Nashville.

The *Tennessee Register* is published by the Diocese of Nashville and welcomes your comments and opinions.

Please clearly mark letters to the editor and send to:

Tennessee Register
2800 McGavock Pike,
Nashville, TN 37214

You may fax your letters or comments to the *Register* at (615) 783-0285. By e-mail: tnregister@ dioceseofnashville.com.

Diversity Demographics.
Race, discrimination, sexual orientation, religion -- does it matter in sponsorship or mentorship of an inmate?

"Prognostication" is defined as a prediction of the future, or indication of what's to come in advance – a forecast. I'm not a mystic or wizard, or fortune teller, but I know something has to be done to start opening the eyes of people's hearts, especially those in political legislative power to begin to treat prisoners as human beings and not just as economic chattel or a set of numbers. Today's inmates need social assistance not "down time" idling and wasting away in prison, but rather to be gainfully employed as a goal after being given what they need to guide them back into society.

But what kind of society are they going to be returning to, and what training (preparation) must the criminal justice system *provide* or *incentivize* so sponsors and mentors can guide prisoners towards re-entering society equipped to function successfully since the current system is a failure?

FACT: FOR A PRISONER, THE <u>ONLY</u> *INCENTIVE* IS TO GET OUT AS SOON AS POSSIBLE – THAT MOTIVATES INMATES 'BIG TIME." YET, WHEN THE INMATE TOES THE LINE, FOLLOWS THE RULES, AND IS "DISCIPLINARY FREE" TO GET THAT TIME TO MEET THE PAROLE BOARD, THE INMATE IS DEVASTATED AND CRUSHED BY THE BOARD WHEN TOLD HE OR SHE IS "PUT OFF" (DENIED PAROLE) AND TOLD TO DO MORE TIME.

Why is that? They EARNED the "good time" to get qualified to get to the parole board with the hopes to be freed early – their incentive for acting right, getting classes, and changing to become disciplined. Yet, because of archaic draconian laws written by weak legislators who were socially beaten down by victims rights advocates years ago to lock inmates up forever, the system, now broken, is bulging at the budget and social seems because the legislatures threw out the one factor all human beings have – we're all human, including prisoners!

Sad how a polar bear at the zoo has more free space, FDA "PETA-approved" menu items and a swimming pool. Yet, the average prisoner locked up in a U. S. prison cell the size of a small public toilet has – if he or she is lucky – the room to their self or at minimum one other "cellee" (roommate) in the cell with them.

Where's the logic?

Wow! *Animals* (polar bears, dogs, etc.) have more square feet in the U. S. in dog kennels and zoos than do human beings. I thought that was only in the movies when I was a kid growing up in the late 60s and early 70s. Not until I went to Attica prison in 1978 with my father and saw for myself the actual size of cells did I begin to see I was ignorant of what *really* goes on in the day and life of a prisoner. My whole perspective began to change. And now after being on "both sides," I declare probably not one victims' rights advocate or legislator that supports such arcane "lock'em up" laws today has ever stepped foot in a prison cell except on some "field trip" to the prison which are all phony and staged for propaganda effect. (I know, we laugh at the visitor "groups" when they enter the prison "pod" (cell block) and the hotshot escort officer – who tries to be coy -- yells, "Visitors on the rock.")

Are we in some Hollywood movie, "On the rock?"

That's the type of stuff *reality TV* shows need to avoid and instead interview responsible mature prisoners, not the "wacky-doodles" that always seem to get interviewed for ratings on prime time shows to justify some questionable criminologist's statistical study, such as on how many prisoners make shanks or tunnel under cell bocks.

Give us (America) a break! Is that what taxpayer dollars are going for – fake studies to scare legislators into believing anything just to throw more money on lucrative contracts to build new prisons and buy more tasers for "security" instead of investing in social and re-entry programs that make a difference to get inmates employed quickly upon release and cut recidivism?

WHEN WILL PRISONERS BE CONSIDERED EQUALS?
(When does "Felonism" stop?)

An old military axiom is, "There are no atheists in the foxhole." As I learned also in the U. S. Army – on the battlefield – there were no *racists* in the foxhole either. Blacks, Whites, Hispanics, Asians, Mixed, etc. all seem to get along when there's a war and a common goal – an enemy – to all "instinctively" agree and focus on leaving gender, race, age, etc. all aside to stay alive. We came together for survival, primarily, for one or more reasons. Not just as Americans, but for self-preservation. A "force" no less, American, but everybody is different. (At least it was that way when I was in the Army 25 years ago, especially having taken an oath to serve as a volunteer.)

Fortunately today that same commonness can still be seen in sports teams throughout the country. There is no war but a link – a common goal -- for the "team" to win against the other team. A simple concept, perspective, philosophy. Everyone has a job on the team to work together following rules and joining up under one banner, per se, or name of the team for reasons (variables) each to his own. Some play on the team for the pride in themselves being the best. Some play for the money. Some play because they like to teach others to be better players. Some just like to win. Sportsmanship and unity for a common cause.

But one thing is for sure, and that is they have pride in an identity of a team, group, organization, race, neighborhood, family – the list goes on and on because that is human nature. Humans are social beings who interact and help each other to make the team work. As for mentors and sponsors of inmates, knowing *who*, not what, is sitting on the other side of the plexi-glass or looking through a pie-flap on a door, can be difficult some times if one is not able to relate to them in order to assess what they need. Assessment, to be less ignorant and to know inmates no matter their background are still human. Inmates want to be on a "winning team," hopefully with a sponsor or mentor that is a team player no matter their background either with the common goal to see the inmate become empowered and succeed.

SO, WHY IS THE CHANGING AMERICAN CULTURE AFFECTING PRISONERS IMPORTANT TO MINISTRY WORKERS, SPONSORS, AND MENTORS?

In his book, "Entrepreneurial Financing: Fundamentals of Financial Planning and Management for Small Business," University of Massachusetts professor M.J. Alhabeeb, presents today's changing diverse America from the aspect of the perspective of a business entrepreneur who must know human behavior in marketing for small business start-ups. He asserts from his research on *The Changing Target Market* that it is not fixed. Rather, it is always changing and evolving according to many variables and influences, such as the population shifts between Asians, Hispanics, African, and Whites. [5]

As populations increase, so does their purchasing power. [6] (See Figure 18.1)

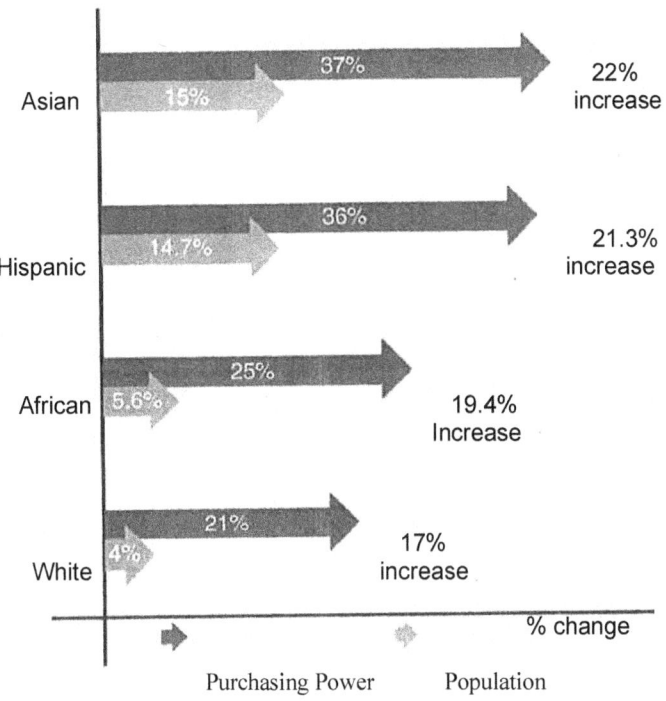

18.1 Purchasing Power and Population Size of Major Ethnic Groups

Another example of those changes is the change in age span and distribution. As the population generally ages, their needs and wants and consumption patterns change. [7] (See Figure 18.2)

To be "successful," small business professionals and leaders <u>always</u> have the latest knowledge about who their target customers, constituents, groups, etc. so they can make *intelligent* decisions. Changes in economic and demographic factors (variables) change and affect the way businesses respond to what the market place has to be prepared for just as *social changes* affect priorities for legislative actions. Factors such as family size and structure, number of married and single people, income, health status, and the like. All these changes would require proper changes in the marketing strategies.

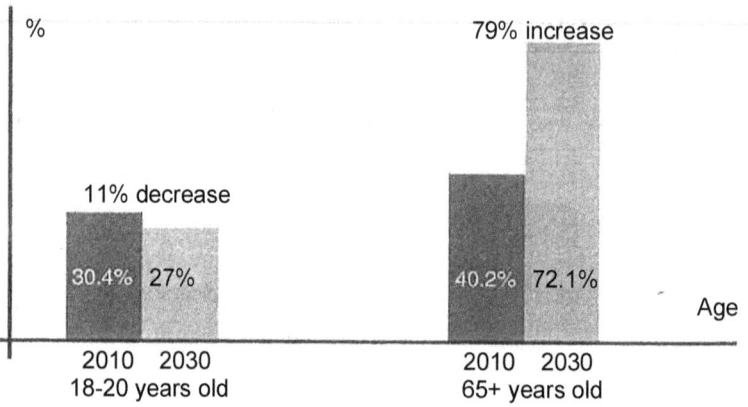

18.2 Rates of Change in Age Groups (the Young Versus the Old) Between 2010 and 2030

Nowhere is diversity in America more complained about race-in-hiring practices (discrimination) than in the labor market. The shift from white male as a single group dominating the workforce to a variety of groups based on gender, race, age, ethnic and national background, and other demographics is changing. [8] Diversifying the workforce is advantageous to all parties, not just blacks and whites, but the rapidly growing population of Hispanics in America. Multiculturalism affects employers, employees, government, prisons, and society as a whole. It is empowering, not only from the fairness and social justice perspective for diversity to be embraced by all, but also from a purely economic perspective as shifts in demographics of American culture having an impending impact on prisoners' needs when re-entering the workforce after long periods of inactivity and skill loss. [9] (See Figure 19.1)

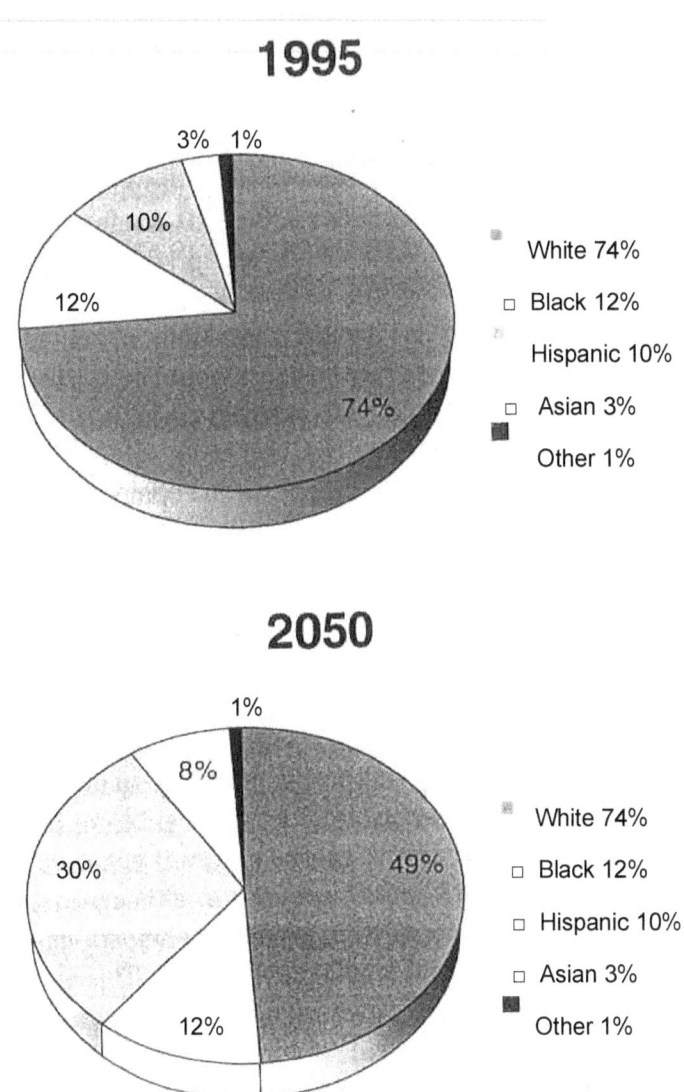

19.1 Workforce Ethnic Makeup Between 1995 and 2050

With diversity, the workforce gets to have more talents, skills, experiences, capabilities and more ways to think and do things, and that would be the major reason to increase productivity. [10]

In short, diversity has a direct correlation effect on increasing worker's empowerment, and as the empowerment represents fairness, freedom, responsibility, and authority to take actions and make decisions, it increases the standard of living conditions of those populations once considered a minority as now through meritocracy, they are recognized as an equal in the society as an inclusive part of the greater whole. This is why prisoners need to be looked at as human beings of the society who are sick [socially] and need help to recover, rather than as the "enemy" to be isolated and kept idle until they are so useless that when they are returned to society, they can't work. (That's called *"disempowerment."*) And if they can't work, they "can't produce," as Benjamin Franklin said about prisoners being in prison too long.

So, let's remember that people of all races and backgrounds CAN get along together. That takes will power, a common goal, attitude and perspective changes, paradigm shifts in philosophies of living, etc. – whatever. This is the time to act [on that] because it is popular, now, in America, for people finally making up their minds and voicing their frustrations that prisoners are to be treated as people too. A position all prison ministers must have if they want to be considered "real" (sincere) – effective.

Prisoner's lives matter.

When prisoners get out of prison, they want to work, provide for their families, pay taxes, and be a part of every community to "move on" and enjoy life again. They just need freedom and a chance. Locking them up until they are no longer productive makes no economic sense, especially when they are kept in prison past their readiness for release [date], which is why outdated parole board rules and long sentences don't work, but rather allowing release for "good time earned" dates – the _best_ incentive that changes a prisoner.

MASS INCARCERATION

Effective criminal control is: "People need to be assessed for their needs rather than treating them as walking threats," says Emily Bazelon in her book "*Charged.*" [11]

"Mounting costs are opening a window for deep reform. [12]

"More than 4.6 million live under court supervision, more than twice the total in jail or prison, another 800,000-plus are on parole. It's a net of social control."

A 2014 *Urban Institute* study found probation was revoked for African Americans more often than for whites. Judges and probation officers baulked to explain why, blaming arrest procedures, sentencing and others for locking up parole violators for petty parole violations not breaking the law."

"A 2016 *New York Times* investigation found "fees" for inmates classes were charged to the state for as high as $5,000 per student per class as "offender – funded" justice with private psychological services or "re-education" corrections services billing the state millions of dollars on obsolete classes and/or classes that half or all the inmate students don't show up. Often these classes are meaningless, serve no value, and don't get any credit towards parole.

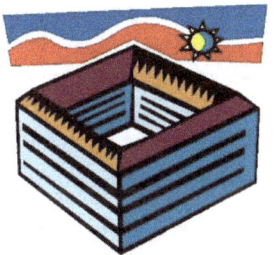

In 2017, a company called Providence Community Corrections agreed to pay total damages of $14 million to about 29,000 people in Tennessee who'd been jailed or threatened with jail because the parolees and probationers couldn't pay their probation or parole fees. Providence, thus went out of business because they were committing outright extortion (See *Alec Karakatsanis, et. al. v. Harris County* (Tenn. 2017) [13]

U.S. Crime Statistics

America's current prison population is:

- 2.3 million nationwide (State & Federal) [1]
- 175,000 in Federal prisons [1]
- 1.3 million in State prisons [1]
- 620,000 prisoners released every year [2]
- 37% RETURN TO PRISON IN 3 YEARS [2]
- Virginia & S. Carolina have the lowest recidivism rates (23%) [2]
- Est. 1 million currently sit in jail awaiting trial [2]
- Total incarcerated & Detention Centers: 4 million (+/-) [2]
- 152 bills were passed in 2019 to block re-entry assistance for Prisoners [2]

---

[1] U.S. Bureau of Prisons (BOP) – reported in article: Could Coronavirus cause a national prison lockdown? by U.S. News (2020)

[2] The Crime Report (Your Criminal Justice Network), Emily Mooney (2020)

WHY EX-FELONS MAKE GOOD HIRES

To make ex-felons released from prison attractive for employers to consider hiring, is the Work Opportunity Tax Credit (WOTC) program and the Federal Bonding Program. These programs give employers the financial incentives to hire ex-felons and get a rebate credit on their taxes. Sponsors and mentors should look into these programs to further give the inmate(s) sponsored hope for a future with a job being hired by some employers. Most importantly, re-entry ex-felons should know these programs and mention them in their job interviews because some employers don't know about them and could use the money the government will credit them.

Work Opportunity Tax Credit (WOTC)

WHAT IS THE WORK OPPORTUNITY TAX CREDIT?

The Work Opportunity Tax Credit (WOTC), authorized by the Small Business Job Protection Act of 1996 (P. L. 104-188), is a federal tax credit that encourages employers to hire eight targeted groups of job seekers by reducing employers' federal income tax liability by as much as $2,400 per qualified new worker; $750, if working 120 hours or $1,200, if working 400 hours or more, per qualified summer youth.

In This Section

- Welfare-to-Work Tax Credit (WtW)
- WOTC Updates
- Work Opportunity Tax Credit (WOTC)

The WOTC is one tool in a diverse toolbox of flexible strategies designed to help move people from welfare to work and gain on-the-job experience. It joins other education and job training initiatives and targeted tax credits, that help American workers

prepare for good jobs; ease the transition from job to job; and create high performance workplaces.

UPDATE: On October 4, 2004, the President signed into law the *Working Families Tax-Relief Act of 2004 (P. L. 108-311)*. This legislation extends the WOTC program and the WtW tax credits, without change, for a two-year period through December 31, 2005. The reauthorization is retroactive to December 31, 2003 and applies to new hires that begin work for an employer on or after December 31, 2003 and before January 1, 2006.

WHAT NEW HIRES CAN QUALIFY EMPLOYERS FOR WOTC?

- WOTC applies only to new employees hired on or after December 31, 2003, and before January 1, 2006
- The new employee must belong to one of eight target groups:

    - A member of a family that is receiving or recently received Temporary Assistance to Needy Families (TANF) or Aid to Families with Dependent Children (AFDC),
    - An 18-24 year old member of a family that is receiving or recently received Food Stamps,
    - An 18-24 year old resident of one of the Federally designated Empowerment Zones (EZs), Enterprise Communities (ECs), or Renewal Communities (RCs),
    Note: All Round I Enterprise Communities (ECs) including Enhanced Enterprise Communities expired on December 31, 2004. Round II ECs are still in existence as are all the EZs.
    - A 16-17 year old EZ/EC or RC resident hired between May 1 and September 15 as a Summer Youth Employee,
    - A veteran who is a member of a family that is receiving or recently received Food Stamps,
    - A disabled person who completed or is completing rehabilitative services from a State or the U.S. Department of Veterans Affairs,
    - An ex-felon who is a member of a low income family,
    - A recipient of Supplemental Security Income (SSI) benefits, and/or

- **UPDATE: New York Liberty Zone Business Employee (NYLZBE)** - This target group was not reauthorized. the WOTCs for NYLZBE hires are available only for 2002 and 2003.

- All new adult employees must work a minimum of 120 or 400 hours; Summer Youth must work at least 90 days, between May 1 and September 15 before the employer is eligible to claim the tax credit.

HOW CAN EMPLOYERS PARTICIPATE IN THE WOTC?

To receive certification that a new employee qualifies the employer for this tax credit, the employer must:

- Complete the one page IRS Form 8850 by the day the job offer is made.

- Complete either the one page ETA Form 9061 or Form 9062

    - If the new employee has already been conditionally certified as belonging to a WOTC target group, complete the bottom part of ETA Form 9062 (and sign and date it), that he or she has been given by a State Employment Security Agency or participating agency.
    - If the new employee has not been conditionally certified, the employer and/or the new employee must fill out and complete, sign and date ETA Form 9061
- Mail the signed IRS and ETA forms to the employer's State Workforce Agency. The IRS form must be mailed within 21 days of the employee's employment-start date.

To get IRS Form 8850, the Work Opportunity and Welfare-to-Work Tax Credits Pre-Screening Notice and Certification Request, and instructions, download from http://www.irs.ustreas.gov/ or call 1-800-829-1040.

You can get ETA Form 9061, the WOTC "Individual Characteristics Form," a brochure, and directories of the State and Regional Coordinators by visiting www.uses.doleta.gov/tax.asp

FOR MORE INFORMATION
Call or visit your local public State Workforce Agency WOTC Coordinator (use the above mentioned State Directory). Call the U.S. Department of Labor Regional WOTC Coordinator nearest you (use the above mentioned Regional Directory). Call the Internal Revenue Service (IRS) at 202-622-6080

For information about EZ/EC/RC locations, visit their web site at http://www.hud.gov/offices/cpd/economicdevelopment/programs/rc/index.cfm or call 1-800-998-9999.

Sample of things Ministers Can Do they don't Tell You.

"Things Ministers Can Do That the Prison System Didn't Tell You"
By M.F. Maraschiello 2018

Like most government bureaucracies, they don't always let you hear, read, or see the "fine print" or don't want to give their secrets for one reason or another, usually so an employee doesn't have to do a lot of work, or serve the public or customer. The same applies to those family members, ministers, or agents (i.e. lawyers, visitors, etc.) who go to prison to provide the prisoner with some sort of assistance, service, or other action requiring involvement. (NOTE: Not every prison, government agency, courthouse, etc. is sympathetic to those who <u>assist</u> prisoners because of the previously discussed reasons for not helping I/Ms.)

What ASSISTANCE Can Prisoners Get?

It isn't surprising that the majority of Americans don't know that prisoners are not allowed – in some states – video streaming and easy-access phone calls but rather <u>only</u> restricted mail in their state's prison system. Propaganda fed to the media, lawmakers, law enforcement, naïve churches and organizations, or just plain fearful people to include family members don't bother to investigate what a prisoner is allowed to receive by way of *free-world* assistance as well. The prison administration, the so-called "seasoned veteran" minister – who sometimes doesn't know the rules and policies themselves, police and court officers, deputies, etc. all have their own bias toward what they believe a prisoner's living conditions, assistance, or what an I/M should be allowed to have. This can lead to inaccuracies about what support or assistance an I/M can get.

GOLDEN RULE: WHEN IN DOUBT, CALL THE PRISON CHAPLAIN.

EXAMPLES OF INACCURACIES (FALSEHOODS).

1. **I/Ms Can't Receive Letters**. FALSE. Some church ministers were told by prison administration underlings they can't write letters to I/Ms because it is "crossing the line" between minister and "friend," and if they write a letter, they will be barred from coming into the prison. This is false. No where in policy does it say that. Yet, there are ministers who refuse to check out the truth, and thus their church services at the prison are low in numbers when the I/Ms find out the minister doesn't care to investigate this falsehood. Why is this important? Not all I/Ms can call on the phone to a church they wish to be a member of or need assistance from. And if the church volunteer (i.e. prison minster) refuses to send letters, then that sends the message to the I/M(s) that the volunteer really doesn't care, and therefore, the minister and their church is perceived to be insincere. The only time writing letters is a problem is when they turn into "love letters," or some other type of relationship other than for spiritual or rehabilitative (sponsorship / mentorship) program-approved motives. When this happens, the minister must *choose* what status they want to be. Otherwise, they will be barred from the chapel.

2. **Ministers can't send money to I/Ms, period.** FALSE. However, this only applies to money coming *directly* from the minister who comes to the prison at the chapel for general services. The minister's church can send money to any I/M for assistance via J-PAY. Individual sponsors and mentors can send J-PAYS, put money on an I/M's phone account, purchase food boxes or *Union Supply Co.* boxes, even purchase things like birth certificates and such. (NOTE. Non-sponsors and non-mentors must use their church general fund.)

3. **Ministers can't take phone calls from I/Ms.** FALSE. I/Ms look to ministers as *bridges* to a strong faith and to be empowered with good advice from their church support group of which the minister is at the leading edge in prison ministry. Communication is critical for factors related to spiritual guidance, suicide prevention, program substance-abuse prevention, family situation (i.e. death in

family), rehabilitation, or any related situation that a minister would like to help with.

4. **Ministers can't conduct events at the prison**. FALSE. Churches can't have Bingo Night and motorcycle rodeos, but they can ask for permission to conduct church baptisms, marriages, feasts, retreats, banquets, book read-in, or seminars at the prison. These are acceptable spiritual-related traditions, customs, or practices that encourage participation and spiritual growth.

Anyone can send a prisoners a Union Supply Company Quarterly Holiday Gift Box.

5. **Ministers can't affect external events for I/Ms**. FALSE. With approval from the prison chaplain and warden, churches assisted by their prison ministry volunteers can do book drives, collect donations for indigents (e.g. money for I/M's who don't have sneakers, eye glasses, or stamps, etc.), contribute to retreats and banquets with tableware, cups, food, writing materials, musical equipment, etc. which can assist prisoners.

6. **Ministers can't put money onto an I/M's phone account.** FALSE. Anyone can put money onto an I/M's phone account whether directly or indirectly. Going to www.globaltel.com and putting money onto an I/M's account can be done. However, a minister is not to send money directly to an I/M J-PAY Trust Fund Account unless they are the approved sponsor or mentor. FACT: How can you communicate with your mentor or sponsor on issues like coordinating for increased spiritual needs, prepare for the parole board, affect re-entry issues (e.g. half-way house), seminary college correspondence course issues, family issues (i.e. your mentor is a conduit for relations with your family), and other aspects unless you can talk to them?

7. **J-PAYS are Identity-Theft Traps**. FALSE. The J-PAY is the *approved secure* way of a Tennessee I/M receiving money to be put onto an I/M's Inmate Trust Fund on-line electronically, or by money order in the mail. **(SEE J-PAY FORM)** No stories of identity-theft – to date – have been noticed to prisoners by the Department of Correction which has been using the J-PAY System, now, for over five (5) years.

8. **Ministers can't send Christian Bibles, Qurans, or other religious books to I/Ms**. FALSE. However, you *can't* just mail a book to an I/M. The book(s) must come from a VENDOR (i.e. bookstore, bookseller, AMAZON, etc.) by policy. Soft-back covers are sure to arrive and make it to the I/M; however, if the book has a *hardback* cover, it may require the cover – with permission from the I/M – to be removed because, per policy, hard-covers are not allowed.

YOU CAN MAKE THE DIFFERENCE!
(The Takeaway)

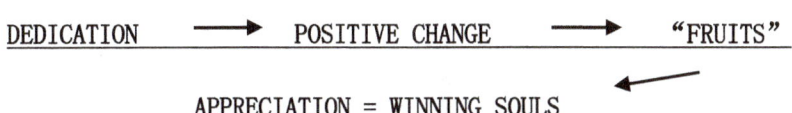

DEDICATION ⟶ POSITIVE CHANGE ⟶ "FRUITS"

APPRECIATION = WINNING SOULS

"Talk" is cheap. It is what you do for prisoners – the "outcasts of society" no one cares about – that opens up their minds to be receptive to faith, especially by *saying* what you mean and *meaning* what you say. Telling a prisoner about God is no good if it is not backed-up with deeds. Prisoners SEE with their eyes more because of the mistreatment they have suffered and the erosion of hope. Showing them love, compassion, and mercy is what it's all about. And when a prisoner sees it, he or she *feels* it and believes it, and they become humbled and appreciative for what you have done. Serving others who have been pushed down by helping them get back up is a noble cause, especially standing up to those who don't believe in what you are trying to achieve. Showing you care is the KEY to an I/M's heart for effective meaningful ministries to produce the fruits God wants to make a difference in the life prisoners whom God values even though the world does not.

Article from *The Maximum Times* 2018 on "Stereotyping"

"DEFEATING *NEGATIVE* CHARACTER EVIDENCE, ASSERTIONS, AND LABELS IN COURT"
By M. F. Maraschiello (RMSI Legal Aide)

SCENARIO: You are in court. The prosecutor or opposition lawyer (i.e. in a civil case) cross-examines you and says, "And Mr. X not only did it, but he *must* have – his father was / in prison. Like father, like son (or daughter)."

Have you found yourself in this situation: Being made to look bad or guilty with a *false* label or misrepresentation?

First, "Character Evidence [1]," like all evidence, has to be "relevant" and meet certain criteria to be admissible. (SEE *Tennessee Rules of Evidence*: Rule 401. Relevancy, and Rule 404. Character Evidence Not Admissible to Prove Conduct; Exceptions; Other Crimes; Rule 608.

Evidence of Character and Conduct of Witness) ALSO SEE: *Tennessee Rules of Court.* Rule 16 Discovery and Inspection, or in some instances, Rule12.2 Insanity Defense or Expert Testimony of Defendant's Mental State and Discovery of Evidence in Pretrial Competency Hearings. In Federal Court, SEE: *Federal Rules of Evidence*: Rule 402. General Admissibility of Relevant Evidence, Rule 404. Character Evidence; Crimes or Other Acts, Rule 405. Methods of Proving Character, Rule 609. Impeachment by Evidence of a Criminal Conviction). "Character evidence is admissible as substantive evidence when character is in issue." (**Blake v. Cich,** D.C. Minn.1978, 79 F.R.D. 398)

These rules, above, won't all be discussed today, but rather how to deal with fighting the falsehoods or misrepresentations used against you by using the number one weapon you have – **the truth**. That is, pointing out lies, misrepresentations, and/or perceived negatives – with the truth, and making them into positives you can use to support your cause.

GOING INTO COURT. The best way to begin is by testifying with confidence and being relaxed. Just because a family member is in prison doesn't make you a criminal or guilty. That person is in prison for the mistakes *they* made, not you. Nor does it mean you are likely a criminal by relation. There has to be evidence – a "history," along with other aspects such as motive, culpability, means, etc., all factors to be weighed, not just who is in your family or association.

THE ATTACK AND DEFENSE The prosecutor or opposition attorney has one goal in court: to make you look bad so they can win. And swaying the court (judge or jury) is their prime objective. And one way to do that is to attack your character and show them you are not innocent (in a criminal case) or "Mr. or Mrs. Good Parent" (i.e. in a custody battle) by impeaching [2] you. Any lawyer is allowed by the rules of court to make an *inference* from the evidence in the record. Further, they can bring up anything they believe is *material* to the case and would help the *trier of facts* (judge or jury) decide the case.

---

[1] CHARACTER EVIDENCE: any evidence of a person's regular behavior, habits, etc. (***Black's*** Law Dictionary., 10th Edition)

[2] IMPEACHMENT: the act of discrediting a witness's testimony with his or her untruthful actions, prior convictions, prior inconsistent statements, or the like. (***Black's***)

That means be prepared for assertions, false allegations, and plain old lies to start coming at you. The probative value of any evidence to help the *trier of facts* go one way or another, can sometimes stick to you, or blow-up in the prosecutor's or opposition attorney's face if they try to cast a shadow on you that seems too far-fetched to be believed. However, if you don't "clean up" or correct their accusation, claim, or assertion about your character, the silence you render is just another point the prosecutor can make you didn't deny or admit to their description of your character. (SEE U.S. v. Harris, C.A.D.C. 2007, 491 F.3d 440, 377 U.S.App.D.C. 49, certiorari denied 128 S.Ct. 1106, 552 U.S. 1157, 169 L.Ed.2d 837. Prejudice outweighing probative value, character of accused. "Even if the district court had believed that defendant was seeking to air relevant demeanor and circumstantial evidence rather than prohibited forms of character evidence, the court was nonetheless free to find the evidence, which cast defendant in the sympathetic light of a dedicated family man who spent the evening before his alleged participation in drug dealing talking with his mother, playing with his son, and caring for his girlfriend, excessively prejudicial.")

FACT: Without evidence, a statement is just an assertion, and nothing to back it up, unless there is some proof. Often, because of silence (called *acquiescence)*, any statement left un-answered or not cleared up goes to the court (judge or jury) to make an "inference" as if the statement were true.

Ergo, leaving inferences to the court is just gambling they will think the same way you do. WRONG!! Never assume a question un-answered will be guessed correctly by a judge or jury. Too many prejudices and biases inhabit people's minds. For example, a juror could hate animal abuse or spousal abuse. And if the prosecutor makes the statement you are one of those, and you or your lawyer does not object and/or respond to the negative, or show proof that the allegation is false, then you leave the juror – or jurors – believing it to be true that you are abusive. Ergo, rebutting the lies and misrepresentations is paramount to a successful and just outcome of your legal matter. A courtroom filled with one-sided lies and void of the truth is most likely to end in a negative result for you, especially to be labeled as a vicious dog-eating killer, super child abuser, or menace to society --- all drawn from the prosecutor's or opposition attorney's inferences because you are silent, and / or some other person comes in with some hearsay [describing your character] that doesn't even make sense.

STRATEGY: TAKE THE WIND OUT OF THE SAILS Like the sails on a ship, it goes no where without wind. So, if you haven't mentioned some of your character evidence that needs to be addressed, and the prosecutor or opposition attorney now struts in front of you, pointing his or her finger, and accuses you of a falsehood or points out something that describes you that needs clearing up, don't panic – **clear it up!!**

Make a negative into a positive, especially if they bring up a past criminal record, or try to tell you that because a family member is in prison, you are a criminal or do that (behavior) too. FIRST, tell the court the truth you have a family member in prison, but how that has no bearing on the case. Do some fighting back of your own and tell how that person has cleaned up their life in prison, and is doing great and ready to be released as a law-abiding citizen you are proud of. **So what they are in prison. MILLIONS** of families have family members in prison because they made mistakes. In fact, by them being prison, they reinforce you to be a better citizen by their example. Whatever negative that is thrown at you, turn it around and make it into a positive for you to use. Not leaving your family member to rot in prison because you communicate with them and support them, shows you are capable of dealing with adverse situations and in control of your life having a positive impact in relationships with people (the incarcerated family member) who needs help which, apparently, you are demonstrating and explaining [your good character], now, in court, that is being evaluated by the judge and/or jury.

So, welcome explaining the truth; it can set you free because it is a strength that tumbles the lies and/or misrepresentations thrown at you the prosecutor or opposition attorney wants you to own.

CATCH PHRASES & CLICHÉS IN THE CLOSING ARGUMENT You've probably heard these on TV shows when the prosecutor confronts a witness as says, "IF THE GLOVE DOESN'T FIT, YOU MUST ACQUIT," or "Birds of a feather flock together," or "The apple doesn't fall far from the tree," and other snarky phrases the prosecutor or opposition likes to use to intimidate the witness or accused and give the jury the belief that he or she has "exposed" or has "found out" the witnesses or accused's *true* character, participation, guilt or whatever. Again, association or knowledge doesn't prove a thing without substantive evidence, whether tangible, witness, real, documentation, or other. So, again, defend yourself with the truth and de-bunk these snarky phrases. Otherwise, as with silence, the jury or judge can infer there is some truth to them. Being labeled a "criminal" or "propensity to commit a crime" can be damaging, especially if there is a history of some other behavior to support the statements. Even a first-time offender can be accused of "possibly committing past crimes they got away with" as a way the prosecutor or opposition attorney may try to sway the jury to see their story sticks about you. And remember, in the closing argument, whatever is in the RECORD – including assertions and accusations you didn't clear up – the prosecutor or opposition lawyer can bring up and say, "See, he didn't even respond when I said he's a chip off his old man's block – criminal minded, with a propensity to commit bodily harm."

DON'T FALL FOR THE TRAPS Remember, the prosecutor or opposition lawyer want to make you look bad – guilty, so they win. DON'T make it easy for them. Don't explode in the courtroom when accused of something totally false or outrageous. Fight back! Do your homework; be prepared. Have AFFIDAVITS of character from your employer, how responsible you are, letters from family, neighbors, medical and psychological records, even education and military records to show the court. These things ARE RELEVANT MATERIAL forms of evidence, whether documentation or direct (verbal) testimony. You have a RIGHT to be adjudged with the truth and sentenced with **ACCURATE INFORMATION**. (SEE: ***U.S. vs. ADAMS***, October 11, 2017, 873 F.3d 512, U.S.C.A., Sixth Circuit.) Hopefully, if you have a good lawyer, they will object in time and you won't have to be under pressure. But if they don't clear things up, it is up to you NOT to leave the jury or judge guessing. If you are asked a trick question or one that is inappropriate, **ask** that it be repeated.

TIP for Court. By law, you can't be made to answer a question you don't understand. So, if the prosecutor or opposition attorney is trying to be slick, pause. And if you lawyer hasn't asked that the question be re-phrased, you ask the judge for the question to be re-phrased. Usually, this makes the prosecutor or attorney asking the question look bad because he or she is trying to be "slick," and judges and jurors don't like an over-zealous lawyer going overboard or being abusive.

BOTTOM LINE: DON'T WEAR A LABEL THAT DOESN'T FIT
No matter on paper or in the court room, a lie is a lie. And leaving it un-contested may defeat your cause because it gives your opponent a dart to throw at you. Remaining silent can be just as equally damaging because the lie becomes true if not challenged. Your "version" (story) and your facts and evidence are *critical* to any case. The court can only decide with what they've been shown. And leaving them to infer from incomplete or false and misleading information is a dangerous gamble, especially if the stakes are high with a life involved. (i.e. child custody or incarceration)

So remember, make sure the evidence fits, and clear up any bogus information. Take perceived negatives and turn them into positives. Labels like "ex-con" and "child abuser" are damaging. But over time, they lose their wind because of your good character you now present yourself as TODAY, not in the past.

Mike Maraschiello is a Legal Aide with some formal legal training since 1981, and has been In prison for over 23 years. He is currently in post-conviction court seeking relief.

Article from *The Maximum Times* 2018 on Separation

FIGHTING THE STIGMA OF A PARENT BEHIND BARS
("Parents in Prison are Family Too") by: M. F. Maraschiello 2018

POINT: Most Parent-Child relationships are important, especially when in the *best interest* of a child. Parents behind bars should not be automatically ruled out, and not assumed to be the cause of a child's unsuccessful life. In today's America more than ever, tens of thousands of parents -- both men and women -- are serving time behind bars. Whether their incarceration is for a major or minor crime, they made a mistake. And the *real* victims end up being the children of parents behind bars.

SEPARATION *KILLS* FAMILIES

Separated from one or more parents, whether it be divorce, death, or some other cause, the children of incarcerated parents carry an additional *stigma* of knowing their parent, or parents, have been labeled by society as *criminals* – bad. Labels such as: "No good,' "evil," "loser," "bum," "jerk," "creep," and many other demonizing names begin to fall on the ears of the children to affect them mentally, physically, and emotionally. But most of all, damage is done to the child's heart as the separation and lack of communication CUT the relationship between parent and child which slowly weakens the bond of love that previously existed. Worse, people who surround the child and try to insulate them from "being harmed" -- by the often FALSE notion that the incarcerated parent is BAD for the child -- are always telling the child what **their** opinion is of the child's parent, and not letting the children decide for themselves. Often, the prejudice leads to the child being taught to hate, rather than understand and recover.

Ergo, separated from their parent(s), the child is isolated and made to feel bad or ashamed of their parent, and thus persuaded to "let them go" and trust in the new set of "parents" or parent – often another family member -- who many times is found not as loving or involved as the child's biological parent(s) now behind bars. After all, who wants to take care of a child "dumped" on them out of the blue?

SO WHAT MY PARENT GOT LOCKED UP!

Often on the advice of child advocates, psychologists, and other social service workers who treat each child as just another *number* in the system, instead of the child having learned the true aspects from their incarcerated parent, the child is given a *sanitized* or obligatory explanation that justifies the reasons WHY the child should no-longer trust their incarcerated parent(s). These so-called *official sources* are often intimidating and unsympathetic to the bond the child had with their parent, and often at the request of the new "caregivers (parents)," insist that all ties be cut with the parent in prison so that they have **total control** of the child, especially when custody rights are their objective. Thus, the child becomes a *pawn* for various things such as revenge, monetary gain, and/ or victim utilization, pitting the children against their incarcerated parent for abuse. After all, the parent must not have loved their child, otherwise they would not have gone to prison. Hence, the blame for every mistake, now, becomes the incarcerated parent of the child - an *easy* target. A convenient excuse for everything, to include how the child is raised without proper discipline, proper love, and appropriate examples of how to become a mature "loving" adult.

So, who is doing *real* child abuse now?

MY PARENT CAN'T BE THAT BAD – THEIR FAMILY.

It is only natural that as a child grows older and begins to ask questions and seek answers, often they will contact their parent in prison or later, to understand what happened that caused the separation. An alarming number of these children find out much of what they were led to believe about their incarcerated parent was actually *false* information justified under the *cliché* "for their own protection." Many of the incarcerated parents ask their kids, "Protection, from what?"

FACT: Tens of thousands of children each year in the United States visit one or more parent behind bars. Parents and family members every day get to phone call and visit their children to keep their love and family intact with support. **FAMILY** has always been the center of life – the apex of society to function. Parents, even in prison, are an essential healthy component to a young child's success and development. Not only is there a physical link, but the social, mental, and emotional ties that make-up a child's future identity is linked to *parental guidance*.

FACT: Eventually, someone is going to bring up the fact you have or had a parent in prison. An *informed* and involved child who understands their parent made a mistake and is now making changes to be a better adult, gives the child *more* self-esteem than leaving the child to believe they are the product of a looser, a bad person -- a criminal.

IT'S OKAY - I HAVE A PARENT IN PRISON TOO.

There is no act of love greater than to show mercy. Forgiving one's parent for making a mistake isn't always easy, especially if years of lies have been told about them being the **"Boogie Man."** Love – and time – can overcome fears and anxieties, especially when the TRUTH is told. Most kids want to hear their parent's apology for going to prison; they want to know it wasn't because of them (the child / children.) The child most of all wants to know that their parent loves them, and wants to communicate and be with them – *normal* stuff, that is okay.

How often is it that people are stuck on some story that turns out to be false? Some kids live their life believing falsehoods and never know the truth about their parent(s). The old example of stealing a loaf of bread to feed the family, versus stealing the loaf for profit truly explains *intent*. And for a child, knowing their parent made a mistake and CHANGED shows the child the parent wants to do right. Better, talking with the child at visitation not only creates a bond with the child, but shows the child that the parent wants the child in his or her life, and to keep that relationship alive to benefit the child. Thus, the child benefits with more self-esteem knowing their parent is on their side with support, and involved in the child's life to fit in society as normal as other children do.

Prison Ministry In Covid America

Assault on Ministers, Mentors, & Sponsors

WHO DOESN'T WANT YOU TO HELP PRISONERS?
By M F. Maraschiello 2018

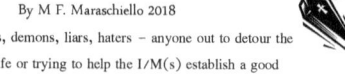

Why Satan and his minions, of course! Atheists, witches, demons, liars, haters – anyone out to detour the minister, mentor, or sponsor from doing good in an I/M's life or trying to help the I/M(s) establish a good relationship with God for hope of reclamation and regeneration back into society.

SIGNS OF SATAN'S EFFORTS TO DETOUR MINISTERS

01. Ignorant people or the prison, government, or court system(s) who ridicule you for your religion for helping I/Ms.
02. Stereotypes, movies, fake news, lies, ignorance, and other fear-causing falsehoods about I/Ms and that prison ministry volunteerism doesn't work, and all ministers are just wasting their time, money, and efforts.
03. Policies, procedures, laws rules, myths, etc. that dissuade YOU from going to or getting into the prison to help I/Ms.
04. Hypocritical ministers or other so-called people of faith or rehabilitative groups who tell you to reject any assistance to an I/M beyond giving the I/M just a token "drive-by" message of salvation.
05. You receive e-mail or personal threats or intimidation from victims or victim rights groups, vigilantes, pro-death penalty advocates, or haters who use the Old Testament "eye for an eye" passage as a reason or platform to believe in giving no mercy, no second chances for freedom, nor for an I/M to pay their debt to society but either by death penalty, castration, "Life Sentence", death in prison, no contact visits, and any other suffering in the process.
06. Your I/M you sponsor gets a disciplinary, is moved to another prison, is slow to change (e.g. fighting addition), or is turned down at the parole board. Anything else Satan uses – including family and friends -- to lay doubt in the fruits of meaningful sponsorship.

> **Note:** It is the ***non-believer*** in God, the ***false*** Christian, Muslim, or Jew who believes <u>only</u> the victim(s) deserve compassion, and that the criminal is deserving of none, nor forgiveness, nor mercy, but only punishment. With this having been said, if there is no balance in justice, then the mal-treatment of criminals is condoned by the society in which they come from, especially if there is no meaningful intervention of which, usually, is only found in the natural religious order of ministers who wish to help prisoners change their behavior and/or condition.

WHAT DO YOU TELL THE PAROLE BOARD OR PEOPLE WHEN THEY ASK YOU WHY YOU ARE SUPPORTING A CONVICT?

(How can you advocate for a child molester, murderer, wife-beater, or crackhead?)

HERE ARE SOME ANSWERS FROM SOME SPONSORS WHO TURN *"NEGATIVES"* INTO *"POSITIVES"*:

1. My God says I am to love everyone and to forgive, not judge; everyone makes mistakes
2. Mr./Mrs. "X" that I sponsor has transformed him/herself and is no-longer the person in the past that did that crime
3. Mr./Mrs. "X" has changed significantly and I am proud of his outstanding prison record, classes he graduated, etc.
4. Mr./Mrs. "X" is REMORSEFUL AND DESERVES A SECOND CHANGE
5. Mr./Mrs. "X" I am proud to call my friend for these past _____ years. I'd trust him today to live at my house.
6. We all make mistakes, some more tragic than others. In this case of Mr./Mrs. "X", he/she has learned his/her lesson and made the corrections in his/her life to make the right choices now with thought to the consequences of actions
7. As a Christian, Jew, or Muslim, person of faith, I am – as a minister – to lead others to a better life with a relationship with God who expects me to reclaim and help regenerate those I sponsor to make improvements so they can lead productive lives once again.
8. My life has been to be a *servant* for God to help those less fortunate. The only difference between the people who want punishment and justice only for prisoners is they forget those same people are coming out of prison some day. My job is to help shape their lives both spiritually and functionally so that they can be re-claimed by the community in better condition than when they came in.
9. I believe if you had a loved one in prison, or were in prison yourself and were involved with an I/M, you'd learn that the situation surrounding the crime – on paper – or in the media doesn't tell the personal side of the story or the facts all the time, and until you do, you can't always judge a book by its cover, nor ignore the improvements an I/M made for life.

Michael Maraschiello

Chapter 4

Building up Prisoners for Success

Success is defined as:

"A degree or measure of succeeding; favorable or desired outcome; also: the attainment of wealth, favor, or eminence" according to the Merriam-Webster Dictionary. [1]

In his book, "*America at the Crossroads*: Explosive Trends shaping America's Future and What You Can Do About It," the author George Barna says that the traditional view has always held that success is about <u>power</u>, possessions, prestige. [2]

In Millennial America, *success* has a new look. The most pervasive elements in the current success formula are achieving personal goals; having good relationships with family and friends; loving what you do for a living; balancing work, family, and leisure; having ample flexibility; experiencing financial stability; and making a positive difference in the world. (See Figure 4.1)

"The dream life revolved around owning a house in a safe and desirable neighborhood, driving a reliable car, and holding down a steady and good-paying job."…"To a large extent, those ideals no longer define a successful life. It's because some of those people take for granted those elements, such as owning a home, living in a free country, or having opportunities in every dimension of life. In other instances, it is because people no longer believe such an outcome is plausible or desirable." [3]

Figure 4.1. **Most Important Outcome for Having a Successful Life**

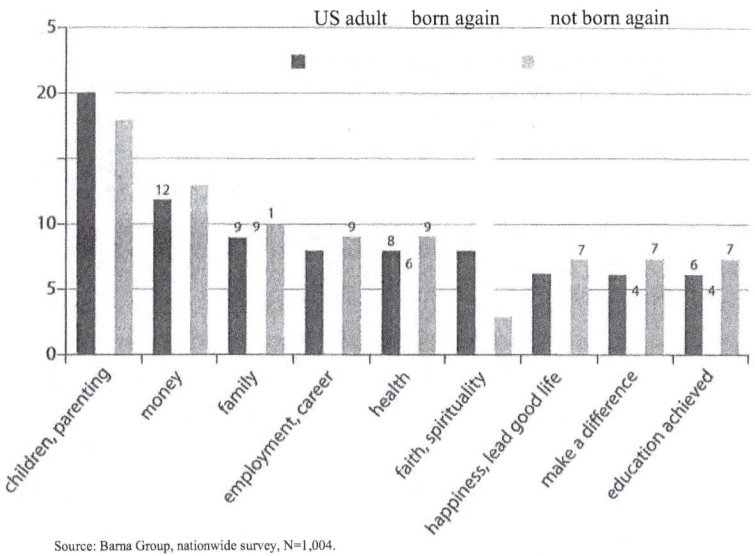

Source: Barna Group, nationwide survey, N=1,004.

1 – *Chapter 15 On Success.* Accenture, "Accenture Research Finds Most professionals Believe They Can 'Have It All,'" news release, March 1, 2013, https://newsroom.accenture.com/subjects/coroprate-citizenship-philanthropy/accenture-research-finds-most-professionals-believe-they-can-have-it-all. Based on a national survey conducted by Ipsos, for Strayer University, N=2,011, in 2014; Jacquelyn Smith, "This Is How Americans Define Success," *Business Insider*, October 3, 2014, http://www.businessinsider.com/how-americans-now-define-success-2014-10#ixzz3g0D4jyvT; "Enjoy Life, Live with Parents: Millennials Redefine Adulthood," Science Codex, July 30, 2014, http://www.sciencecodex.com/enjoy_life_live_with_parents_millennials_redefine_adulthood-138600#ixzz3g0JesUBB; *Heartland Monitor Poll XIV*, Allstate/National Journal, https://www.allstate.com/resources/Allstate/attachments/heartland-monitor/hearltand-XIV-data.pdf.

People need to recognize the *value* of prisoners as human beings capable of change and positive contribution to society for investment to begin to be reflected in budgets for social plans and criminal justice reform for the future. Otherwise, Millennials will not be able to accommodate such high costs for incarceration with little return for the money when elderly prisoners are reduced to stay on the tax payer's backs for sustainment due to the present prison system [failure] of generating illiterate and un-employable men and women not only too old but lacking self-sustaining skills with which to live. This is where the burden falls to the faith groups (i.e. churches, mosques, synagogues, etc.) and community groups to lobby for changes in state and federal government to seek funding for programs less expensive than incarceration in favor of probation and community service. Services even for those currently deemed "violent offenders" in the broken system where men and women are often not violent, but committed one violent offense (label) as their defining "stone around their neck." That label of "violent' has multiple definitions; however, the worst is the misrepresented one often given by a overworked and ill-advised judge through a public defender not recording the actual full and true character of the convicted person's history causing un-due prejudice. Many pled guilty to terrible charges only to come into the prison system with the consequence of now wearing a label that does not fit them. This is seen in undisciplined juvenile cases having assaultive behavior charges dropped and pleading guilty to such offenses as burglary. They then go to prison as a "non-violent" offender and go before the parole board as "non-violent," yet, their disciplinary record and the number of assaultive and aggressive incidents they have and their attitude all indicate a violent pattern or streak of behavior. Yet, another person – who never was violent -- can be in a vehicular homicide that killed someone and get the label as "violent," and be viewed by all as just a person with an alcohol problem. Yet, for purposes of classification and the way the parole board looks at him or her – the drunk driver -- as "violent," even if they have no record of violence at

all while incarcerated. This, then, is a classic example of a failed classification system of justice and parole board because the *real* violent person in the first example, gets a "pass," and the drunk gets viewed as a violent criminal less likely to make parole because he or she is labeled "violent." The current state of the prisoner is what a person should be judged by, not who they were years ago because that person may no-longer exist – a product of *felonism.*

Barna adds that researchers, however, have added a few pieces to the puzzle, citing components of success people often ignore. The personal traits recognized as contributing factors include consistent and deliberate practice that ***develops knowledge and skills***, resulting in expertise; self-control; grit; and time invested in working hard. It turns out that a few external factors **empower** success as well. Those include having a competent **mentor** and intense engagement in a breadth of activities and relationships. [4]

"Recent Studies indicate that increasing numbers of people are turning to **technology** to facilitate their personal success, especially when it comes to experiencing a balanced life. People are relying on technological solutions to enable scheduling flexibility, expand the dimensions of the workplace, foster better communication, and increase personal efficiency. [5]

> FACTS: 77% of professional believe technology facilitates schedule flexibility, which is important because 80% of professionals say flexibility is critical to achieving work-life balance. [6] And 90% of American adults believes success is more about happiness than power, possessions, or prestige. [7]

Barna continued to add that Americans expect to enjoy success without making the challenging personal investments required for it to happen. This he wrote about concerning the "brokenness preceding wholeness," in which he said, "Unless we understand and embrace our own brokenness, we are insulated from so many of God's glorious and desirable promises." [2]

I believe as Barna that rejecting brokenness prevents us from:

- Living the promises God made to us (2Cor. 6:14-17; Heb. 6: 9-12)
- Evolving into a "new creation" God envisioned us to be (Rom. 12:2, Eph. 4:24)
- Having true freedom from sin's grasp, self sin, and the counter culture
- Realizing God's omnipotence (Job 38; Gal. 6: 7-10)
- Putting God first (John 4: 23-24; Rom. 1:23)

Barna continued with expressing that his research with American adults who are people on the journey to holiness emphasized the importance and accuracy of that contention. He stated on page 173 of his book that, "People become isolated from God and resistant to brokenness because of emotional blockages or pain. (i.e. issues of the heart); spiritual ignorance, confusion, or self-indulgence (i.e. matters of the soul); intellectual distortions and misunderstandings (i.e. challenges of the mind), or behavioral and physical obstacles (i.e. manifestations of strength). Our adversary (Satan) is an expert at blending potential seductions in these areas into a minefield that maims and destroys us." [2]

That's why we need *godly* ministers – Christ-like disciples -- to put people in these conditions back together and make them whole again with Christ's loving power to heal, educate, enable (empower), and transform [us] so the joys of the promises God has for us all can be ours to experience in the family of Christ as we draw nearer to Him. The simple philosophy that works is to take on the attributes of Christ experienced in a personal relationship that says:

> "I need help to change because I can't do this life myself by my way of living and thinking."

This is why ministers and sponsors must incorporate Christ's attribute of speaking directly to people in a parable-like candidness in order to

be effective at reaching prisoner's hearts in the language of care they can understand and believe.

That is, you have to speak a prisoner's language to teach them a new one. The same with teaching a person a new way of living life rather than the way the sponsoree or mentoree has been living it which got them to jail or prison – the wrong path.

NO COMPUTER SKILLS = NO SKILLS
(AND NO GOOD START)

The impact of the Internet and the World Wide Web on Education and Re-entry Prisoners. Are they skilled?

It's a "no brainer," that if you want to survive in this modern world, you have to have computer and smart-phone skills or you are "economically unviable" and tech-illiterate, to say the least to function in America today. From job applications to online banking, your tech skills can make you or break you. And for thousands of prisoners deprived of the skills to keep up, they are woefully ill-prepared to go out and have the necessary tools and skills to fend for themselves to say the least and stay off the recidivism charts.

Several good books are out there to deal with things like the internet; however, not only does the internet provide access to extensive text and multimedia resources, it also allows teachers and students and people to communicate with other teachers and students all over the world. And in doing so, it will enhance stability and assure that economic survival will take place.

Once such aspect of the internet communication is **"Netiquette,"** which is short for Internet etiquette, is the code of acceptable behaviors users should follow while on the internet – that is, the conduct excepted of individuals online. Netiquette includes rules for all aspects of the internet, including the web, e-mail, FTP, newsgroups, and message boards, chat rooms, and instant messaging. (See Figure 4.2, below)

From Book: "Integrating Technology in a Connected World" (Teachers Discovering Computers), 7th Edition, B. Shelly, G. Gunter, and R. Gunter, Course Technology, Cengage Learning (2012)

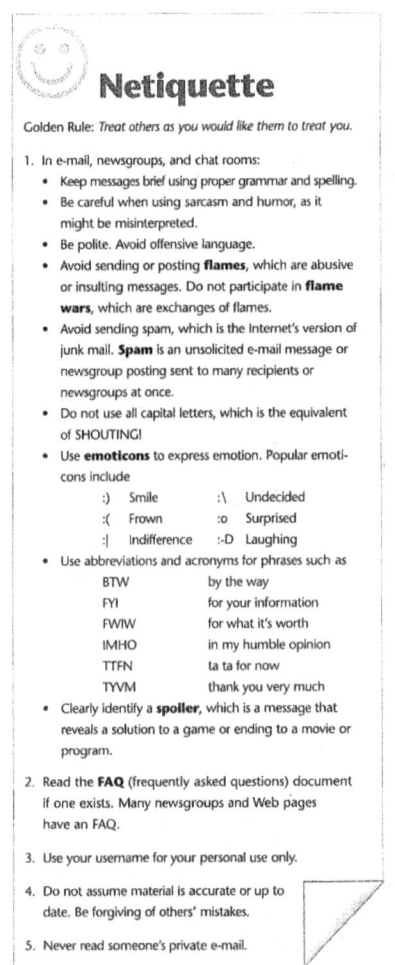

Figure 4.2

      The authors of *Integrating Technology in a Connected World*, state that the present – and the future – is all about the Internet in our "e-world" (electronic world) with the world wide web that puts us in touch with people and places at the click of a button. That students no-longer learn from a text-based communications system but rather are in need of being literate in the use of powerful multimedia communication systems of today. Learning tools must be presented to educate students to learn basic skills such as researching data, tech hardware, and performance measurement applications to know they have acquired (learned).

> **FACT: Almost all prisoners have absolutely no access to the Internet or a cell phone or Smartphone, nor even know simple e-banking or how to use a touch screen due to many states' draconian "corrections" policies or procedures which – in the long run – send inmates out of the prison system illiterate or electronically disadvantaged with the basic skills for personal responsibility, success, and financial freedom.**

In Appendix 2, an inmate survey I conducted shows a snapshot of computer skill illiteracy of a sample of one prison's inmate population.

EDUCATING BEHIND BARS WORKS

According to Elizabeth Northrup in her article, "A College Education for Prisoners Reduces Recidivism,", the key to changing the rate of recidivism, or tendency to reoffend, lies within the prison education system. [8]

"70% of those incarcerated are nonviolent offenders. On average, 650,000 are released every year in the U.S. Low employment levels for that group cost between $57 billion and $65 billion annually in lost economic activity, according to a study by the *Center for Economic and Policy Research*. Experts say low reading and technological literacy, as well as reluctance among employers to hire former convicts, means many drop out of the labor force altogether."

"Whether you are letting Hollywood shape your image of prison by watching the myriad of crime dramas on network and cable TV, or you have a more personal connection through a friend or family member who is incarcerated, most people would agree that prison is not somewhere they would choose to end up. And once someone has experienced being imprisoned, you would imagine that there is a strong desire to not return once released. However, the recidivism rate, or relapse of criminal behavior, is close to 60%."

"As a society, we can argue whether or not prisoners should be afforded the privilege of a higher education behind bars, but the numbers clearly show that **education and training in prison works.** According to Gerard Robinson, a scholar at the *American (_____) Institute:*

"Economically, it doesn't make sense to keep people incarcerated as long as we have with no great results. The right thing to do is not only give them a second chance, but to also admit the fact that many of them didn't receive a first chance at school." [9]

Reiterated again, Governor Bill Lee of Tennessee's motto when it comes to prisoners is that: "Incentives drive behavior." What motivates prisoners to change are incentives with "time off" for good behavior, and meaningful skill training (education) while incarcerated. These are where the public will get more "bang" for the buck and less recidivism. Not outdated "BS" classes for prisoners to learn "sensitivity training" and nothing about the latest technology so they aren't behind the "hiring curve" when they get out and the only jobs left for inmates are "ditch diggers" and "bucket toters." (To say the least of the lowest paid jobs available to recently released convicts.)

Remember, released prisoners want to thrive, not subsist on the "welfare state" social assistance roles.

MERCY: PRISON RELEASE REFORM

It's time prison ministry volunteers came to the rescue of prisoners and return them to their communities and families before they degrade so much, that they are unable to function in society but for daily subsistence because "the system" has created socially-incapable people who can't work to support themselves.

In his article, "A Truly Just System Must Do More Than Protect The Rights Of The Innocent; It Must Also Respect The Humanity Of The Guilty," From "Who Belongs In Prison?," Adam Gopnik writes that nothing has changed more in the past couple of decades than attitudes towards the crisis of incarceration in America. What was largely an **invisible** civilization of confinement – millions of men & women locked up for, cumulatively, millions of years – is now a commonplace concern. Everyone running for the Democratic nomination pays lip service to the needs to address mass incarceration, and what was once essential political instincts – to side with the police & the prosecutors in every instance, to "get tough on crime" -- have become, at the very least, negotiable. We have gone from "Lock'em up!" to "Lock'em up?" to "Set'em loose!," all in a relatively short time. One reason for these changed attitudes is …for the first time in decades, ordinary citizens could care more about the consequences of imprisonment than they did about the threat of violence." [10]

"Even if all the prisoners had done what they were imprisoned for, the normal question remains whether anyone deserves to be put in a bathroom-size cell for the rest of his or her life."

"The cases that test our convictions involve offenders whose crimes have had real social & human costs."

"The pressing issue is not whether white-collar criminals should be punished more or less than others; it is whether the practice of locking anyone up in a closed penitentiary for long periods is an *effective* way of punishing or preventing criminal behavior."

"The quality of **mercy** has never been more highly strained than it is in America today."

"Perhaps the most radical & challenging of new approaches to incarceration involves the move to cap all prison sentences at some designated limit."

"The evidence is overwhelming that, even with the most seemingly noxious criminals, age & time wear away danger: little violent crime is done by middle-aged people, and eliminating all hope of release is one of the crueler, if unfortunately not at all unusual, punishments we imposed."

"Justice without compassion is something other than civilized…we have to want to humanize the treatment of those we think "belong" in prison with the same energy with which we agitate for those we don't. De-incarcerating our society…involve[s] making harder, & more foundational moral choices."

Christ wants us to be kind and merciful to all people of all races, colors, creeds and – yes – conditions, like those who have "fallen down" and were sent to prison. God pardoned all our iniquities, and heals our ills. We just have to believe. As the psalmist says, 'He redeems your life from destruction, crowns you with kindness and compassion. Merciful and gracious is the Lord, slow to anger and abounding in kindness. Not according to our sins does he deal with us, nor punish us according to our iniquities (crimes)." (Psalm 103: 1-2, 3-4, 8, 10, 12-13)

As Jesus said, we are to *love* even our enemies. (Matthew 5:38-48) Often prisoners are hated simply because "the mob" or – in today's electronic world -- "the media" glorifies and/or condemns someone on the [fake] news which generates social media-hyped frenzy to slander, attack, or otherwise hate someone or some group, especially if they have been arrested.

Can you explain to a prisoner how it feels to be mocked, spit upon, jeered at, falsely accused, or slandered by a mob or the media and paraded into a court room of screaming people asking for your blood?

Try and relate to someone like that. (Jesus knows.)

So, for the prison ministry to care for others, Jesus said to his disciples, "You have heard that it was said, *An eye for an eye and a tooth for a tooth.* But I say to you, offer no resistance to one who is evil…You have heard that it was said, *You shall love your neighbor and hate your enemy.* But I say to you, love your enemies and pray for those who persecute you, that you may be children of your heavenly Father, for he makes his sun rise on the bad and the good…so be perfect, just as your heavenly Father is perfect." What's Jesus talking about here that I should know to help me become a better mentor or sponsor, or what's needed to help my sponsors and mentors do more for prisoners in my prison ministry?

Simple. It's the Holy Spirit dwelling inside us – an undeserved gift. Omnipresent, as we abide in faith in Christ, we then act or behave in the way God intended us to by loving others more as we would want

to be loved. However, our carnality prevents us from fully partaking in God's love as we fall short in our daily walk. The world culture filled with Satan's snaring minions and temptations often cause us to stumble due to our human weakness.

Nevertheless, we are to endeavor to persevere as Christ did and his apostles did to show others the way by guiding and help people in the discipleship process Christ demands from a merciful heart and **His** character. We, as mentors and sponsors, are to show prisoners – our "brothers and sisters in Christ" -- unconditional love even when *the world* calls them "enemy."

EDUCATION IN PRISON

GOD'S GRACE AND GLORY IN INSTRUCTION

Mike –So what kind of instruction do prisoners need, or anybody in need, to heal or get back up on their feet?

The Bible best summarizes the importance of individuals regardless of ability in I Corinthians 12: 14-27. Verses 23 through 27 show our human frailty:

"And the parts that we think less honorable we treat with special honor. All the parts that are unpresentable are treated with special modesty, while our presentable parts need no special treatment. But God has put the body together, giving greater honor to the parts that lacked it, so that there should be no division in the body, but that its parts should have equal concern for each other. If one part suffers, every part suffers with it; if one part is honored, every part rejoices with it. Now you are the body of Christ, and each one of you is a part of it."

As prison ministers, mentors, and sponsors – educators, we need to determine what we value, then, in educating prisoners. What is

successful instruction and learning that will captivate or motivate an inmate in need of change to start accepting the *plan and process* of transforming his or her life. This is a "coaching process" to guide inmates onto the best path for them in instruction. Not as a dictator, but as a teacher and friend equally together to facilitate the inmate's new character to be released for success. No inmate should feel pixilated or confused because you are doing things way over their head. Basic needs and such, as we'll see addressed in Part II, are usually all that's needed first to "kick start" an inmate into becoming serious about making changes and not to lose hope.

One approach to helping inmates is Differentiated Instruction to spark men and women to practice their God-given gifts to their fullest capacity beginning with accepting and knowing they are a part of the Body of Christ. And yet, the world in which we live in that is constantly testing us with Satan's threat is always ever present. However, by the power of the Holy Spirit, in the strong Body of Christ, we can tap into our unique gifts God gave us and defeat the "viruses" and "diseases" [of the world] so we can live as God intended us to.

No matter if you are a prisoner or a free-world person who is struggling to "break free" of the chains of sin or a situation that seems hopeless, all you have to do is believe you have a Savior, Jesus Christ, who can empower you with His Word and his disciple mentors and sponsors who – like you – are a part of the Body of Christ all working together for the good of all through God's redeeming grace available to all no matter your iniquity, crime, sins, or situation.

As stated before, an education is a major incentive and effective tool to curb recidivism. Education influences: social factors, neighborhood conditions, peer groups, family wealth, employment opportunities, and other things from the empowerment an education brings.

In a report by Wolf Harlow, she suggests a relationship between education, unemployment, and imprisonment. [11] Harlow found 38% of inmates who completed 11 years or less of school were not working before entry to prison. Unemployment was lower for

these with a GED (32%), a high school diploma (25%), or education beyond high school (21%). In other words, improving the social and economic conditions for all people might result in lower rates of unemployment and a smaller prison population. This further translates into "the higher a person's educational attainment, the less likely he or she is to be in prison." [12]

Reviewing more of Harlow's findings from the Department of Justice, it was found that 41.3% of those Americans in prison have some high school or less as compared to 12.7% of the prison population HAVING SOME POST-SECONDARY EDUCATION. Young inmates less well-educated than older inmates were more likely than older inmates to have failed to complete high school or its equivalent. Over half of inmates 24 or younger had not completed the 12th grade or the GED (52%), while just over a third of those 35 or older did not have a high school diploma or GED (34% for those 35-44 and 35% for those 45 or older.) (See Table 1.1)

Educational Attainment	Total	Prison Inmates				
		State	Federal	Local Jail	Probationers	General Pop.
Some H.S.	41.3%	39.7%	26.5%	46.5%	30.6%	18.4%
GED	23.4	28.5	22.7	14.1	11.0	NA
H.S. Diploma	22.6	20.5	27.0	25.9	34.8	33.2
Postsecondary	12.7	11.4	23.9	13.5	23.6	48.4

Table 1.1 Educational Attainment for Correctional Populations and the General Population

FORGIVING POWER WORKS

In the last couple of years, forgiveness has been a hot topic in the news. We've seen some police officers wrongly shoot un-armed men such as George Floyd, only to leave families grieving and tensions flare to vent the frustration for changes to be made.

But what about when forgiveness is applied?

Take, for example, the young woman (police officer) who tragically shot and killed a beloved family member in his own apartment. The family – practicing Christians – displayed the love of Christ and forgiveness to the world in a powerful way. They did what we as Christians are called to do … FORGIVE, as we have been FORGIVEN! Right in the courtroom, they told that former policewoman she was forgiven and hugged her. It was a display of courage as well as an act of letting go of the pain and loss of their beloved family member, and a signal for healing for the former officer to let the guilt go away to be replaced by hope for change of a better future. The same with the grieving family.

Can you forgive a prisoner the same way? A sex offender? A killer? The "dope man" who sold drugs and got a teenage girl pregnant?

In the New Testament (NT), and particularly the Gospels and the ministry and teaching of Jesus, we see the importance of forgiving others. Perhaps the best known of Jesus' statements regarding forgiveness is in the model prayer in Matt. 6:12: *"Forgive us our debts, as we also have forgiven our debtors."* On another occasion when Jesus taught them how to pray, He said, "And forgive us our sins, for we ourselves forgive everyone who is indebted to us." (Lk. 11:4) Matthew 6:14-15 further emphasizes what Jesus said in verse 12. The language in these verses is clear … If we forgive others, then God will forgive us; but if we refuse to forgive others, then God will not forgive us. Some people complain that this makes God's forgiveness conditional, but that is what Jesus said. It is true that forgiveness from God is through His grace and Mercy … we cannot earn forgiveness by our on merits. Forgiving others does not **earn** our forgiveness from God. God's forgiveness, however, cannot be separated from human forgiveness, and our forgiveness from God does depend on our willingness to forgive others.

In Mark 11:25, Jesus was even more specific when He said, *"And whenever you stand praying, forgive, if you have anything against anyone, so that your Father also who is in heaven may forgive you your trespasses."* It isn't possible to pray with bad feelings about another person in your heart. {Feelings of anger and bitterness} are like am impenetrable wall that separates individuals. Such feelings also separate the person who holds them from God! Jesus said if you hold anything against another person, forgive that person first, and then you can pray to God. It only makes sense that if your heart is not right in one way, then it will not be right in another. It is only by removing these bad feelings from your heart that you can ask God to forgive you of your own sins.

In Luke 6:37, Jesus connected forgiveness with being judgmental and critical of others: *"Judge not, and you will not be judged; condemn not, and you will not be condemned; forgive and you will be forgiven."* We all know that it is easy to be hurt by others and to be judgmental and critical of their behavior. In this verse, as in the Sermon on the Mount (Matt. 7:1-5), Jesus tells us not to forgive them at times, but that is what Jesus wants His followers to do!

C.S. Lewis in *The Weight of Glory* made this insightful comment: *"To be a Christian means to forgive the inexcusable because God has forgiven the inexcusable in you."* The apostle Paul wrote a similar thought to the Ephesians: *"Be kind to one another, tenderhearted, forgiving one another, as God in Christ forgave you."* (Eph. 4:32).

So, many in the "world" don't understand biblical forgiveness a Christian must exhibit. Forgiveness is a vital part of the Christian experience and necessary in terms of our relationship with God, and demonstrating to a prisoner, that we have a loving God who accepts us in our brokenness to make us whole again. (Matt. 6:14-15) Let the Christian family of the killed black family man that forgave the white female cop be a powerful reminder to us about our great responsibility to extend mercy and grace as it has been extended to us!

BUILDING PEOPLE UP BY EDIFICATION:
"Walking the Walk, not Talking the Talk" but Showing Jesus' life in words with action.

When I first gave a sermon on this subject of *edification* back in September of 2019, specifically targeting my audience of fellow inmates in the prison chapel, I used a basic "takeaway-message" approach that centered on the core foundation that our lives must be built on a cornerstone [philosophy] of first making a strong *spiritual* house (spirit-relationship personally with God) which would sustain a holy life modeled on Christ's way of living.

Literally, edification means "building up," it approximates encouragement and consolation (1 Cor. 14:3; 1 Thes. 5:11), though with edification focus falls on the goal, defined as being established in faith (Col. 2:7) or attaining unity of faith and knowledge, maturity, and the full measure of Christ (Eph. 4:13). Edification is the special responsibility of the various church leaders (Eph. 4: 11-12) and is the legitimate context for exercise of their authority (2 Cor. 10:8; 13:10). The works of building up is, however, the work of all Christians (1 Thess. 5:11). Spiritual gifts are given for the edification of the Church. Of these gifts, those which involve speaking are especially important (Acts 20:32; 1 Cor. 14; Eph. 4:29). All elements of Christian worship should contribute to edification (1 Cor. 14:26). Prophecy and instruction are especially important (1 Cor. 14:3, 18-19). **Edification is not all talk, however, but involves _demonstrative_ love. (1 Cor. 8:1) and consideration for those weak in faith (Rom. 15: 1-2).**

So, how do *you* build people up?

How are Christian mentors and sponsors supposed to build people up?

Don't prisoners need to be built up after falling down?

Saint Paul says the most important thing is to be aware of Christ's life of encouraging (1 Cor. 14:3) others to change, follow Him, and worship God.
How is that done?
Consider this:

> Do you learn when you are alert and sober,
> or sinful and unwatchful to gain knowledge,
> experience, and wisdom in how best to live
> worthy of God's approval, not yours or man's?

Let's look further at what *edification* means and where you get knowledge and wisdom from to make a difference in helping someone.

"Edification" is simply to **_improve_** one's morality or intellect to gain knowledge; to be educated or guided, to learn from being taught.

You can get that knowledge from books, teachers, a parent, the internet, the Holy Spirit, and especially from our BEST example, the "chief cornerstone," Jesus Christ. "Wisdom" is simply the best application of the knowledge to benefit from.

Now, consider yourself lucky to have at least one good friend or family member in your life who will stick with you through thick and thin.

Can you name someone whom you *trust* for edification? To help you in your life?

● What character points or attributes do they have that make them stand out as good people to help you learn and get through things in life? (Eph. 4:29)

● Do they show mercy to people and forgive them for mistakes? Have patience, kindness, provide hope, show love, lead others to Christ? (Heb. 13:21)

● Do YOU inspire people wherever you go like Jesus did? The prophets? (Rom. 5:9 God-saved)

● Do you glorify God in what you say and do or don't say and don't do? (2 Thes. 1:12)

● Do you listen to the Holy Spirit telling your heart to think about what **_Jesus_** would do in the same situation you are in? What to tell someone else? How you can be a solution-maker instead of a problem taker or faker?

PROBLEMS WITH SUCCESS NOT FOSTERED IN THE MULTI-CULTURAL SCHOOLS LEADING TO YOUNG PEOPLE COMMITTING CRIMES DUE TO BEING ILL-EQUIPPED FOR LIFE ROLES IN A DIVERSE COUNTRY

As described in his book "Taking Sides: Clashing Views on Education Issues," author Glenn L. Koonce says that today's public schools use a balanced learning curriculum. Academics and social media are now inter-twined for modern goals for effective learning outcomes. [13]

"Solution of improvement are non-conventionalism and constructive reform."

"Today's school system has radical reform critique of government-sponsored compulsory schooling has depicted organized education as a form of cultural or political imprisonment that traps young people in an artificial and mainly irrelevant envisionment and rewards conformity and docility while inhibiting curiosity and creativity. Potential is not tested to expand knowledge and skill and expand the chance for higher student success in life."

"Teacher's goals are to master the art of bringing a variety to the curriculum according to the needs of any given set of students is the challenge that such diversity can bring. This is done BEST by using instrumental practices that differentiate instruction." [14]

From my experience, training, and studies, I believe Koonce is right. Further, I believe in the bifurcated classroom of homework balanced with take-home mobile device or tablet electronic devices utilized to give students the familiarity and skill with e-transacting which is the present and future of society interaction for living and working. Not a ephemeral way of teaching only to what is of temporary interest. And for prisoners, tablets are a must, especially during COVID, because their learning will not be interrupted for prisoners to become better citizens which society expects.

In his book, "Critical Issues in Education," Eugene F. Provenzo, Jr. says that "Most important postmodern issue affecting education is multiculturalism." [15]

Provenzo said, "Education's main goal is to encourage the growth of competent, caring, loving, and loving people. The problem is that there is a presumption that multi-cultural education automatically takes care of racism."

Plato, commenting on education, said that "Involvement fosters the thought process." He argued for students to receive individual interests, abilities, and stations in life for development.

Aristotle said, "form the child to become virtuous – to do the right thing or act in a moral way (philosophy).

Thus, education is good for society. St. Augustine went further saying, "Developing a philosophy of education in which learners must be aroused by the teacher to discuss what they hold within themselves."

In the multicultural classroom in America today, not only are the ideals of famous white, European, and Asian philosophers being given time to reflect upon, but also those of African descent, such as W.E.B. Du Bois (1868 – 1963). A graduate of Fisk University in Nashville, Tennessee who earned a Ph. D. from Harvard University in 1895, Du Bois championed black rights. His doctoral dissertation, *The Suppression of the African Slave-Trade to the United States of America, 1638-1870*, was published in 1896. Du Bois originally believed that social science could provide the knowledge to solve the race problem, however, became convinced the way to solve it was by agitation and protest head-on. [16] This method to fight racism clashed with the predominant and most influential black leader of the period, Booker T. Washington, who preached a philosophy of accommodation. Urging blacks to accept discrimination for the time being and elevate themselves through hard work and economic gain, thus winning the respect of the whites. Du Bois started the Niagara Movement in 1905 which opposed the platform of Booker T. Washington and later morphed into the NAACP, founded in 1909. Du Bois' new "integration" movement was primarily of middle-class blacks and progressive whites.

Unfortunately, his Marxist overtones and leftist overtones cause much friction which lead to his becoming completely disillusioned with the United States so he joined the Communist party in 1961, and moved to Ghana, renouncing his American citizenship. [17]

The two philosophies of solving racism (Du Bois' and Booker T. Washington's) show that for over a century there has been a failure to solve the problem by accommodation or by radical protest. What is evident, is that protests get the attention when action takes place for the United States legislators to begin enacting reforms into laws that affect change. These laws directly affect people of color more close to home because they have suffered the injustice of inequality more so that than majority race inside the borders of the country. And until the laws meet up with the beliefs of the people, there will be friction for the next group of people demanding more rights or equality for their race, color, or creed in society.

It is important to know that because it is the classroom where the minds of children are indoctrinated with the knowledge they are supposed to have to function successfully in society-at-large and be able to live in peace and harmony. That is important because many in prison never received an education that helps them assimilate or be comfortable as themselves to be free of prejudice, hate, or other forms of disagreement and know that they don't have to be treated as such in a country that has rights for all its citizens to be free of such deplorable conduct hold one back from their potential as a human being and a citizen.

Thus, these are the politics today that amidst racism and other political issues of the day which will not be fully addressed in this book, they all factor in when dealing with those in prison who, most likely, came from broken homes, were abused, are of a minority or even mixed race, a religion despised or no religion, but what ever the environment they came from, the dynamic of uplifting an inmate's life to change and still find potential within themselves is the fruit of the experience to make a difference in their life so they can have the freedom of living in society once again as others are doing.

That's a "big prize" a prisoner wants to be involved in – going home, or to a freedom-made place they can call their home, as many have told me where they came from was no home.

Today's prison ministry mentor or sponsor can't be someone who is ignorant. They have to be aware of the politics going on around them. Politicians worry because of demographic shifts in the landscape. Coexistence among the various cultures and subcultures can be risks to the political futures of politicians if they are not voting on the right laws affecting parole or prisons or social initiatives communities need help with to protect them from out-dated draconian laws and practices designed to keep men and women in prison for too long a sentences without proper treatment while they are locked up. For educators, awareness of this means better use of organizational, political, and diplomatic instructions for our children to raise more law-abiding children to become law-abiding citizens. This implies teaching *values*. Values which come from god, from our parents, and supposed to come from our educators to be accepted across the board to shape the minds of the learners – the "dreamers" who want to grow up and experience life to their potential.

Yet, we are seeing a downfall in American culture, and a downfall of religion with a shift to a Science-man-for-answers way of living without God. This is called *Modern Anthropocentrism* – the view that God disappears from the world resulting in downfall of religion and a hegemony taking over which is all authority to a government, state, or body devoid of god(s).

Ergo, the traditional teaching in the past in American schools under world *postmodernism,* today, has changed the experience of teaching in our schools to the new dynamic to meet the needs of the society versus the individual child/ learner. This is the classic *Marxism vs. Capitalism* debate that has been going on since the early 1900's arguing that the government knows what's best for the individual, not parents, not clergy, not teachers but the body-in-charge. And the process of learning is dramatically affected to shape political opinion with conditioning through technological usage of media-based visual and other computer smart ware replacing old-route repetition. Long gone are the tried and true scientific or critical methods of learning for one's self to research and find answers, but rather what "junk" the government or "group-think" body says, must be taken as gospel.

With this Multiculturalism vs. Monoculturalism war, "exposure" (teaching children everything – which is impracticable in a modern classroom) is not a "cure all." However, no child should be made to feel invisible given their background or differences as to the rest of the class room of students who all want equal access to an education that will give them the tools to sufficiently function in a modern technologically-advanced society today as in Plessy v. Ferguson, (1896). [18]

In *Plessy*, a case of an American citizen one-eight African blood and seven-eighths Caucasian (Mr. Plessy) was removed from a white-only train car after declaring himself "black." The State of Louisiana had a "separate but equal" law given the train had no blockage of transporting people with black-only and white-only passenger cars. The Federal government's Supreme Court was to adjudicate the case under the 13th Amendment (Abolishing Slavery Enforcement) and the basic civil rights of Mr. Plessy who was a born and raised citizen of the United States of America.

Mr. Justice Harlan opined, "In respect of civil rights, common to all citizens, the constitution of the United States does not, permit any public authority to know the race of those  entitled to be protected in the enjoyment of such rights. Every true man has pride of race, and under appropriate circumstances, when the rights of others, his equal before the law, are not to be affected, it is his privilege to express such pride and to take such action based upon it as to him seems proper. But I deny that any legislative body or judicial tribunal may have regard to the *555 race of citizens when the civil rights of those citizens are involved. Indeed, such legislation as that here in question is inconsistent not only with the equality of rights which pertains to citizenship, national and state, but with the personal liberty enjoyed by every one within the United States."

Justice Harlan goes on to say, "The words of the amendment (13th), it is true, are prohibitory, but they contain a necessary implication of a positive immunity or right, most valuable to the colored race, -- the righ to exemption from unfriendly legislation against them distinctively as colored; exemption from legal discriminations, implying inferiority in civil society, lessoning the security of their enjoyment of the rights which others enjoy; and discriminations which are steps towards reducing them to the condition of a subject race."

Plessy had a very important argument which rose to give credence to his case in which the segregation of a train car should extend to street side walks and roads making the argument for segregation absurd and undeniably unreasonable to stand up to the law.

In short, *Plessy* makes note that bad legislation interferes with freedom for categories of people. Not only the issue was 'equal access" the first order of the case to ride a train, but the case brought out the very "thinking of the time" that not only were there segregationists still in the Halls of Justice and on trains, but also there were truly wise men and women harking for justice both in the courts and in American society which – at the time – was not fully accepting integration but moving in the right direction however so slowly.

This case is important because it shows changes in society are reflected in the way people address them for the legislators to take corrective action. Whether by get-in-your-face protests or by meaningful writs in the form of legislative bills, the shaping of American society takes place and moves forward. The same with understanding the needs of prisoners, a category often oppressed and discriminated against. Depending on how and what you teach or don't teach, every group cannot be taught, nor every side of the story, which is why it is up to students beyond the class room or what is on the evening news for people to learn the facts through involvement and gain the higher-knowledge level of truth for one to be more apt to master a specific study or discipline. As mentor and sponsors, what we teach the inmate in our relationship has a huge impact on their decision-making and the way they perceive becoming better citizens for a brighter today and tomorrow. Postmodernism refers to an increasingly radical change in the relations of the nature of the nation-state, the development of new technologies that have redefined the fields of telecommunications, of informing people through social media, and the interdependence on globalization-building cultural norms which increasingly influence Americans now to look away from the past and to a different Millennial future American young people want to form for themselves. That challenges us to argue modernist and scientific assumptions. We can't assume what we don't know, which is why relying on history is important so we don't make the same mistakes. This is why prisoners come back most of the time because they forget the history of their lives and don't learn from their mistakes. An issue one has to come to terms with for a prisoner if they want to move forward. The same principle for solving the problems in other disciplines including multicultural wars and the differences between groups.

COMPASSION: *The Soul of the Christian Heart*

by M. F. Maraschiello, MCE (2019)

Did you ever wonder what makes a *Christian* a Christian?
It's quite simple, really. It's the outward expression of the inward
grace God gives the true follower of Christ to reflect *His* love
towards others in the giving of self over to altruistic and compassionate acts of mercy. (Acts 11:26; 1Pet. 4:16; 2Cor. 4:4-6)

The Calling to service. As responsible God-fearing Christians, we are not only expected to do our individual part to establish a personal relationship with God and take on the attributes of Christ, but also make time to assist others less fortunate in the kingdom to help them with not just their circumstances that may be of need, but also in their spiritual needs as well. (Titus 3:1-3; Heb. 5:8,9) Each person has talents God expects us to use in the kingdom here on earth to maintain the covenant with God in a father – child relationship with our caring God as the head of the church. (Rom. 1:7; Ps. 103:13)

Therefore, if we recognize our strengths and passionately work on our weaknesses, we can improve the quality of the relationship we have with God and others in our homes and community to strengthen the tie with God and our fellow citizens of which all who seek peace can experience greater happiness and prosperity in the world. And at the core of this is compassion. (Rom. 1:16; Col. 3:12) Treating others with kindness and slow to anger while seeking correction or the teaching for the benefit of wisdom through knowledge and experience gives way to mercifully treating others who do not know or have the "skill set" to make the changes in their lives to recognize it is the true Christian at work seeking to build up the kingdom and not criticize it or tear it down with hate speech or marginalization of others because of their disabilities or circumstances. (Rom. 2:1-4; Mt. 14:14)

What does Christ have to offer me in my life today?

No one is without sin. (Rom. 3:10; 1Pet. 2:1-3) However, Christ offers His way of life as the alternative to death and hopelessness in whatever problems we are experiencing today. (Dt. 32:-36; Ex. 22:27) Christ won the victory at the cross to overcome ALL adversity, and to give others the strength and encouragement to look into ourselves to make available to God our trust in Him via true faith to believe that we have the POWER to change our situation. (Mark 16:16) All throughout the Bible's New Testament Gospels are the miracles and words of Jesus Christ who teaches the type of character attributes we need to reflect in our own lives to receive the promises Christ has for us. (Eph. 6: 11-20) Not only in prayer does God hear us, but His omnipresence overshadows everything we do as He see everything anywhere and at all times. (Sir. 18:13; Matt. 5:16) He knows our situation and promises better lives for us because of his great love and compassion for us He reflects from His heart, especially sending his only son, Jesus Christ, to die for humanity and our sins. (Rom. 10:9-10)

Thus, by learning about Christ and "how to live" as he did, allows us to be in the position to make smart choices – Christian Choices – which reflect Christ's mercy and goodness that comforts and manifests the necessary benefit of *His* love and zealousness for righteousness to multiply the good works we do which bear fruit for us all in the long run. (1Pet. 1:13-15; James 1:22)

So what is the "takeaway?"

By taking into your heart the "compassion" that Jesus has, and looking out upon others less fortunate than you, you can feel the love in the giving of yourself as a witness for Christ and the church which creates a self-motivating POWER of hope and accomplishment to work towards solving the problems in one's life and/or that of assisting others to do so to build up the kingdom and help keep the relationship we have with our God who cares for us. (1Pet. 3:8-18; Jude 24) A God reflected in our daily "walk," given in to His love we have accepted as the way to conform our daily behavior wherever and whenever the call is made for us to help our brothers and sisters in need, or when we come together to worship and give thanks for ALL He has done for us in our lives. (Hos. 11:8; 1Cor. 10:33)   End.

Compassion
Dt 32:36 will vindicate his people, have C
Ps 103:13 as a father has C for his children
Hos 11:8 my C grows warm and tender
Mt 14:14 had C fir them and cured their sick
Ro 9:15 I will have C on whom I have C
Col 3:12 clothe yourselves with C, kindness, etc
Sir 18:13 the C of the Lord is for every living
Ex 22:27 I will listen because I am compassionate
Jas 5:11 how the Lord is compassionate and merciful
Sir 2:11 for the Lord is compassionate and merciful

HELPING PRISONERS GRIEVE
– A VOLUNTEER'S JOB: Knowing What to Say

If you want to see real suffering, frustration, and bitterness, experience a prisoner who just found out his or her family member just died and the prison staff could care less telling you "Oh well, it is what it is."

We're not all therapists, nor have all the answers. But we can still have compassion and listen to the heart beat of a person who is grieving and may be in need of assistance get communication going to visit the grave site, funeral home, or watch a video download of the funeral at the chaplain's office. It may even be to even call the chaplain to find out *why* the inmate isn't being allowed to access the phone.

Plainly put, you – as a volunteer – are to show love and support, and find out what the inmate's status is as to what they need. **HUGS.** Health talking – about them. Less talking and more listening. Holding a hand or other forms of comfort give the person the feeling you care. Understanding you are there for them, not looking at your watch. **Get** in touch with who they need you to contact. Reaching out to family gives feedback to the inmate you are more than just a visitor but a friend. Stand firm like Christ as a pillar of support for them that they will get through this and heal. God is in control.

Remember, YOU can touch and talk to the inmate. And in prayer, you both can communicate to God to get through it all.

TYPES OF CHILD ABUSE
(Article taken from *The Maximum Times* 2018 by M. F. Maraschiello)

Note: This may be what your inmate you are seeing may have suffered.

Abuse is normally intentional; however, *negligence* is now considered abuse equal to or less or more (depending) intentional – and criminal!
1. **Physical** – Visual (i.e. bruises, scars, deformities, etc.) or un-seen (sore areas, healed broken bones)
2. **Mental** – PTSD, TBI, developmental (from starvation – brain has grown abnormally, etc.) other
3. **Emotional** – Responses to situations – inappropriately; numbness, outbursts, etc. can be indicia of abuse.

Severity of abuse, today in American Society, is no-longer a factor. American culture and norms have taken abuse to be ANY type, way, form, or severity meaning there is no severe, plain, little, extreme, mild, or general abuse. There is only abuse.

ABUSE OR DISCIPLINE?

- TELLING AT A CHILD TO BE QUIET ON AN AIRPLANE
- TELLING A CHILD "NO" -- WHO ASKS FOR CANDY AND THE KID SAYS THEY WERE HUNGRY
- DENYING A CHILD TO SIT IN THE FRONT SEAT OF A CAR, BUT RATHER THEY MUST SIT IN THE BACK SEAT IN A CAR SEAT.
- DENYING CHILD A *ONE-A-DAY* VITAMIN AT BREAKFAST BEFORE SCHOOL

- ARGUING WITH YOUR SPOUSE IN FRONT OF YOUR CHILD
- FORCING YOUR CHILD TO GO TO THEIR ROOM FOR USING PROFANITY
- TELLING A CHILD "NO" -- WHO ASKS FOR A NEW PAIR OF SHOES
- TAKING A TOY AWAY FROM A HAPPY CHILD WHO WAS STICKING IT INTO AN ELECTRICAL SOCKET
- BAD-MOUTHING YOUR EX-SPOUSE ON THE CELL PHONE IN FRONT OF YOUR CHILD
- IGNORING YOUR CHILD'S HOMEWORK
- DROPPING A CHILD OFF AT A BABYSITTER WHO IS MORE CONCERNED ABOUT "MAKING OUT" WITH THEIR BOYFRIEND
- FEEDING A CHILD JUNK FOOD
- ALLOWING THE CHILD TO GO WITHOUT A BATH OR SHOWER FOR 2 OR MORE DAYS
- WATCHING PORNOGRAPHY WHILE YOUR CHILD IS IN THE NEXT ROOM
- NOT KNOWING YOUR CHILD'S BABYSITTER WATCHES PORNOGRAPHY WHILE BABYSITTING
- LETTING YOUR EX-SPOUSE WORRY ABOUT YOUR CHILD'S MEDICATION

<u>HAVE YOU BEEN IN OR SEEN THESE SITUATIONS HAPPEN?</u>

REMEMBER, CHILDREN <u>SEE</u> EVERYTHING. THEY LOOK TO PARENTS AND ADULTS – YOU -AS THE EXAMPLE OF HOW TO ACT. DON'T ASSUME THEY – AND OTHER PEOPLE (I.E. NEIGHBORS) -- DON'T KNOW WHAT IS GOING ON.

CHECKLIST INTRODUCTION
(Article taken from *The Maximum Times* 2018 by M. F. Maraschiello)

"What does Your Inmate that You Sponsor Need?

Today's society demands expanding volunteership in prison ministry work to focus on <u>*reclaiming*</u> prisoners through effective mentorship and sponsorship as previously discussed in other sections of this guidebook.

Ergo, putting a *band aid* on an open chest wound just doesn't work. Wherefore, it is the purpose of a checklist to help guide the sponsor to provide *meaningful* support, encouragement, and guidance to the I/M in order to help ensure that sponsored I/Ms have the <u>***best***</u> opportunity to make positive changes. Additionally, the checklist serves to inform the I/M of the steps to take to achieve the goals the checklist has for the I/M's unique situation or needs to meet those objectives to be a better person ready for re-entry back into society as a productive citizen.

<u>SOME MORE FACTS WHY INMATES NEED A SPONSOR.</u>

Did you know some I/Ms can't read? Never finished high school? Never held a solid job? Don't know how to write a resume', can't use a computer, nor

Continued

do they know how to do a job interview or even search the web for a job?

QUESTION: Is a person like that, above, "handicapped" in today's fast-paced society?

Imagine for a moment the *retardation* a prisoner suffers being locked-up from society with its revolutionary technologies and changes in culture occurring as the decades go by. How is an I/M to keep up with such things unless they have a *bridge* or link to a computer and people on the outside [of prison]? Who will "step up" to build the bridges so I/Ms can come back into society with the right skill-set of emotions, attitude, faith in God, and abilities to successfully function normally?

There is no doubt from the news and television sources we [as] Americans see all the time that the government or "state" does little or nothing to prepare I/Ms for release so that they can be successfully re-integrated back into society. Such things as rent money, money for driver's license, money for food, etc. are not a part of the state's re-entry concerns, but rather warehousing and security of the prison is the state's total focus when it comes to budgeting programs for reducing recidivism and assisting I/Ms on their way out the door. The "Real Ville" takeaway is that I/Ms come into prison usually in better condition than when they leave. By the time they are released, they are embittered against the system [of government] for the degrading conditions of prison, the lack of concern for their personal family situation which prison usually enables destruction and family separation, and the hope and will to work and continue life to find happiness in society is thwarted when the I/M leaves prison too old with a mountain of debt from court costs and fines. Also on the back of an "ex-felon" -- laws and parole rules so restrictive that they are sometimes *worse off* than living in prison where "three hots and a cot" (meals and a bed) are guaranteed, un-like a free-world person who gets to work for a living and a roof other their head without petty *violations* to worry about.

As pessimistic as it sounds, above, this is basically what a defeatist view sounds like for a person who does not have: 1) GOD – number one in their life, and 2) A sponsor or support group who is monitoring and providing *effective* assistance and guidance to the I/M in prison so that they don't fall victim to the above system failures that don't foster a prisoner's development and preparation for successful release back into society with the proper job skills, attitude, faith in God, and emotional and mental faculties to re-adjust properly and be a functionally-independent person any community would wholeheartedly welcome not as an "ex-felon," but as an otherwise *normal* human being.

WHO NEEDS A SPONSOR'S CHECKLIST?

Probably 90% of all I/Ms need a checklist and a sponsor to drag the prisoner – literally – out of prison due to the "red tape" and flaws of the prison system, especially for those I/Ms going up for parole.

FACT. Having a sponsor *increases* the probability of parole for an I/M because the sponsor may be the **only** person speaking for the I/M at the parole board who puts a FACTUAL POSITIVE face on the I/M, probably for the first time..

A CHECKLIST USED AT THE PAROLE BOARD? ARE YOU *FOR REAL*?

QUESTION. How is a sponsor's checklist important to putting a positive face on the I/M?

Simple. The sponsor uses the checklist as a *talking platform* [document] of the *merits* of the I/M's time and achievements while in prison. The sponsor's verification of the chronological list of merits of the I/M's accomplishments and positive changes that an I/M has made show the "transformation" – with the sponsor's help – which gives testimony to grounds for warranting the I/M receive votes for release on parole. Additionally, the checklist serves to answer the parole board's own criteria or "factors" for parole consideration. (SEE "Common Sense Parole Factors": Parole Board Guidelines sheet, 2018) The checklist gives the sponsor the talking points in support of the I/M, and to, perhaps, rebut or "take the wind out of the sails" of any derogatory statement or falsehood about the I/M going up for parole and the case for their readiness for release and ability to comply with any and all policies, laws, and rules the parole board has for the I/M on parole. (This includes eroding the old "threat to the victim and society-card" [excuse / reason] the protesters often employ out of their *hater's playbook* to deny parole.)

NOTE. Not every I/M goes up for parole. Some "flatten" – serve out their sentences full amount of time -- and just walk out the front gate with, literally, a check for $70.00 dollars and the clothes on their back headed for poverty or "skid row."

RELEASE FIRST-TIME OFFENDERS WHO HAVE PROTESTERS?

As previously addressed in this guidebook, this is the number one concern for an I/M. And for a first-time offender, having a sponsor is critical, especially for an I/M with a violent crime who is facing "protesters' at the parole board hearing. Without a sponsor to advocate for the reformed I/M -- and if the I/M is ill-prepared -- retribution, hate-speech, retaliation, revenge, cries for additional punishment, and even lies and false accusations or innuendo can dominate and **_"poison"_** an I/M's chances for a FULL and FAIR parole hearing.

FACT. When the I/M has no sponsor, involved family member, or support group advocate at the parole hearing, the parole board _usually_ sides with the protesters, and hardly ever believes the I/M to be truthful, especially when the I/M is speaking about themselves as worthy of parole, and facts related to the crime, compared to what the victims say happened.

TAKEAWAY. Having a sponsor at any I/M's parole hearing or at court utilizing a checklist and having the knowledge about the I/M's prison record, life, faith in God, and changes they merit for parole, ensures that the I/M has a **_voice_** to herald <u>positive</u> facts about the state of the I/M as to their character, repertoire of skills, and chances for success back into society. Without the sponsor, the I/M is open to attack, and the focus of the parole hearing turns back in time encompassing the crime committed long ago and what the I/M **was** rather than is [today], with the protesters saying just about anything to intimidate or threaten the parole board with negative consequences (i.e. e-mail the governor to have the parole board chastised) if the board votes for anything other than a denial for parole.

Hope

The Scripture, "With God, nothing is impossible," is interwoven in all three major religions of the world.

PROOF OF REHABILITATION – NOT A COMPLETED CHECKLIST?

FACT: With the passage of time, people change. This is the purpose of rehabilitation. The parole board gives absolutely no credit to the rehabilitative programs or efforts completed by I/Ms even with the assistance of mentors and sponsors who are – ironically – asked to support and help rehabilitate I/Ms. These noble sponsors -- at their own expense, time, and effort -- take the extra step(s) to pick up what [prisoners] society has cast away, and what, regrettably, is observe in the process the failure of the criminal legal system to help foster meaningful effective rehabilitation and parole for the reduction of recidivism and the preparation of I/Ms for re-entry into society.

Bottom Line: All the more reason why a sponsor and an I/M need a checklist TOOL to use to help both the I/M and the sponsor have a better chance to track the I/M's transformation into a better person and prepare them for release whenever that time comes.

CAVEAT. Tennessee law states that parole is a privilege, and not a right, which means bias and prejudice can creep into a parole member's subjective decision-making process, and deny an otherwise parole-worthy I/M from receiving parole. Yet, that should not stop God-fearing men and women from volunteering to sponsor I/Ms needing a bridge to maintain faith in God and have hope. Faith in God is the _key_ to maintaining hope while in prison until such time the outcome -- one way or another -- of an I/M's situation [of freedom] is resolved or not. Ultimately, it is God who is in control with HIS plan [for us] that we must accept. However, while at the same time, we must persevere because it is during such extreme times that we are tested that we learn enduring character so that we can face even bigger challenges in life whether free or incarcerated.

A Simple Prayer We've All Come to Know.

Why Prisoners Need Prayer

Lord,

"Grant me the serenity to accept stupid people the way they are, courage to maintain my self-control, and the wisdom to know that if I act on it I won't make parole."

- *The Convict Foundation (2018)©*

Pictures: Author's Father

(Maraschiello Collection)

CW4 Victor J. Maraschiello, (WWII Vet) - 46 Years AD/GD/USAR Probation Officer, Erie County (Buffalo, NY) - 34 Years
First took the author to Attica Prison, NY in the 1970's. Then, as a part of his college thesis on Erie County Probation and Paroles, the author spent time at the prison and in the courts studying law, Sociology, and Psychology and attended ECC, Canisius, and SUNY campuses at Buffalo and Amherst, NY.

Author at the controls of a UH-60A Blackhawk, below, 1989.

A pilot in the United States Army, and an FAA-certified Commercial pilot, after the war, the author wanted to fly for the police department.

(Maraschiello Collection)

Author. Just after the 1991 Gulf War.
(Maraschiello Collection)

Police Officer Maraschiello, Nashville, TN (1994)
(Maraschiello Collection)

The Author – an incarcerated veteran in June 2020. (Maraschiello Collection)

"Prisoners are always in a struggle for their lives, which is why they need to be rescued and lifted up." - *M.F.M.*

EFFECTIVE MINISTRY MENTORSHIP / SPONSORSHIP

Doing all things through Christ - The *Best* Teacher

On Leadership.
"Members of the church were called on to demonstrate the power of Christ's redemption in their own lives by exemplary conduct, embracing every area of life." – Romans 12: 1-13:7; Col. 3:12-4:1).

"I can do all things through Christ which strengtheneth me."

- Phil 4:13

"All scripture *is* given by inspiration of God, and *is* profitable for doctrine, for reproof, for correction, for instruction in righteousness: That the man of God may be perfect, thoroughly furnished unto all good works."

- II Tim 3:16,17

Takeaway: Equipped, Accountable, Successful. All in three simple verses.

Chapter 5

LEADERSHIP

How to enter and leave the prison ministry with a look at the fundamentals behind it

Over the years, I've seen many volunteers come and go either to a church religious service, therapy session, or even come in at visit for the first time at the Visitation Gallery (VG) where you can tell the volunteer(s) are apprehensive, uncomfortable, or otherwise may not want to be there. And with the COVID-19 epidemic, I've seen more volunteers exit the prison ministry for that and other reasons as we'll discuss.

Since "COVID," many dropping out of the prison ministry did so with the "silent treatment." Not accepting calls, no responses to letters or even third-party e-mails -- utter shock to some prisoners who had thought their sponsor was "cool," "tight," or "professional." Even some volunteers who promised to write letters to the parole board before the hearing failed to do so, as some inmate(s) found out at their parole hearing.

Is that conduct Jesus would approve? What if someone promised to stay with you "all the way," or do something for you and didn't do it?

Reality check

Folks, let's face it -- prison is not a *normal* place to be or visit, especially for a "first-time" volunteer who may be going it "solo." I've seen some volunteers at the VG sit like a rock all stoic and then jump at every radio buzz or door slam reminiscent of those old 1990s *Scream* and *Friday the 13th* "slasher" movies where they were scared by every sound. Going to a prison is either overwhelming or no big deal depending on the circumstances and the pre-conceptions one has had from propaganda, poor training, or other influence(s).

I remember when my youngest daughter came to visit me for the first time when she turned eighteen years of age. She'd been prejudiced to believe me to be all these terrible things from the brainwashing and hate she'd received for almost fourteen years. She was tense as I hugged her, then she sat rigid in the chair next to me with her soft drink bottle. In retrospect, I was glad she wore her grey U.S. Army "PT" (Physical Training) sweat pants and hoodie, so she didn't have to be so uncomfortable and apprehensive meeting me for the first time – her father, who posed absolutely no threat to her. Yet, because I was in for killing her mother in a rescue attempt of her that went wrong that she didn't know from not hearing the truth all these years, her fear of me and the years of prejudice to believe I was "bad," was still an overwhelming force to persuade her conscience to be on guard and distrust me. She didn't realize nor understand that I would not even be permitted to have a "contact visit" with her unless I was already determined by psychological services of the Department of Correction to be deemed "minimum" security, as having demonstrated no violence, ever, in prison, nor had I ever made any threat to anyone especially her whom I loved. (I will discuss later some of the reasons why it is important for children of parents in prison to have a relationship with their incarcerated family members because it helps the children – like my daughter – come to close their wounds and heal. She – a victim – deserves healing, and the fastest way to do that is to have open dialogue and communication with the parent so they can get the answers – and truth – for closure and moving on in life as a "survivor" to find happiness and success in life again. Something, unfortunately, she was not taught while growing up.)

Visiting. So, do you believe Jesus, today, would "suit-up" in body armor with combat boots, pepper spray, tactical-gloves, baton, and face-shield to see *His* prisoners?

Of course not. Depending on the maturity level of the volunteer and how well they handle stress, are trained – educated by their prison ministry *leader*, and their love of Christ to help people, going to a place with an otherwise high concentration of allegedly violent sociopaths in close proximity may be a time only God knows what to expect given divine activity at work for which you expect good things to happen. Right?

Consider, for example, going to a *maximum* security prison to check out your church's prison ministry "A-team" in action. Before going, did you ask questions about what to wear? What you can take there? Whether your Bible will pass through the metal detector okay? How much "prep" (training) you need? Or, did you just agree to go there and "wing it" like some observer at an autopsy where you don't participate and/or make waves?

What's your *reason* for going?

The most important first part of prison ministry is, "Were you *called*?"

Being "called" is a mystery for each of us; however, it entails an inner drive based in believing God has identified in you a enthusiastic desire to do something. It gets tricky because you may feel you have a calling to be a "Mars explorer," but the odds of you getting to Mars anytime soon are pretty slim. Just as being called to be in the prison ministry, you have to have the calling, then the resources, qualifications, training, and then availability to then perform the tasks and be involved.

Now that the simple version of being "called" has been defined, let's look at the reason for being uncomfortable and taking steps to alleviate that before going to the prison so you can have your mind clear to observe your prison ministry at work instead of focused on the problem (fear(s)) distracting you.

I got a kick out of my oldest daughter's reaction when we first re-connected when I told her I was not the "Flying Chupacabra." Living in Southern California on the Mexican border, she heard of the "goat sucker" (el Chupacabra) that swoops in and snatches dogs and children then eats them. (I never heard her laugh on the phone so loud before; it was humorous, but sad.) This mythic four-foot tall giant bat that trolls the skies to attack innocent prey wherever an opportunity presents itself was – as with my youngest daughter's "belief" that I was somehow described as such – a demon. Again, as I will explain later about the "myths" of prisoners being deterrents to normal "healthy" relationships, this too is a type of false representation about visiting prisoners. Falsehoods that are a roadblock for some people taken in by such nonsense about inmates that it impedes us from what necessary work Christ expects us to do, and from having normal healthy relationships with people.

Imagine that! Just tell a little lie about prisoners being dirty, filthy, *demonic* creatures then go visit them. Jesus today wouldn't have one fear at all of going because he *knows* what the truth is and doesn't believe in lies; He's God, and is omniscient.

Well, I've yet to meet a Chupacabra myself, nor a prisoner who is, especially at the VG. I have not in my life time ever heard of a single visit at the VG with a first-time person ever experience an inmate going berserk; it just doesn't happen.

Like FDR [1] said, *"All we have to fear is fear itself."* And he's right! Mostly, it is the visitor with the "problems" -- not the inmate -- who doesn't know the inmate is usually overwhelmed with feelings of enthusiasm and the hope they don't blow the first encounter [visit] by doing or saying anything inappropriate. The typical first-time visitor usually comes in "bug-eyed" and fidgeting their watch that is so noticeable, not to mention the stiff-necked straight-faced look that exudes thoughts of "get me out of here" or "I'm nervous."

Funny, but sad, as many first-time volunteers believe the Hollywood hype those prison movies, TV shows, and police novels put out what I call "pulp trash" because a lot of it is fiction. That's not to say some of that doesn't happen because some of it does; however, back to reality. If you are in a VG folks, every prisoner there ***earned*** the privilege to be there because of *excellent* prison behavior that is non-violent and non-threatening. Everyone one of them, especially if you are in a prison with an "open" VG, meaning you sit in lounge chairs similar to those arranged at a typical airport lounge with vending machines and microwaves to purchase snacks from.

Starting to get the picture? About some fears of going to a prison *not* being something to fear at all?

So, whatever the first visit to the prison is going to be about (i.e. mentorship, sponsorship, preaching, observing, visiting a family member or friend, etc.), whether in the prison VG, chapel, or auditorium, gym, or even the recreation ("Rec") yard, going to see your ministry team, sponsoree, mentoree, family member, friend – whomever, it is one of two purposes:

1. Going there to observe dangerous zoo animals, or
2. Going there to witness (meet) people who need help

Am I clear? Are the fears you may have being questioned now?

Your reason for going – or leaving

Please know that God has your back! Don't worry because God has everything under control; the Chupacabra won't get you! Reality will set in and the fears and stereotypes will melt away for some volunteers. For others, the reality may be too much and "buyer's remorse" may begin to wear on the volunteer's conscience. The once noble thought of going to the prison to be a part of a "ministry" may now be something less desirable or viewed with less excitement first based in *naïveté*. The urge to join a ministry may have been a knee-jerk decision based on peer pressure, pride, or self-induced ego syndrome (believing you are a "Knight" [in armor] for Jesus) believing only you can change a person from good to bad or free them from evil by your divine knowledge of God and secret talents only you possess. No matter if the honeymoon is over, you want out having changed your mind, and don't quite know how to tell your pastor, ministry leader, or even the inmate(s) you were visiting, relax! God will give you the right words if you just stay focused on what Jesus would do.

Inmates know the "Golden Rule." Do you?

I'm reminded of when my mother pointed her finger at me when I was a child every time she used the *golden rule* on me when she caught me doing or saying something wrong to someone. Funny, how that same rule of "*treat others as you would want to be treated*" still applies today. Yet, for some people, when it comes to *prisoners* – a class of people considered a part of Christ's "least ones" needing extra care or compassion -- they seem to somehow forget that and treat inmates in a selfish way.

Consider this: Whether you are a man or a woman, the *golden rule* applied to prisoners prequalifies them as *human beings* with feelings that may be the same as yours. Hundreds of scenarios can be played out why and how people visit prisoners, usually with caution at first, because they don't know what to expect given one's limited understanding of what the prison[er] is [like].

Let's compare going to visit a sick friend in a hospital to show your loving support and compassion. You show up in the parking lot of the hospital which is white, colorful, and has stuffed flower beds all ornately groomed to make a nice impression that your friend is in a good place. You put on your PPE mask expecting it to be the norm when you go in and are greeted by the smiling friendly receptionist whom you ask for the room number of your friend. You use your mobile device one more time to call your friend to see if he or she is awake, then walk up the stairs or take the elevator to their room and go in, quietly, so as not to disturb the other patient(s) if it is a multi-occupancy room.

Pretty cut and dry realistic scenario, right?

But did you stop and think about the *germs* you are bringing in on your feet and clothes? That you can catch a disease or spread it? That your health is in jeopardy when you visit a high-concentration area of toxicity, then take home the diseases and germs to others? That other people there might not like seeing you and your friend enjoying a nice conversation while they have tubes stuck in them and vomit pans on their chests?

Gee! Describing going to the hospital doesn't sound so nice now, does it?

Now let's take visiting a prisoner – the "convict," the criminal who has been given the "Mark of Cane."

Walking up to the prison entrance you are met with roving dog patrols now searching your car behind you for guns, drugs, and cell phones. There were some flowers, but the concertina wire and drab 2-color scheme of grey and black really doesn't make you feel joyful entering the prison. The guard with a gun is still watching you as are the cameras. You enter the building and must go through a metal detector. With your PPE mask on, you are asked to show proof you passed your COVID 19 screen test. No one is smiling at you when you came in. By now you made it into the building, and make your way to the VG and take a seat. (Most *minimum* security prisons, even maximum security prisons for their minimum "staff," have lounge areas for the minimum security inmates to have "contact" visits where you sit as if at an airport terminal lounge.) You then wait a few minutes until your inmate you are visiting comes in. They know you are coming because when you came in, the officer at the desk notified them that you arrived. Once together, you meet and have your visit talking, getting some food you have to pay for out of the vending machines, or walking around the VG looking outside from the windows being sure you don't step on any small kids running around with toys. If you went to the Prison Chapel to visit or other location, you would simply walk there with, perhaps, other visitors headed the same way to attend a religious service or event.

So, what's the "takeaway?" It's impossible to explain every scenario for a prison minister visiting a prison, but the point is it has one thing in common with visiting a hospital:

You are going to visit a person that has feelings – another <u>human being</u>, not a diseased animal. And that person expects to see you care.

You've read now where I often like to use the "zoo analogy" where visitors come to visit prisoners – even disenfranchised family members – and just come to sit and stair at them, feed them, then depart leaving behind the inmate feeling nothing happened but a cold impersonal visit just to satisfy a conscience, debt, or other justification but not going for the benefit of the prisoner.

Sounds like a trip to the zoo, right? Where you get off the bus, maybe with family, other students, or friends, stop by the elephant exhibit, throw some peanuts, then you get bored and it's time to go back on the bus with a memory of the zoo that is quickly forgotten.

Pretty typical for some trips to the zoo, and often a typical first and only trip for some who went to a prison one time.

Case-in-point. My friend who's family only began to contact and visited him at the prison because they wanted something – money. After twenty-some years, all of a sudden his sisters start calling him because his father had left him the "lion's share" of an estate in the will. Now my friend is their "favorite convict" whom they want to know how much he's getting!

I don't have to spell it out, but let's be real here! Just because men and women are locked up in prison does not mean they lost touch with decent human behavior or conduct of acceptable norms or mores of the society that are even based in Christ Jesus' way of preferred living. Many scholars of Christian prison ministry would agree there are some *better* people in prison of higher character, education, and worthy of respect acting more "Christian" and more mature than a lot of people who are living in the *free world* right now. I've seen people turn their backs on prisoners after they did nothing having been falsely accused, only to now wear a label that discredits them. Then, the *culture* further condones them via social media – a scourge -- used maliciously now in Millennial American theophobic culture to further slander those convicted.

In short, by design, I hope I have stirred some thoughts given to visiting or communicating with inmates and the expectations you may have about them. "Getting it right," meaning making sure if you are to be an effective prison minister, mentor, sponsor, counselor, friend, etc. to a inmate, one must be above all **_human_** in your approach, with a heart and mindset of Jesus.

K.I.S.S. (Keep It Simple Stupid) -- the Golden Rule.

Is that too hard to grasp: That being "human" dealing with humans cuts right through the elephant grass of confusion and just be real – be yourself – when dealing with another human being who is stuck in a prison and needs some help?

If you went to the hospital, don't you think that friend in there that was sick needs help from the doctor(s)? Staff? Nurses? You?

Wouldn't you want to be treated as an *equal* if you were visited by someone? Not looked down at like the typical Jew or Roman of Jesus' day looked at the Samaritans?

Well, there you go! It's the same thing visiting inmates, folks:

> Treat inmates the same way you would want to be treated. You get their respect that way to accomplish both your goal of wanting to help, and their goal of picking their life up with hope and a better present and future from your talents. Why? Because you are not treating them like an animal at the zoo, but as a human being God created <u>just like you</u>.

Using good discernment (judgment) leaving the ministry

For those with *second thoughts* who feel prison ministry just isn't their *thing* or "calling," bowing out is okay. Don't be afraid to tell the inmate(s) you've been visiting or communicating with, that you are leaving or ending doing ministry work; it's bad for everyone's moral, especially the inmate's.

Think back when you were in grade school. How would you feel if your teacher of two years all of a sudden just left without saying good-bye because they married and moved on? Or their parent died and they had to become the other's caretaker? Or they joined the military and were headed off to military training? Or your son or daughter comes home from school and they don't understand why their teacher left without a word?

Wouldn't you feel a bit insulted or hurt being owed a reason? Your son or daughter? What kind of example – "witness" – is that teacher for a child? Don't *normal* people expect *normal* actions and explanations with common courtesy or decency from people in leadership or authority positions?

HIGH EXPECTATIONS. As a volunteer sponsor or mentor, your mere presence invokes clout, especially if you are a *Christian* minister – an authority figure (*witness*) of Jesus.

To an inmate, your character (i.e. integrity and honesty) ranks high among an inmate's expectations. How you "step away" from a relationship is just as important as how you first stepped into it. That is because the next volunteer coming behind you will be judged on the score card you were graded with on your performance as a sponsor or mentor.

Case-in-point. One inmate I will call "Marty" had requested a mentor from the local church before he was going up for parole. The woman wrote Marty a letter, put money on his prison trust fund account, and then started visiting him at the VG each week. Then, she stopped. Three months went by; no letters, no visits – nothing. Finally, Marty asked me what to do, and I told him to contact the church. The church's prison ministry leader checked into it. To his amazement – and ours -- the leader told us she "disappeared." The look on all our faces was one of disappointment. More so, Marty, who felt deeper pain having had vested some time and hope with this volunteer to help him, only to have those hopes dashed and the credit of that church and his "faith" went way down.

Was that an example of *Christian* volunteerism?
No.

Given "hindsight" is 20/20, and speculation is all relative to the situations of intrinsic and extrinsic forces at play, that volunteer in the above incident could have just sent a "Dear John" letter to Marty saying she changed her mind about prison ministry and was leaving to do something else. No big deal. Right?

Most prisoners understand volunteers have a "life" outside of the prison. Volunteers come with all sorts of backgrounds, capabilities, resources, talents, educations, health conditions, marital statuses, handicaps, cultures, and financial status to say the least.

Regardless, however, a volunteer still should "bow out" gracefully and not leave the representative Christian faith in such a manner that it is questioned or seriously tainted. Marty didn't lose anything like his home, driver's license, or bank account, but he did lose confidence in the ministry that volunteer represented – ***Jesus' ministry!***

Why? Because the volunteer's inappropriate behavior can leave their church's ministry and leadership being damaged -- discredited, as it was supposed to be reflecting the positive discipleship or stewardship principles set by our Lord, Jesus Christ. Giving the "silent treatment" to Marty didn't score one for "Team Jesus." Rather, it created **doubt** in Marty damaging his already weakened faith now believing that a successive ministry volunteer could follow in the same sour footsteps especially if poorly trained by the responsible *senior* minister. And a successive poor volunteer would certainly raise the red flags that the senior minster, then, is more concerned about the management of the ministry team than sending out *qualified* ministers who are entrusted to do the work Jesus expects them to carry out. After all, what good is an army of soldiers if they can't fight or do their mission? Isn't that what Christian mentors and sponsors are supposed to do? Carry forth to the prisoners, evangelistically, both the Scripture and deeds for the salvation of souls and provide care to those in dire situations? Carryout Christ's [com]mission?

As my friend and former Vietnam-era Green Beret friend and Catholic Deacon Ted Welsh often says in his prison ministry work, "What good is a book to a villager with an empty stomach? He can't eat it."

Effective Ministry begins with Leadership

I hope I'm driving home the point that prisoners are human beings – people, like you and me with hearts and minds; not animals, insects, or amoebas. People get caught or were blamed for a crime then convicted or pled guilty and were sent to prison. Some deservedly, some not. Prison is where people are sent *as* punishment, not *to be* punished. However, some people don't understand that concept; they don't or won't. That's human nature. But in *Christian ministry*, men and women of faith are supposed to be *called* to a divine mission to serve as Christ did and to minister to the sick, the poor, the widows, the orphans, and – yes, even to prisoners, the tax collectors, prostitutes, sex traffickers and the wealthy – *all* called the "children of God." With particular attention given to the "least ones" of which **prisoners** are among that group to specifically be visited. (Matthew 35: 36)

Our task, therefore as Christian leaders, is as Saint Paul said which is to simply "witness" a Christ-like character to whomever we are mentoring or sponsoring in prison. In *1 Corinthians,* Saint Paul talks about Christian leaders showing people who need to hear about Christ's character, in us, reflective of Christ. And by seeing how Christ working in our lives is fruitful, this encourages others to believe Christ is real and therefore Christianity an attractive faith – the ***only*** way to salvation by imitating Him through us. Further, it is this "*transformative* process" that prisoners need, and Christian volunteers need to promote. As mentioned before, discernment over judgment is needed not just to determine what a prisoner(s) need, but rather *interpretation* to find out what prisoners need the most.

WITNESSING IMPLIES A LITTLE DETECTIVE WORK

As we witness, we not only bring Jesus, we bring ourselves to show those [like us] we are amongst you coming as a friend and teacher, not an overseer or dictator. Knowing the fundamentals of basic discipleship and applying them "in the field" is for one purpose – build up the body of Christ through bringing the Word and uplifting people's conditions. Seeing disciples in action rather than hear a bunch of words creates a lasting impression of unity and strength knowing that Christianity is about taking care of community, especially those in need the most. Therefore, historically, a church can look back and see where it is having successes and where it is failing by the quality of service it provides for the community. Historical accounts combined with present situations show data a church can use so that it remains vibrant or makes improvement for it to remain strong or thrive in the future.

Changes in generations

I've talked about Millennials and the multiculturalism now making America an increasing "melting pot" as was used to describe the cultural landscape changes a hundred years ago when Europeans and Asians were coming in by the tens of thousands each month into America. Now, it is the flux of Latinos from Central America and people of Islamic countries coming to America to live. Hence, old generational concerns in the church fade away as the new generation of Americans form new priorities and concerns for living to include what values they place on God, country, and social justice. Churches that do not review the history and present status of their church moving towards progressive new trends, can find gaps occurring between old church leadership wanting to cling to traditional programs, policies, and values in conflict with the new generation seeking a different approach with a church's direction. The old generation was brought up on the "authoritarian" principle. The old families drew a broad black line between pastor (priest) and parishioner. So long as the church had what they called "faithful followers" – parishioners without courage and ambition – they were happy and content in their spiritual life. The church, in effect, had many docile members who just followed the church in an orderly manner called the "good old days" -- where parishioners seldom questioned their church leadership for fear of breaking the established system of their day.

Without a doubt, that "old order" of church thinking has all but come to an end today. Any church that has this above description is either dying or already dead. The children of these churches have a totally different perspective of how their church or group is supposed to function, especially providing for the common good of its community of member parishioners. Today's generation of church members generally want to be independent thinkers and not robots in a "hive-minded" church. Gone are the days of churches only concerned about the *church* (local) rather than its contributing and non-contributing [community] members. Voted-in radical changes to church dogma, un-observed church policies, and plain giving in to worldly pressure to relax Scriptural principles by the new generation of church leaders can very easily creep into a church and destroy it. This can happen quickly or unsuspectingly over time if the current leadership is not doing their job of monitoring the church's present conditions and assessing meeting the objectives of the church to meet the needs of today's society rather than continue only focusing on old generational needs. Learning the lessons of history show that clinging to dying stale practices don't make for a better church. New generations brought up on different sets of values will see those old generational values as radical and may reject them, only to consider what works for people today to fill the needs of people. Times change, and so must the churches, to keep up with what's needed.

Consider a well dug for a village provides water. But if there is no crop, what good is the water?

Trouble and distress follow suit, and the church that does not change with the times and still maintain the Scriptures, no longer looks like the same church. This is understandable because not every society is the same in a global world now. And when people don't see a church helping its people, they question that church's viability and reason for it to exist.

In conclusion, the fruit of a church is its people being provided for through that faith. That *sells* the church – period! Just as Jesus performed miracles, as did his disciples, so too are our churches to provide modern-day miracles of providing "life" to people (e.g. to prisoners) by visiting them and giving them the hope and attention they need based on today and for tomorrow so they are prosperous as Christ wants all to be. This is the opportunity we as Christians have to decide on making choices that attract people to the faith, not discourage them. Prisoners look up to ministry volunteers and church leadership for help. Sadly, there are church leaders and volunteers who look down at prisoners not with humble intentions but rather without a conscience 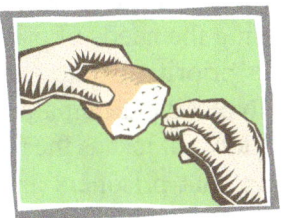 of a duty to serve and yield to reasons that don't promote Christ but pride instead. And not changing with the times for an evolution of prison ministry objectives and priorities of service for the millennium prisoner, means an old system of rigid "we-they" attitude still persists, and not one of "Body of Christ" with the prisoner -- a wounded part -- needing help to heal is taken care of no matter what the need. Applying a "band-aid" treatment on a broken leg is not going to give the casualty a chance for survival. But assessing the fundamental needs, like a doctor – for Christ – can give the spiritual medicine and social medicine to a prisoner who Jesus said is worth saving and deserves our effort to save that limb or the person from the spread of infection and loss of life. Remember, evolution is a continuation process, and churches have to evolve to meet the needs of the present day and future. Those churches that are pragmatic and connected to the climate of the day, reading the culture of the landscape by taking barometric readings, will be successful because they will have the information to be effective and provide meaningful assistance. Those who don't stay up on current events and *measure* their church's performance will inevitably fail due to lack of membership of the new and coming generations for failing to keep them connected to a church that has meaning and an *relevant* faith worth keeping and utilizing as passed down through example of its impact on daily lives for success today. Our faith is like a powerful tool, used with its life-giving light to keep us vibrant spiritually, physically, and socially for us to use our god-given talents and make the world a better place for all. And by knowing our faith looks out for the "least ones" (e.g. prisoners), we know we are of value by the care our faithful brothers and sisters in Christ take care of us, in spite of a world that hates us and considers us (prisoners) as disposable garbage. That is why church leaders must speak out against internal as well as external voices and practices which condone suppressing the needs of prisoners and move prisoners from the bottom of the priority list to the top. Until this is done, prisoners will continue to receive the smallest part of the budgets – the crumbs – and be looked down at just as the rich man looked at Lazarus. Only until people realize that prisoners are just people who made a mistake – sinners – that got caught and are sentenced to prison for crimes to be "re-educated and re-socialized," will there be any justice for them. And the times are changing for this "revolutionary idea" to begin making church leaders begin to think about it because the old ways of "doing business" in the prison ministries no longer presents an attractive means of care. Rather, it tells prisoners your church is a failure. As my father used to say, "Sorry doesn't pay the doctor bill." I took that to mean that whatever the church fails to do is just an excuse like the band aid on a broken leg. Or like Rev. Ted Welsh's saying about books don't feed empty stomachs of villagers. To be effective the church must adapt and provide for what is needed, not what they perceive to be the needs based on old church policy. Asking prisoners, being aware of what's needed for parole, what is needed for an education for a job skill – all require some good old fashion "home work" for the volunteer to know what's needed.

Like Military Intelligence during the 1991 Persian Gulf War, I had to call AWACS before flying my assigned route called the "air corridor" to get the latest "Intel" (intelligence reports) about enemy threat activity in the area as well as "friendly zones" so I could accomplish my mission. Needless to say, the same applies to any organization today including churches or organizations which provide support for inmates which is:

THE PRUDENT CHURCH LEADERSHIP NOT ONLY KNOWS *WHEN* TO ADAPT TO NEW PRIORITIES, BUT ALSO KNOWS *WHAT* TO ADOPT. THIS ENSURES AVOIDING THE PITFALLS OD CHANGE BEFORE ITS TOO LATE.

So, continuously working on your ministry's plan ensures mission success. Just because some volunteers of thirty years ago are today without the wealth and position they once had to do more, doesn't mean that they failed in their church obligations for the ministry. What some volunteers lack in monetary resources they make up for in skills to find resources and/or educate inmates and other volunteers on a multitude of subjects regarding supporting prisoners. Be aware that church members are harder to keep than to accumulate as time goes on when, as today, posts on social media can smite what your church or organization is not doing for prisoners as Jesus would expect. The fault lies, again, in leadership because time and study prevents poor planning to meet objectives today and tomorrow by staying on top of current events – the "Intel."

Consequently, when the needs of prisoners changed, instead of a ministry or support group changing their old methods and adopting new methods for the new phase of social justice, they continued in the same old way. As in a basic business model of management, "business as usual" -- if outdated and obsolete – is a sure recipe for disaster in any organization. It would show no wheels of opportunity spinning in a positive direction for the business to have any chance for success. A principle true today for any church, organization, or ministry that believes it can be successful if it doesn't adapt to the changing times.

Thus, again, leadership must have it's eyes and ears" open to address the needs of people within its sphere of responsibility, otherwise it loses sight of the mission it was formed for and tasked to accomplish. Leadership principles for today's mentor and sponsor to take to heart and apply in their mission to provide for a prisoner(s) they have accepted to help safeguard with Scripture and the witnessing for Jesus by actions pleasing to God.

LEADERSHIP Training

In my research, I came across a book by D. A. Carson, PhD, called, *The Cross and Christian Ministry: Leadership Lessons from 1 Corinthians* which talks about the importance of leadership in church ministry. Carson too uses the early church leaders, like Paul, as an example to show how they had been forming the early evangelical stewardship in the church, making sure those disciples and the "local leaders" of the various churches were all in sync with the teachings of Jesus Christ. Paul's core message in (v. 4:16) is imitating Christ to teach those who need God. [2] "Christian leaders must prove faithful to the *One* who has assigned them their "fundamental task." (v. 4:1-4) Paul's logic is easy to follow: Those who are servants of Christ are the ones entrusted with the knowledge and have the Holy Spirit within them reflecting Jesus to the people." [3] They are called to please the Lord, suffer as He did, and are not influenced by the church, the world, or any FALSE "apostle." Discernment, over judgment, is key for no man knows what God knows. (Matthew: 7-6;

1 Cor. 4:5) The "good Christian leader" refrains from presenting him or herself as if they had the corner on the truth, or all the gifts, or exclusive authority or insight. Leaders are only God's servants, given talents from God, and should be humble, industrious, and evangelize

as a "builder" of God's temple which dwells in all people. But God cares about his church, and he holds its leaders accountable. Why? Because if leaders are too greatly elevated in the popular mind, they can do almost anything, and large numbers of their followers will trail along unquestionably. [4] Paul warns the Corinthians in his epistle that destruction of leading God's people astray is wrong, and only God's wisdom must be boasted about, not anything of the world. (1 Cor. 1:19-31; 2:10-11)

In today's prison ministry, effective leadership is key, beginning with the Scriptures and men and women honed in the teachings of Christ who reflect his character. A leader must use discernment and pursue what is best for the person they are counseling (evangelizing) – witnessing to. [5]

Dr. Carson writes that St. Paul found it necessary to address several Corinthian misconceptions regarding the nature of genuine Christian leadership. These believers were adapting too many models from their surrounding world. [6] As can happen today, as it did then in Corinth, "bad leadership" as exemplified by inserting worldly-influenced cultural influences into the faith is tantamount to a usurpation of Scripture and an overriding hijacking of Christianity representing false doctrine of Jesus Christ that is counter-productive. Those believers at Corinth were infatuated with Sophist teachings (relativism, skepticism, morality, etc.), many of whom prized form above content, prestige above humility, stoicism above passion, and organizing philosophy (wisdom) above frank confessions of ignorance and the limitations of human knowledge, rhetoric above truth, money above people, and reputation above integrity.

These same "influences" then are no different now that can divert the goal of the gospel truth to the world today by missionaries, disciples, teachers, or leaders of the church. In that environment then, Paul, as was discovered, had to return to the basics and explain what it means to confess Christ crucified. But he also had to chastise his readers about the evil in their tendency to lionize certain Christian leaders and ignore others. Thus, in 1 Corinthians 3, Paul insists that

Christian leaders (ministers/ elders/ bishops/ pastors) are *servants* of Christ first and not to be accorded allegiance reserved for God alone. [7] This is bad because the Corinthians were still basically stuck on the carnal mind of the world culture or "milk," as Carson says, and not practicing nor living the lifestyle of Jesus Christ. [8]

As I said before, Christian leaders should be witnesses and wear the gospel of Jesus Christ wherever they go. This was echoed by Dr. Carson in his book as well when he said:

"A leader is a role model that reflects the Gospel." [9]

We know that Christian leaders are supposed to be servants of Christ because Paul tells us so (1 Cor. 4:1). It's the heart of the commission that was entrusted to the disciples to carry out the secret things of God (1 Cor. 2:7). This was the *wisdom* of God, not the wisdom of man. As Dr. Carson points out, what is meant by being a servant of Christ is to be obligated to promote the gospel by word and example, the gospel of the "crucified Messiah." [10] This, of course, is reflected in Paul's statement that we Christian [leaders] are to be imitators of Christ (1 Cor. 4). Yet, "pride" can be a Christian leaders worst problem, if they don't recognize and acknowledge that their strengths and talents come from the grace of God not by man or the world. [11]

So what are the strengths and good attributes of a leader?

As a former military man, teacher, and pilot I can give you the *world's* definition of attributes such as: reliable, confident, guide, manager, builder, conductor, commander, influencer, performer, has respect, is honest, industrious, zealous, pragmatic, wise, and a number of other traits and character points in a good leader.

To Paul, as Dr. Carson points out in his book, Christian leaders are *"evangelists"* – teachers – who must be filled with the Holy Spirit." [12] Not only teachers but servants, like Jesus, who suffered under the cross and are not afraid to bear it and suffer – take the risks for the faith – as Jesus did.

What – take risks like Jesus did? Is that what a Christian leader does? Bear insults for helping prostitutes? Get yelled at on social media for helping a sex offender find a halfway house? For preaching the Word of God to a bunch of atheists? For giving an ex-con a job? For eating at a restaurant with two ex-murderers?

Is that what Christian leaders do?

Folks, <u>ministering *is* leadership and stewardship all in one</u>. And Jesus is the "Senior Minister." His standards are high because He paid the price at the cross of salvation which is FREE to all. As leaders, it is our job to get that message of freedom and hope out for God's glory, not our own. People don't get closer to God because of the leader's influential status in the community or their self-recognized abilities, but rather because of the Holy Spirit of God through them as we see in Jeremiah 9 quoted by God himself:

> "Let not the *wise man* boast of his wisdom or the *strong man* boast of his strength or the *rich man* boast of his riches, but let him who boasts boast of this: That he understands and knows me, that I am the LORD, who exercises kindness, justice and righteousness on earth, for in these I delight," declares the LORD.

Ergo, leaders must have "clout" to be effective to spread God's standards of *His* world. [13] Human standards are of the world – a *fallen* world. No Christian leader worth his or her salt would fathom to partake in spreading the world's false doctrines over the Word of God and the teachings of Jesus Christ. And giving incorrect interpretation of Scripture or a bad example of living to a prisoner that is not in keeping with the teachings of Christ is equally wrong.

This then, my friends, comes to the role of a leader to be that of shepherding and stewardship because "faith without works is dead"

(James 2:17). And part of that work is for Christian leaders to stay focused on Jesus' words and acts of mercy because "Christian leaders must prove faithful to Jesus" (1 Cor. 4:1-4), not faithful to each other, the senior leader, or the church. Being a Christian leader is one of being in a position of trusted authority, and Christ is counting on the leader to harmonize all, including disciples, to know Scripture and act as Jesus would to carry out the mission of bringing light to the world which – for the subject of this book – is for the benefit of prisoners in the category of "least ones" needing help (Matthew 25: 31-45).

Let's go back to Saint Paul and the Corinthians on the subject of leadership and who is following who. Dr. Carson points out that in Corinth, some Christian leaders were:

> "...*going to be written off simply because they preferred to follow some other leader as a "guru."* [14]

To elevate one leader and offer her or him allegiance that belongs to God alone is bad enough, to write off all authority in any other Christian leader not only betrays a woeful lack of courtesy, but places the self-appointed judge in the place of God, according to Dr. Carson.

As in Corinth, as can happen in today's leadership circles within a church ministry, some leaders can find themselves "clichéd up" as a [cancerous] cell, elevated in a conventicler manner, controlling the senior leader (pastor/ priest/ bishop/ elder), and therefore usurping the place of God making decisions based on what's good by *their* standards and not God's. Leaders need to realize that the church is not the head nor the pastor the hireling, but rather Jesus is the supreme head – the focus, of whom the church and all Christian leaders are to follow. [15]

Folks, being in a prison ministry isn't all happy smiling people riding the carousel with cotton candy and gum drops. It's a sad and often seen as the least funded and least participated ministry at the bottom of the church or organizational budget for some groups with little enthusiasm and optimism for desired positive results and effects. And, as Dr. Carson says, to praise a form of leadership that despises suffering is therefore to deny the faith ... leaders in the church suffer the most." [16]

To sum up Carson's book, the overall goal is to point out that genuine proactive Christian leaders, as exemplified in Christ and written about by Saint Paul, are to reflect – 'witness' the light of the gospel of the crucified Messiah to the people of God for **_consistent_** Christian living. Christian leaders dare not overlook their responsibility to lead the people of God in living that is in *conformity* with the gospel. This is why Paul urged people to live a life worthy of the calling they have received (Ephesians 4:1). It is why Paul prays that believers may live a life worthy of the Lord, the crucified Messiah, and may please him in every way (Colossians 1:10). "And if the people of God dig in their heals in disobedience, there may come a time for Christian leaders to admonish, to rebuke, and ultimately TO DISCIPLINE THOSE WHO TAKE THE NAME OF CHRIST BUT DO NOT CARE TO FOLLOW HIM... That is the part of the responsibility of Christian leadership." [17]

Do you see where this is all going? That we can't rely on our leaders alone for the right way to minister, but rather depend on Scripture, the Cross of Christ, and the Holy Spirit within us for direction. We have to be very careful we don't follow blindly the "senior saints" appointed within our church who want everyone to follow his or her rules contrary to discerning what Christ wants and Scriptures say for the ultimate goal of the salvation of men and women's souls. We have to be *effective* witnesses reflecting Christ, bottom line. [18] Following *His* example guarantees we are providing others the correct reflection of himself through us. "World Christians" – like Saint Paul – went everywhere to evangelize and trained evangelists to reflect the lifestyle of Christ, sticking to the Scriptures as a witness. Today, that same manner is applied globally, even amidst a culture bent on tempting Christian leaders and believers to question Scripture and the necessity of Christ in today's Millennial multicultural society of ever increasing atheism, agnosticism, junk science, and relativism propaganda being dumped on our children in public schools today. Sacrificing the gospel and giving in to the ways of the world would de-commission Christ's entire mission within the framework of God's plan for his creation – mankind – which Christian leaders must fight for our Christian rights to be free from the chains of sin which Christ broke for us at the cross.

Simply put, we as Christina leaders in our church ministries – especially prison ministries -- are to uphold our God's Scripture and Christian values for the sanctity of life because ALL MINISTRIES MATTER. Sanctity of life is not just for the unborn, but for the living as well (i.e. sick, prisoners, sex-trafficked victims, etc.) who need the light of Christ in a world or situation of darkness where only divine intervention is going to give people the hope and relief they need because our faith [practiced] says so. To Saint Paul, the requirements of a leader are: builders and teachers who are: (a)(1) Not a current convert (1 Tim. 3:6) and (2) Able to teach (1 Tim. 3:2); and (b) Trustworthy [19] This is why strong leaders are necessary – to carry out the work of Christ – period! Not some church leader's conception of what prison ministry is all about as I will explain.

"SELF-CHECKS" DON'T WORK: GET OUTSIDERS TO EVALUATE IF YOUR MINISTRY IS ALIVE OR DEAD.

Did you ever hear the phrase, "Cleaning house?"

To some people, that is a nice thing to do. Stay at home on a Saturday afternoon with the family while you clean out the garage and the kids and your wife vacuum the house and wash the windows and such. Then, after it's all done, you all celebrate with a backyard barbecue and a "high five" for a well-spent productive day.

Or, to others, cleaning house is bringing a wave of nasty visions of a boss at work who is firing employees because they failed to perform their jobs and lost the company – and the good-working employees – a paycheck or two.

Well, in prison ministry, like a business, the military, or any organization, the phrase *cleaning house* is both good and bad. Good that you get rid of the "dead wood" or ineffective people who won't or can't perform, and bad because you may be one of them. Or, a practice or "luxury" of past dogmatic in-house ways of doing things may have come to an end, such as taking the yearly budget money earmarked for prisoner purposes and using it to fund a new copier machine or food processor for the church kitchen which doesn't benefit the prisoners the money was supposed to be spent on.

Sound far fetched? Not really. In probably half or less of some prudent churches around America, money earmarked for the prison ministry budget goes directly to prisoners for things like: shoes, books, TVs, smart tablets, toiletries, halfway house rent, driver license fees, bus fare, first month's rent, eye wear, tooth fillings, gasoline to pick them up when they get released, first payment on a vehicle, birth certificate fee (as high as $30.00), phone calls, flip phone, or even a month's rent ($400.00) for a prisoner's spouse who was going to lose her apartment. All real funded items I personally know of that were done by effective church prison ministries over the years, and then some. Yet, in other churches, their budget money hardly ever scratches the surface to provide meaningful assistance to prisoners for things such as mentioned above. Token pizza parties and free bibles – all "write-offs" for churches with federal non-profit 501(c)(3) status – may make some ministries feel "mission accomplishment." But for prisoners with significant realistic needs for re-entry, a church's support can do better, especially if what they provide for are properly documented for the deductions at tax time -- the whole point of the 501(c)(3) status for religious "public" benefit for rent assistance, paying driver license fees, food, clothing, and even burner phones and kitchen or food pantry items that all benefit church initiatives to help the poor of which prisoners qualify. (A less publicized little-known "secret" some churches don't want prisoners to know, especially that what they get from church volunteers isn't coming out of their pockets -- like some claim -- but rather the receipts for the pizza, shoes, zoo-zoos and wham-whams, etc., goes back to the church for the tax exemption write-off.)

These types of prisoner responsibility avoidance practices are not "high-five" moments for Jesus, but rather lame excuses for prison ministry work claiming to help people uplift their lives. Pizza parties don't help an inmate going out the door with a job or pay the first month's rent at the halfway house. A prison minister should be happy to provide what he or she can to a needy inmate who may have nothing, when released. Unfortunately over the years, I've seen where some churches pick favorites – preferred inmates to assist over the rest for support, while really needy prisoners looking to that same ministry get crumbs for support. This situation is most unbecoming of a Christian to say the least. Eventually they get exposed and the bad sponsors or churches are ferreted out because – in the eyes of the church elder leadership – this kind of behavior gives the church a false sense of providing support and a reputation of that church a "black eye." (Note. In over twenty-five years of being incarcerated, I've seen this happen, including many fellow inmates telling me they've witnessed seeing the same inside church "elites," "service custodians," or "servers" made up of inmates getting preferential treatment, while the rest of the inmates get the cold shoulder. This applies to even non-religious groups as well that come in to "support" prison advancement, re-entry, or counseling programs. Personalities of some volunteers sometimes don't mesh, and volunteers pick and choose who they want to give assistance to, while leaving some more needy prisoners to flounder in the system.)

Not all prison ministries are like this, nor are non-religious organizations doing this all the time; however, it does happen. Not all organizations and ministries have the resources and volunteers trained to adequately provide for all the needs of prisoners. It's human nature; however, for people to drift towards people they feel comfortable with.

The sad thing is that identifying and just picking the "easy route" isn't helping those who need help if you are the only face your church or organization has to offer that prison, jail, or halfway house. To make a decision to treat some of the prisoners around you as "second class" is a poor witness of Christ, and certainly a deploring example others will soon see by the way you interact with men and women who are "tuning in" to everything you say and do expecting you to be able to help everyone. The purposeful act of deceiving an inmate can be hidden from him or her; however, you can't fool Jesus. He knows the quality of love and support a prisoner needs and for which your church or organization sent you out to take care of which is what a true leader is supposed to safeguard from happening.

So, how does this make a prison ministry more effective?

"Cleaning house" usually involves the board of elders, senior clerical members, bishops, etc. who usually begin to see complaints. Usually problems about funds disproportionately spread out over a period of time when the ministry is no-longer generating the shining model of Christ's mercy and compassion it first began with, or never had, and their prison ministry is now discovered to be a liability producing no fruit. The first "knee jerk reaction" is usually to get rid of any suspected quisling prison ministers in a round up manner similar to quietly going after suspected pedophiles priests and pastors who failed to perform their first obligation and duty to be responsible to Christ and the Church. These "de-frocked" ministers are the "ex-leaders" – the *supposed* examples who don't represent Christ nor their church. And if they set the wrong example, then those who are under them are equally flawed to some degree, and if not vetted, they will put out or perform exactly like their model leaders who they believed to be doing the right thing. This is the problem of "silent obedience" to authority, and what harm poor leaders and *groupthink* can lead to.

Intrinsic Failure. A fallen or failing prison minister would be one that is doing something themselves, like being an alcoholic and getting a DUI. They never show up at the prison on time and may miss part or all of a session or service and are so tired they fall asleep in the chapel pew. (Unfortunately, I've seen a few.) Other intrinsic signs can be some leaders telling falsehoods to prisoners such as they can't write letters to inmates, or that a church music or singing group isn't allowed at a service, or even to step up and call their family when an inmate's father or mother died and the chaplain is not available. Worse, not writing a letter to their sponsoree, such as during the pandemic when no visits were allowed because of fear of spreading COVID through contact. One sponsor said to his sponsoree that he was his "brother" and "with him all the way." Yet during COVID, when the prisons stopped volunteers from visiting their inmates, he didn't even write or give the inmate the address of his church or home to write him.

Is that meaningful witnessing, caring, and due diligence?

Those are all examples of the prison ministry volunteer choosing to keep their distance – a sign of not being "all in" as Jesus was, but as I will discuss in a later section what is called "drive-by" ministering, which is a level of ministry some people perform not quit willing to be a true prison minister to provide what is necessary for caring for prisoner's needs.

Extrinsic Failure. A fallen or failing prison ministry may have "duck and dodge" type support above the head of the prison ministry leader. This is "the church management" a.k.a. "the elders" of the church organization *controlling body* (leadership) which delegates the authority of the prison ministry leader to do or perform what "it" (the church elders) only want the prison ministry leader to do.

For example, this may be telling the prison ministry head that none of the prisoners are to be given church bulletins or flyers which the rest of the congregation get because it lists the resources available to the congregation the church elders feel the prisoners should not have access to. Another example is when church members "in good standing" who are highly-respected in certain closed circles for their major financial contributions to the church; however, who specifically earmark their money for charity but not for prison ministry. The same with food, clothing, and other donations that pour into a church's resource pile which the church elders wish to keep from the prisoner's knowledge. Worse, when prisoners hear of grant money and 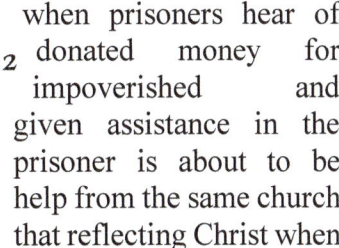 donated money for projects to improve impoverished and marginal people being given assistance in the community, and a prisoner is about to be released and asks for help from the same church but is rejected, how is that reflecting Christ when the prisoner -- a member of the community --is in need (e.g. needs a place to stay), yet is turned down?

Jesus in, Jesus Out and Group Think

If after release prisoners from your church ministry are not showing up to your church thanking you, that's a sure sign your ministry is in trouble, or you never had an effective ministry to begin with as you and/or your church or organization expected it to be.

Jesus left miracles in many places to announce "the way" is to *follow him*. If your church's or organization's ministry leadership is not performing, people are going to notice it because it doesn't reflect Jesus Christ or the spirit of His teachings. This is where the failure of prison ministries lies: Doing it your church ministry's way other than the way Jesus said to do it.

"I did it my way," Frank Sinatra sang in one of his songs. When we start doing it the leader's way or the elders' way and not Jesus' way, that's where the failure lies. Prisoners are not stupid, nor outsiders who can see "Groupthink" in action, of which I studied in college back in the early 1980s at the University of New York at Buffalo. We learned the *Bay of Pigs* invasion by President Kennedy was a result of his order for Cuban mercenaries to attack Castro's Cuba supported by U.S. military forces, only to be wiped out because of *groupthink* – [which was] no one speaking up to Kennedy and telling him the truth about the intelligence of plan was wrong. The result: a failed operation because of Kennedy's "advisors" – his board – were afraid to speak up and say and do the right thing for fear of "rocking the boat" and being targeted for ridicule and, perhaps, jeopardize their job position within the administration.

Is your ministry experiencing *groupthink*?

Does everyone agree with the church pastor, elder, bishop, or leader without question? Nodding your heads around a table like bobble-headed dolls afraid to speak up and present ideas that provide meaningful assistance, especially for prisoners in a prison ministry where prisoners one day will be freed and possibly come to your church? (That is, if you and/or your church or organization *really* want them to when they are released.)

BACK TO WHAT JESUS WANTS FOR A MINISTRY

If your prison ministry is just for the "hash tag" effect meeting a requirement from the downtown corporate office, or looking good on a publication to the management head, or filling a space in a bulletin, or to puff yourself and your church up to show it on your résumé, then you should re-think your priorities for having a prison ministry altogether. If the love of Jesus Christ is not there for the prisoner -- NUMBER ONE, and not for anything else but to the benefit of prisoners, then you don't have a prison ministry.

It's a "no-brainer" that Jesus considers prisoners to be a part of **<u>your community</u>** of brothers and sisters. Diaper money for incarcerated moms and shoes for incarcerated men are not the only needs for prisoners. Nor do budgets for flower gardens and paving the church parking lot for the second time in 2 years help the community as a whole when it is good for another 5 years only to make the outside *physical* appearance of the church "look good – while the inside social barometer shows some of your parishioners are in bad economic and social shape.

Ergo, what's the point of a church that looks good on the outside, if there is no one inside of it? Isn't *the church* really the people, not the building or the management? Who is serving who? Is money that could be used meaningfully for prisoners wasted on other projects bursting with excess? That streamlining other project costs within a church budget could see sufficient funding of prison projects? Is that a responsibility of effective leadership? To "call the ball" and bring it to the attention of church leaders for better prison project funding for your ministry? Not just give token dollars or donated items like "zoo-zoos and wham-whams," but rather real ticket items that give prisoners meaningful changes in their lives. Meaningful items such as paying for a professional counselor to mentor inmates who are members of your church, pay for the first month of rent for a re-entering inmate, pay for one of your church retirees to drive a re-entry prisoner on the first day out of prison to places they need to go (e.g. VA, SSI Office, Unemployment Office, DMV, a bank (to open an account)), and even to get a burner phone so they are not just wandering the streets like a "bum" with no purpose or no way of calling for help, especially if they are handicapped or medically disabled.

Do those sound like *Realville* prisoner concerns?

If you don't think so, then, perhaps, you don't have what it takes to be a prison minister. One who is to help provide ***paths*** for a prisoner to uplift their condition whether someone else agrees with you or not. JESUS is the one who says these things are important, and your reason and responsibility for visiting them.

So, what's your *barometer* of your ministry's health?

Priorities, folks. That's what it is all about. If compassion and mercy are in your heart, then also **prioritize what prisoners need**. Many had a life of "*lemons*" and now are thirsty to make "*lemonade*." Some are getting out as old as in their late 70s with no money, no health, no job, no family, no church – nothing; they can't function. Many can't even begin to know how to use a kiosk or a smart phone. They may not have any living family members either.

<u>**Prison ministries are supposed to be your community's *Church Support System* for those who need help with situations of social justice.**</u>

Your church leader just has to go to the prison on a night to see how the other effective church ministries are doing by the number of attendees at those services which are swelling with prisoners because those sponsors and mentors are ***actively involved***. They take each prisoner seriously as a man or woman, and spend quality time with them. Not sitting in a circle for two hours talking about the "pit of hell" waiting for them if they don't turn to Christ to be healed, but rather relating to them and witnessing as if like from a father or mother to a brother or sister or son or daughter who needs to know that they are wanted, loved, special, and of value the way Jesus sees people.

That's what brings in the "souls' to services – a church that honestly cares with deeds of support, not words alone.

FACT: MANY PEOPLE DON'T REALIZE SOME PRISONERS CAN QUOTE BIBLE SCRIPTURE BETTER THAN SOME TV EVANGELISTS BECAUSE THEY HAVE BEEN STUDYING IT FOR YEARS AND ARE ALREADY *SAVED*. THEY NEED MEAT, NOT JUST THE MILK. PRISONERS KNOW PRISON TIME CAN BE *PRODUCTIVE* TIME.

So, remember we discussed that prisoners are people who have needs. Needs that should be addressed. Not addressing those needs makes prisoners – just like other human beings – look elsewhere for support, it's human nature.

Again, as my friend Deacon Ted Welsh says, "What good is a book to a villager with an empty stomach? He can't eat it."

For example children of parents in prison are in very much need of contact with their biological parent(s) who may be in prison. NO OTHER is more likely to fight for that child than the biological parent because of the natural bond. Yet, there are those who try to separate them from a parent, say in a divorce or other legal matter. Sadly, that child suffers in life because that child is searching for answers maybe only the incarcerated biological parent may be able to help them with. Especially to help that child heal from their wounds of separation and loss of an otherwise normal life. That child grows up with voids often learning abnormal social behavior because the family unit was destroyed. Then they end up in situations they can't quite understand or handle emotionally and/or psychologically which cause them undue anxiety and depression or other things like substance abuse and thoughts of suicide.

What's this got to do with prison ministry?

Let me tell you, I've probably just described 90% of *everyone* in prison who has experienced the above scenario, including myself, in one relation or another to a similar situation. I've had to deal with my own daughters' separation, and counseled hundreds throughout my life beginning in the early 1980's when I was a Special Needs Teacher, including counsel my wife who was a victim of severe rape before I met her. Prisoners experience loss of relationships and separation – it's a fact! 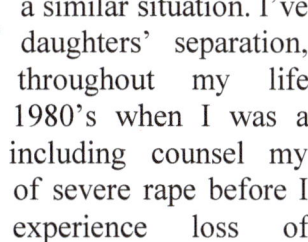 And depending if that person is young when they broke the law and didn't have an upbringing in some way that provided them the basics of normal development, the psychological and emotional damage that could be present can be enormous. So damaged could a prisoner be that putting the pieces back together or making new ones can be a challenge for some, if not all prisoners. Yet, with the help and grace of God, and perhaps a good prison ministry that wants to provide some help for that "sick" (damaged) prisoner, maybe giving them more than just some bible verses and some paraphernalia will uplift that inmate's present condition to one Jesus, not you and your church, would be proud of.

Success isn't pretty, but you hear about it. Remember, you and your church don't do things to please you, your church, or the prisoner. You do things that please God. A prisoner asking for a vacation trip to the Bahamas when released isn't going to happen. A bus or plane fare may. Realize, not all prisoners are what the horror stories are, making them all out to be "grifters" and "con artists" who will take your 401K account or max out your credit cards. But it is the discernment of the leaders in the prison ministry and the decisions of the volunteers to do what is pragmatic -- what works – that is meaningful. This is what an *effective* prison ministry looks like:

- One where prisoners inside the prison flock to your service or class and can't wait to see and pray with you.

- You've witnessed and lead inmates to Christ.
- Inmates at the prison are writing letters to your bishop, pastor, elders, or church newspaper and telling them what a great job you are doing.
- The warden proudly drops by and is satisfied to see engaged/ involved inmates and volunteers.
- Inmates are breaking the doors down to the chapel because there are no seats open at your service.
- Inmates you helped are getting jobs when released.
- You've helped restore an inmate to his/her family.
- You've helped an inmate get an education.
- Your budget and ministry body is getting bigger taking on more responsibility to serve.
- Other ministry or organizations are calling you for advice or to accept donations and support your team.

Don't forget, "bigger isn't better." Just because your church is big, doesn't mean it is doing Christ's work as it should. Closing the door to LGBTQIAX, foreigners, republicans, democrats, prisoners, whites, blacks, Asians, communists, socialists, Marxists, gang members, haters, racists, drug addicts, those once infected with COVID, etc., does not show God's love! The door has to be open to **_all_** God's children in our *multicultural* world now, to every "sinner" to show people the way of the cross to salvation no matter their status. [20] Times have changed where, today, the *world* requires "World Christians" like Saint Paul to bring the gospel to those who need it. As diverse as the U.S.A. is getting, it will be 50% Hispanic by 2050 as it is estimated. A large portion of that population will be Spanish-speaking and Catholic, according to sources. I'll use an acronym my friend, Dr. James Kelly used to apply to people and apply it to the prison ministries: Y.C.W.Y.T.A. - "You choose what you think about." Meaning, churches and ministries need to think about what they need to do before choosing to do or not do them which can have negative consequences not only on prisoners, but on your church and ministry as well. "Token ministry" with slogans and intentions of only preaching "The Word," may be okay for people that need to hear and begin to come to Christ needing the "milk." But for the people who need the "meat" in deeds and actions to help them uplift them with their education objectives, housing, re-entry, parole, and other aspects such as the relief from parking tickets to get their driver's license, the time for deciding to loosen-up the funds to help these "least ones" improve the quality of their life with these survival assistance needs is a priority over cruise ship specials for divorce' "meet-n-greet" trips, or buying new vans when the current ones are still good. Making a fundraiser for prison relief funding to sponsor a prison's few church members who have no outside support and need assistance for re-entry is a great way to say, "Our church supports prisoners ... they are church members too."

How would you think that prisoner who is a member of your church would feel if he or she was being released after 20-some years a member, and your church didn't even offer him or her a ride to the unemployment office the day they were released?

Do you think she'd / he'd want to be a part of your church when – at the time he or she needed you the most -- your church wasn't there to support him or her?

Would Jesus looking down from Heaven after seeing that say, "Well done, noble servant?" Or, would Jesus shake his head in disappointment?

Ending being a volunteer or saying "no" to their request(s).

Wrapping up how to look at, assist, and otherwise examine a volunteer's appropriate treatment of inmates and leadership training, if ministering just isn't your thing, just do what Jesus would do – leave love behind when you go. "Leave on a positive note," as they say. That is: be kind and gentle, which is as appropriate as you can get if you tell a prisoner it isn't working out and you are terminating support. If you found a replacement, that's even better. At least you didn't leave the prisoner adrift. Being a prison minster, sponsor, or mentor can be tough. But if you are going to stay in it or be a leader in some way, be sure to do the right things that would please Jesus. Handle telling a prisoner you are exiting like handing them a balloon rather than shoving a brick in their face or giving them the silent treatment. Everyone can take a balloon easier because you can see it coming at you as compared to a flying brick. The same thing with telling a prisoner "no." It's not "rocket science," just what's works – the love of Christ and your best foot forward. Honesty works and so does candor because they expect that from a volunteer who represents Christ.

For example. Many volunteers are retirees. As previously mentioned, some volunteers are personally on fixed budgets, and even some churches and organizations are poor with only their hearts to give. An inmate won't be offended even if you wanted to buy him something he needed, like a watch or pair of glasses, but you did not have the resources and even searched for resources but still you were out of luck. Tell the inmate that you tried; that's what they want to hear and know. Maybe even refer them to another person, especially when "mission creep" occurs, when you have several prisoners that are really desperately in need and you can't do it all. "Outsourcing" and going on the Internet (e.g. social media) may bring help for you from others out there who can or would like to help you. Such as with "tag-a-long" students coming into the prison from the local colleges to volunteer and want to get in on compassionate assistance. Regardless, not all volunteers have access to resources; however, some do.

"Miracles do Happen."

I must hark this story of one incredibly zealous sponsor last year who found a truck valued at nearly $6,000 dollars and donated it to a prisoner getting out on parole. His generous spirit of giving gave this prisoner a huge gift [of God] because he was going to a halfway house. Everyone here at the prison immediately felt uplifted knowing there are incredibly kind people – like "J" (his name for which I will keep anonymous) who blessed this one inmate with a truck on his way out on parole so he could go back and fourth to work. Not only did that sponsor's "street cred" go up, but also the ministry he was involved with for making a significant meaningful impact on that prisoner's life to help keep him from becoming homeless and without means to become self-sufficient and a part of the community. The acts of showing God *works* with deeds from mature Christian leaders such as "J," give hope for others to also believe they can be blessed with a miracle which proves God's loves for us all.

So, as most scholars of Christ's discipleship ministry today would agree, prison ministry is:

Doing what you can -- love.
That's all Jesus asks.

After all, *He* did all he could for us and then some at the cross. *He* "set the bar," and is the one judging your performance -- or exit -- with the prison ministry as to how you – a servant -- showed *His* love and compassion for *His* prisoners ("least ones"). Prisoners don't see your work as "charity," but rather love-in-action – justice from above God is credited with for restoring (uplifting) the least one's through the power of Christ with the sponsor's or mentor's hands.

Are you praying about answering the prayers of prisoner today?

Volunteer Assessment – It Pays Dividends!

Finally, as stated in this book, the prudent volunteer has a vision or idea to help others at a prison, jail, rehab center, or juvenile hall depending on whatever peaks one's interest to help a person in need or those who are providing ministry or organizational work serving others.

Here's a short description of what strengths are needed for such volunteer work, as quoted from the book *"Business Fundamentals for the Rehabilitation Professional,"* by Tammy Richmond & Dave Powers: [21]

> "Entrepreneurs are also leaders and managers. Grady defines leaders as individuals that "inspire, direct, guide, and teach others." [2] They possess the ability to create and communicate a bigger picture that encompasses effective and efficient utilization of people power, and innovative and established service models, and they challenge themselves and others to do the job better. They lead with organized management. Managers are individuals who can "increase efficiency, promote stability, assess situations, and select goals. [2] They administer and maintain the bigger picture by implementing structured daily operations and policies and procedures.
>
> Can you see the commonalities between the entrepreneur, leader, and manager? Successful business owners and rehab professionals:
>
> - Possess essential skills in there area of services
> - Understand the basic principals of management, marketing, and finance
> - Are disciplined and organized; act ethically
> - Engage in team building
> - Are action-oriented and self-motivating
> - Have self-confidence and effective communication skills
> - Have passion and perseverance
> - Know when and where to seek assistance from experts. They seek opportunities that will provide services or products that will deliver value and benefits to the client."

---

[2] Grady D. From Management to Leadership. In: McCormack G, Jaffe E, Goodman-Lavey M, eds. The Occupational Therapy Manager, 4th ed. AOTA Press, 2003:333-345.

Therefore, those seeking to be ministry leaders or "volunteers" need to be aware of what qualifications one needs or attributes to best be effective, as with the approach to volunteering the way a business entrepreneur envisions a "project" or "venture" they are virulent about doing. A, to provide the assistance to those in need just as health care professionals in communities who seek wellness for others. (See Figure 5.1, below)

VOLUNTEER'S ASSESSMENT TOOL

Here is an assessment tool that can help volunteers identify strengths and weaknesses and what to improve on for effective mentorship / sponsorship.

Considerations Work	Yes	No	Needs
I have a desire to help people, and am forgiving.			
I belong to a group, church, or network with resources.			
I have a vision of assisting.			
I have a good example-setting spiritual life.			
I have a good example-setting personal life.			
I have current knowledge of criminal justice issues.			
I have resource and networking skills.			
I have good communication and computer skills.			
I have current knowledge of social justice issues.			
I have a current knowledge of mental health issues.			
I am not afraid to stand up for those *the world* hates.			
I have patience to listen and gather information before acting.			
I am proactive to learn current innovations about my volunteer work and continue self-improvement.			
I don't resist criticism and change which could better my volunteerism.			
I can assist people of color.			
I can assist people who are LGBTQIAX*			
I can assist foreigners.			
I can assist gang members.			
I can assist child molesters.			
I can assist member of the opposite sex.			
I can assist murderers.			
I can learn to trust the inmate I am assisting.			
I am not afraid to give my contact information to my inmate so if they have a problem they can contact me or someone from my group for help.			
My purpose for assisting is not for self (e.g. romance) but to uplift someone.			
When I go to the facility, do I do more than just talk to make a difference in the life of inmate(s) that reflects God's definition of meaningful assistance?			

* LGBTQIAX (Lesbian, Gay, Bisexual, Transgender, Queer, Intersex, Asexual/Allied, Xir (Zeer) "Both")

Figure 5.1. These are just a few key issues to ponder about volunteering to assisting those in need.

Michael Maraschiello

Chapter 6
"The 4 Levels of Prison Ministry"
(The Four Types of Volunteers)

"Christ died to make people holy. Let's live to set people free."
- M.F.M. 2018

OVERVIEW

First, no one who hasn't the stomach to forgive has no business in the prison ministry because the target community – prison – is comprised of law-breakers – people who are deemed: criminal, uneducated, un-redeemable, worthless, losers, drug addicts, hustlers, murderers, homosexual, rapists, perverts, sexual abusers, bullies, thugs, gang-bangers, and any other negative stereotype creating the FALSE idea that all prisoners are undeserving of mercy and forgiveness – the __*real*__ test for a Christian, to say the least.

WHEREFORE, overcoming the stereotype of a "convict," "ex-con," "inmate," or "prisoner" is a challenge because of the indoctrination in education circles and propaganda by the excitement-chasing media, Hollywood, and groups opposed to a those called to forgive the incarcerated "offender." Not every stereotype fits, as each inmate is unique, with their own story. Each prisoner came from somewhere, has an education, and may have a family or job history. (This is addressed later.)

The bottom line is that the demographics, economic, religious, and social environment of an inmate has a tremendous importance as to the level at which *prison ministry* is effective for a volunteer to fit in and make a difference in an inmate's life – presently, and in their future.

CHOOSING THE RIGHT LEVEL OF PRISON MINISTRY

Everyone wanting to join "Prison Ministry" soon finds out that it is not what they first imagined it would be. Myths of prisoners behind dirty plexi-glass with nappy messed up hair barely able to speak proper English wearing dirty clothes are typical of what "excuses" detour the potential prison ministry volunteer. Ergo, the *calling* must be a serious consideration as not all people can preach or teach to others especially to the group so identified, above. That's why it is a good idea to first observe and then "get in where you fit in," and then go from their.

THE 4 LEVELS OF PRISON MINISTRY

1. EXTRINSIC INVOLVEMENT

This first level is usually the most participated or first step a volunteer approaches prison ministry because they may *never* go to the prison, talk, or see an inmate. One simply stays at a distance from home, church, work, etc. and does ministry from a far – unattached, and able to quit at the drop of a hat. The volunteer may feel and/ or have the idea they are contributing greatly because they wrote a check, sent a card to a prisoner, purchased a Bible, or coordinated some benefit (e.g. a *retreat* or book club) for an inmate(s) their church or organization has targeted. It may even involve writing articles or making some other project for the ministry achieve its goal in one way or another.

Regardless, this level is *one-directional* -- basically "plain white toast" and impersonal. Often the volunteer remains anonymous, and never knows if their intended effort made a difference or not. Usually, the benefit does have some plus for the inmate; however, this level is seen as disingenuous and more as a *"hash tag"* approach to ministry work. Rather than a true sacrifice from the heart as Jesus said should be done, these volunteers think that this is all they have to do, like buying a pack of peanuts to take to the zoo and feed the elephants. (The last time I went to the zoo, I observed it took a lot more than a one-ounce bag of peanuts (e.g. several hay bales) to feed a two ton elephant.) The proportion of help given just does not fill the amount of help needed. Often the ignoring of the real needs are obvious at this level. And with COVID-19 and social distancing fears, many will stop here and consider their "duty" done.

2. INTRINSIC INVOLVEMENT

The second level of prison ministry is *intrinsic* involvement. This involves actually going to the prison with the idea and feeling that the mission of simply "saving souls" by getting inmates to repent is the crisis to be addressed. This is a mistaken theory to base one's ministry work to help prisoners. At this level, an ominous assumption exists that all prisoners don't know Christ, don't follow Christ's teachings, and must have church volunteers to turn the inmates from sin and going to hell. Again, this is a one-way approach. Often the volunteer is a dictator preaching only such a message that begins to resonate within the inmate church service or "group" that it begins to sound like the "we – they" (bad vs. good) finger-pointing the courts, police, and juvenile counselors keep saying but never say any thing else. And when the seats at the chapel, gym, or in the classroom begin to thin out, it is often too late to hold the inmates interest at this level because the dictating volunteers never accept positive feedback and ignore criticism of their ministry believing they are right and the inmates are wrong. Many of volunteers at this level come to the prison time and time again for years sometimes, only to one day never return when they figure out their stale repeated message to "the lost" to [repent] is nothing more than a hollow message – words, with no offers of care to uplift inmates' conditions behind those words. Again, it's sorely impersonal. Yet at this level, a *physical* face is put to the ministry from which the volunteer (observer(s) or preacher(s)) come to the prison. It is when the physical appearance is made that people see *who* they are by the way they interact and whether or not they represent Jesus' *expectation* of a compassionate shepherd. This is, perhaps, the nation-wide *majority view* of prison ministry volunteers who come to a prison.

That the goal of the ministry is nothing but "salvation preaching" -- driving "demons" out of criminals -- with <u>only</u> the Word of God so that the inmates may find a faith.

> **Really? Just say a few words and "presto" -- that will save their souls from hell and a life-style of damnation? That's all a prisoner needs? Words?**

Many times, fellow inmates have confirmed what I've seen where volunteers – whether their message was effective or not -- often leave the prison with a false sense of accomplishment. Many times volunteers who don't care if their message is effective or not – don't know why the attendance at their services are so low at the prison. (I know, because some have asked me why attendance had dropped off in their services.) Often, it is because they preach the same old *shtick*, and inmates who need the next level of Christian mercy (care) decide to go to another prison church service or ministry organization in search for the "meat," having graduated from the "milk."

Ergo, at this level, although a step up from extrinsic, it is giving some of what they need; however, not as meaningful as it should be. To begin to be effective, prison ministries need to assess themselves from time to time and make adjustments to their messages and programs of assistance because each individual "sheep" (inmate) is unique in their spiritual faith level (Christian maturity) and need the next level of care in their personal life. And what worked for a ministry in 1990, surely has changed by 2020 in Millennial America.

FACT: This is often as far as <u>most</u> volunteers will go to help prisoners, even if it's for Christ. This is often called the "drive-by" approach to ministry, like going to the fast-food drive in and quickly getting the 99¢ Happy Meal; it barely works. The excuses – whatever they may be – are often justified by reasons such as: no time, no finances, horror stories and myths, or the one told bluntly some times – "we only bring the Word." Even legal reasons such as fear of being sued by an offender's victims for helping the inmate with anything can be the volunteer's reason or excuse for a lack of genuine Christian assistance to prisoners.

Can you imagine that? Some people can be bought off by Satan to believe that they are just helping prisoners with only words? God's Word is powerful; however, faith without works is dead. (James 2: 17) And at this level, where the *wheat* can be separated from the *chaff,* inmates will see whether or not the volunteer is sincere or not about helping people not only come to Christ, but help them in their **human** personal condition as Jesus demands.

3. REHABILITATION, RECOVERY & RE-ENTRY

That brings us to the third level: Rehabilitation, Recovery, and Re-Entry of inmates. This is the "meat and potatoes" of prison ministry – what it ***really*** takes to help a prisoner survive with hope from his or her Christian faith and church, reform, and then successfully re-enter society. If anyone thinks just faith and praying for everything is all a prisoner needs to make-it in prison and prepare for the future of living in society after they are released, then brothers and sisters, you are in for a shock!

SOME ALARMING FACTS: Some state prisoners make as little as 8¢ per hour after deductions. That's about $10 a month. They have to purchase their own toiletries, shaving gear, shoes, etc. They have to pay for phone calls and postage stamps are 55¢ each on such a pittance old "heads" (old convicts) used to call a "slave wage." Even envelopes cost money. They have court costs in prison, when they get out of prison, have no Internet provider, nor a phone to secure a job when getting out. Worse, for a place to stay, they may not get parole because the half-way house the parole board wants them to go to requires a non-refundable security deposit of up to $650 (first month) before they even leave prison.

Who can pay for that on 8¢ per hour?

Thank God there are some real Christian volunteer "heroes" who step up to the calling and make a significant difference in a prisoner's spiritual and personal life to assist them and prepare them for getting out. And a "blessing" for the volunteer if the inmate they are mentoring or sponsoring is already *saved*. It is then the personal life needing the care -- clothing and out-fitting of the inmate to get ready for release -- that is the focus of this level. Zealous organizations or churches rally their resources and members in a "team-approach" to try and give the inmate the things they need while continuing a healthy spiritual life. Such things may include: purchasing a birth certificate, an educational course, a car payment, picking up the inmate when released and driving them to the Department of Motor Vehicles, VA, Good Will, Unemployment office, dentist, etc. before dropping them off at the half-way house. Even more important, especially during COVID social distancing, e-mailing the parole board or speaking on the phone or SKYPE to confirm support is there for the inmate to help guide and sustain the inmate towards independence when released to be a productive citizen once again.

Feed my Sheep." (John 21:16)

Simply put, even the sheep need to be washed in the river and made clean. Dirty sheep attract bugs and flies. A shepherd's care of his flock is known by the way he goes after his lost sheep, then takes care of them with food, sheering, shelter, and protection. Just as a parent looks out for a child, or a friend looks out for a friend, so too do prisoners re-entering need a hand up, not a hand out. A community's church's ministry is viewed as "successful" by the *quality* of the sponsored prisoner that maintains him or herself properly, especially if they never return to prison. This is a true sign that effective prison ministry is being conducted. Of all the levels, this can be the most challenging because it involves TIME and EFFORT. An inmate's life is at stake, especially if they rely on the church and outside organizations for help their family or friends can't or won't provide. It is a ***community-approach*** that is needed to, theoretically, "rescue" or re-claim the prisoner from prison. Assisting the inmate with a plan for success begins with the Holy

Spirit, having empowered the inmate to be on God's plan for him or her with the volunteer's mentorship, and for the community of shepherds to organize and re-claim the "lost sheep" who have great value.

4. ADOPTION: TRUE LOVE

This fourth level is above all the best because it signifies true *agape* love, fellowship, discipleship, and trust with an inmate who is taken into a sponsor's family and life. The bond Christ had with the *Father* is exemplified in prison ministers who take on the role of the Father and adopt the prisoner – ALL THE WAY!

At this level, all aspects of the *Armor of God* (Ephesians 6:11) are here to ensure the relationship between volunteer sponsor and the inmate are strong and protected. There are no *weak* Christians at this level. Here, **TRUST** is at the core of the relationship between the inmate and sponsor, who interact at visitation, on the phone, share pictures, tell jokes, make on-line purchases, fear no "identity-theft" myths – NONE of the *prejudices* are present.

Why? It's because unconditional love is present with a discipleship relationship. Like the lost sheep that has value, the shepherd has but one goal for the sheep: To be healthy and thrive with the rest of the flock. The sheep is to the shepherd, as an inmate is to a family -- society.

FACT: Not all prisoners have family. A church volunteer may be the *only* family an inmate has.

No matter what, accepting an inmate into one's "world" is a huge step, and not for the average sponsor. It is; however, the MOST EFFECTIVE means to ensure an inmate maintains a relationship with Christ because the Christ – in the sponsor – visits and totally has

committed to loving the inmate as a family member enjoys being a part of a family or an authentic agape relationship. The worst thing a sponsor can do, however, is give a prisoner FALSE hope, with meaningless promises of care and support. Discouragement like that has a devastating effect on weak prisoners, especially coming from an out-side free-world sponsor. (Remember, prisoners are subjected to lies, deceit, and rumors constantly which erode hopes and increase fears.)

Simply put, this level shows a person *cares* about another. Like I've quoted repeatedly what Rev. Ted Welsh often said,

"What good is a book to a hungry villager...he can't eat it."

So much so that they place faith in the prisoner who then sees they have self-worth which gives them hope. That is why JESUS insisted we go to prisons so prisoners have hope and do not feel they are abandoned. And men and women are worth more than sheep. By loving a prisoner, you show GOD loves them.

You are giving back to God a soul that you saved from being lost. It does not matter what a prisoner was convicted of, but rather how much mercy he or she is shown by the society in which we live. Is our community a bunch of judgers? Or, do we forgive our fallen members and help them back on their feet.

Where are you today?

Consider what level of ministry are you at or willing to sacrifice and partake in. How much mercy are you willing to give? Can you forgive those who need help? Can you dig into your wallet? Or do you just "talk the talk?" Where are you today to carry Christ's message and make a difference in someone else's life? To help the socially wounded, the physically ill, the forgotten, the abandoned, the convict?

The first part of being in an effective ministry is to be aware of the levels, and know that "feeding the sheep" requires more than just words or a postcard. It requires fortitude to stand up to Satan's minions also trying to stop you from doing something Christian -- and good. Not everyone is cutout to be a shepherd, and not everyone in prison is "bad." People fall down and want to get up. And whoever brings a person back from sin and saves a soul – like the *parable of the lost sheep*, there is a reward for them waiting in heaven. (Luke 15: 1-7) Bringing back a person from the dead is a true miracle, and Jesus and his apostles performed all sorts of them depending on the need. One of the hardest things was to show others about forgiving a sinner and bringing them back into society from prison, especially against "the system." "Haters" and opposition groups are constantly with us, bent on stewing victims instead of transitioning them into survivors which does nothing good for the victim, prisoner, or society.

So, do you have the guts to go to a parole board and testify about your sponsored prisoner whom you visit and call, "Friend?" Or are you afraid someone will find out you support prisoners with heinous crimes, and people will protest you or your church or organization on social media? Are you even afraid to put your name and return address on an envelope or card sent to a prison for fear someone will know you are trying to help prisoners?

Saving lives *is* a noble and necessary cause. Prisoners will eventually come out of prison; it's a fact, folks! Restorative Justice is the *new* approach in COVID America; it's here to stay.

Consider this: If no one preaches to the prisoners, who will then? And if Christ doesn't come to them, who has the victory? Satan?

The Issue: If you're going to do prison ministry work you need to do it right! If you want to save souls from hell, then the prison ministry may be for you. Many are already saved and just need the social and restorative justice, like that given to the man helped by the Good Samaritan. (Luke 10: 29-37)

Not only did the Good Samaritan help the beaten man to the inn, but he paid the inn keeper out of his pocket to care for the man. (Wow! A total stranger who had compassion for another stranger. Is that awesome love or what!)

> **Do you have what it takes to care for another as the Good Samaritan did? To treat another as a brother or sister – a neighbor -- as Jesus instructs when all others are watching you and/or disagree of that level of care?**

Summary Up to Now

Effective Prison Ministry as discussed in the "*Four (4) Levels of prison Ministry*"—in Real Ville terms-- is basically a calling for the right people with the right attitude to line up with the right theology, and to reclaim not only the soul of the prisoner, but other aspects that see that the prisoner or "inmate" is *reclaimed*. That is, treating the inmate with respect and *value* as a human being who has gone astray and needs help to guide them with God's love, compassion, and mercy, to make the changes in their lives to become a successful member of the community when they are released. (For those that can be released.)

Jesus Christ taught that the rich man is no different from the poor man, the highly-educated are no different from the uneducated, the infirm are no different than the healthy, the *free* no different from the incarcerated, nor did Jesus pick "favorites' along race, color, and creed, Jew and Gentile – Jesus was no discriminator of persons, he taught we are to "feed the sheep, " – *all* of them.

In this basic guide there is the generic tools and information to assist ministers with providing the level of ministry they are equipped, resourced, funded, or have the time to sacrifice for a prisoner(s). This depends on the prison and the level of security and relationship the prison chaplain has with the church or individual (preacher, mentor, sponsor) wishing to provide the prisoner(s) which will determine the level of ministering.

Ministering vs. Sponsorship / Mentorship. Prison *ministering* is different from prisoner *sponsorship or mentorship*. The main differentiating factor between them is that sponsorship and mentorship are contingent on whether the volunteer minister wants to do more for the inmate(s) and gets approval to "sponsor" them as their mentor, Bible Guide, academic guide, or other additional assistance other than bringing the word of God to the inmate. For example, a prisoner that comes to a church service and is *saved;* bu has no family and is going up for parole, may need a "sponsor" to speak for them at the parole board, check on the inmate to see if they are staying out of trouble at the prison, taking self-improvement courses, victim-impact courses, trade schools or other classes for a job when re-entering society, etc.. All can be huge factors from a sponsor who takes an **active** interest in an inmate to see they doing what Jesus expects them to do. Sponsors can visit their inmate at selected times approved by the warden even sometimes mentoring during *count times.* Not only can sponsors meet in the chapels, classrooms, or designated common areas, but some elect to fully give their attention to one inmate and visit them at the visitation gallery (VG). At the VG, the sponsor and the I/M can relax, talk without other prisoners' obnoxious behaviors interrupting, and eat vending machine food like a semi-normal person without the feeling of being "behind bars." (FOR further information of the benefits of visiting an I/M at the Visitation Gallery, **SEE Article:** *"Prison Visitors Extend Mercy And Hope To Those Behind Bars",* The *Tennessee Register,* October 9, 2015, in the next section.)

Restorative Justice vs. Retributive Justice. "*Reclaiming*" – is a Heating Ventilation and Air-Conditioning (HVAC) term, and is defined as "taking *good* refrigerant out of the system so it can be used again.' Like HVAC reclaiming, inmates can fit this metaphoric example with great accuracy. Many in prison just made a mistake or mistakes – a crime(s), and pled guilty. (Usually to something higher than what they would have gotten at trial.) The difference is for millions of people who broke the law and didn't get caught, is that those behind bars *did* get caught. And today in American culture, for the most part, [the government] states are in favor of *retributive* justice over *restorative* justice. That is, *retributive* justice is the old "throw away the key" mentality, whereas *restorative* means placing emphasis on rehabilitation and restoration and education programs and incentives to help the *errant* make the necessary changes so they can get out of prison as a "recovered" person. Albeit, in addition to conditions and treatment of I/Ms in confinement, the I/M is forever labeled an "ex-felon," which suggests a purely retributive act of punishment, revenge, and retaliation, categorizing the marginalized "criminal" to be *permanently* considered "no good" and of no redeeming value by the state (world). **Translation:** Unless church volunteers step up to being "shepherds," there is NO mercy or forgiveness for prisoners, mistake makers, errants, and sinners in today's world.

So, whether the world's justice or God's, man will always have to make a decision which "justice" will influence them to make decisions. As long as there are prisoners, there will be a need to bring the light of hope – Christ who is the light of the world -- to them so that they can live life in victory as abundantly as HE intended.

So, Who are these Witnesses to Mentor and Sponsor?

As Adolph Saphir (1831 – 1891) put it, Jesus is our "Guide and Companion." [1]

He said that Jesus is always with us, and we should never weaken from the meaning of this assurance. He says, "The incarnate Son of God, who is at the right hand of the Father, is our constant Guide and Companion. As truly as He saw His throne to succor and receive him; so truly do His eyes rest now upon each of His disciples; so truly is He present wherever two or three are gathered in His name; so truly does He enter with the assurance of His peace into every heart that loves Him. Jesus is with us – for the Holy Ghost has not come to supply Christ's absence, but to accomplish His presence. And as Jesus is God and man, so with human sympathy and tenderness is the Lord of glory with us." [2]

As stated before, the presence of God within a relationship based on Christ can be mysterious as prisoners see Christ reflected in the mentor / sponsor-relationship based in Christ's love. This is because the Spirit brings the presence of the Lord unto our souls. But is it therefore real?

In Matthew 28: 20, it say "... *And lo, I am with you always, even unto the end of the world. Amen.*"

It is here that Saphir states where we get our strength. "Leaning on Christ, our difficulties vanish. *"Have not I commanded thee?"* said God unto Joshua, *"Be strong and of good courage; be not afraid, neither be thou dismayed: for the Lord thy God is with thee whitersoever thou goest"* (Josh. 1:9). ³

So, Jesus is aware of our afflictions, as should true mentors and sponsors be of prisoners. His is not only divine compassion, His is brotherly human sympathy. He remembers His earthly experience; He understands the tears and fears of human hearts. While we are suffering below, Jesus is upholding us by His priestly intercession sending angels in the form of good Samaritans, deacons, mentors, sponsors – true brothers and sisters – to the discipleship "calling" commissioned in Heaven. High above, where sin and sorrow cannot enter, lives our God and Brother. But He is also with us, having never forsaken us, and in our suffering, can deliver us from evil even if we feel our soul is not worthy or want to give up. All He asks is for us to have faith, open the eyes to our troubled hearts and let Him in. (John 14:1)

Prison Ministry Members are a Part of the Community Organizing Team

Religion and philosophy have tended to provide frameworks for the conduct of social welfare. These are often handled by community organizers also called welfare services or social work. ⁴

Community organizers can be church or non-church group members in any purposeful capacity. Their basic concerns of social welfare – poverty, disease, the and elderly – are at charitable or dutiful assistance to those daily existence, incarcerated in disability and dependent young the core of responses to render who struggle for a including those prisons, jails,

mental institutions, and holding facilities. The well-being of these categories of distressed people in need of assistance is of importance because it defines a society as to its moral obligation to have stronger "healthier" people look out for its "least citizens" that require assistance or emergency measures. The sick, the disabled, the at-risk – the vulnerable -- all affect a society who pay taxes or render resources to address these people, especially social services who place a high value on keeping families together in their local communities. [5] Volunteers for hospitals, nursing homes, after-school soccer programs, school lunch programs, elderly share-a-ride programs, kid's little league or other activities, etc. all help people in the community who have obstacles or less means of living. And this help costs time and money – taxpayer's money and/or revenues from other sources.

Wherefore, organizations and/or ministries set-up to address these socially at-risk groups must have a priority if we are to rescue disadvantaged people from further distress, and from making the rest of the community ill, harmed, or fail if their condition of need is not slowed, reversed, or "healed" with effective involvement (i.e. mentorship and sponsorship) and the funds to fix them early before its too late.

The "Bottom Line."

The "takeaway" is that Christian Sponsors and Mentors who are first *disciples* of Jesus Christ are, in fact, to be "teachers" who inspire inmates to change and become transformed in all aspects to live a "new life" based upon Christ's example as seen through the mentor or sponsor or friend in that role. Where the "heart is" of the mentor, sponsor, or friend of the inmate is will certainly come out in the inmate's life in changes of behavior and in the way they are prepared for the parole board and re-entry back into free-world society. And a sponsor's or mentor's "faith" will be tested, as it is no easy task to "drag out" a prisoner from prison given all the hurdles, prejudice, and policies a prisoner and volunteers are subjected to. wearing the label of "felon" or "ex-con."

Trust. Trusting in God to lead you by being edified by the blood of Christ and His example and that of the Apostles who mirrored Christ's attributes and proclaim the victory and power of Christ to overcome your situation and that of the world's one person at a time. Trusting "man" – a mentor or sponsor – can be a difficult situation especially when many weak, "tag-a-long," or "wannabe" mentors and sponsors come and go. They decrease a prisoner's faith rather than increase it because the prisoner(s) feel lied to and abandoned by so-called "men-of-faith" or "women-of-God" who make promises (talk) but don't show Christ's love [in action] (walk).

What Jesus did was powerful. What He said, what he taught, what he shared, and what He left behind for the world to be built up, not torn down. False hope let's down a prisoner, fast; it hurts. Christ came to save God's people by offering them life, not destroying them. The only thing He came to destroy was **death**. By His life, we can learn to live. That's the 'take away' -- the <u>cornerstone</u> built upon solid ground we too can build upon to help rebuild another human being's life – a prisoner. One whom Christ valued enough that when he visited, he didn't wave at the inmates and toss some peanuts as if at the zoo then leave. He compassionately gave *His* meaningful love – period – with sacrifice and care. That's being effective.

Michael Maraschiello

"Keep Climbing"

*With each step up,
the past gets farther
and farther behind you.*

*With each step up,
new views
of more and more
possibilities
keep coming into sight.*

Keep Climbing!

(Poem taken from *Heartline* Series card, © Hallmark Licensing, LLC, Kansas City, MO, (2019)

Sample Add for Church Bulletin and/or Website for Prison Ministry Assistance

Individual Inmate needs assistance.

> **PRISONER NEEDS TUITION ASSISTANCE**
> The *Generic Church Prison Ministry* is sponsoring an Inmate, Miss Ima Prisoner, at the 123 Prison in American City to get her Associates Degree in Personnel Management with ABC College via correspondence. A former Iraq War veteran, Ima will be assisting our church when released. If you would like to contribute to this worthy cause, we are trying to raise the $1,600 tuition for her. Contact Rev. Eye Care at: www.gcpm.com.

Group ministry needs.

> **PRISON PROJECT ASSISTANCE NEEDED**
> The *Generic Church Prison Ministry* is helping sponsor a Holiday Food Box Project at the 123 Prison in Rockville, TN. We are trying to raise $5,000 to buy the 1,100 each inmate a pair of socks, a toothbrush, and 2 tubs of cheese as our church's pledge for the multi-church project. If you would like to contribute, please contact: Rev. Eye Care at: www.gcpm.com.

Note. Adds to support your prison projects or an inmate's education are all socially and spiritually worthy because you are uplifting their condition. "Poverty" is not just of the physical sense, but also of the spirit, mind, education, and with social skills to interact and function. Helping people in need **NEVER** grows old, as poverty is always with us, especially for prisoners, who usually have very little. You and your church or organization should be looking for all sorts of resources because the needs never run out.

MICHAEL MARASCHIELLO

Sample Church Service Flyer & Poster to Make and send the Chaplain at the Jail/ Prison you Visit

SOUTH MOUNTAIN BAPTIST CHURCH
of Buffalo, TN

2020 2021

Sunday Morning
Church Service

Come here Divine Scripture and a related "real-world" message for Christian's to thrive in today's society as presented by:

REV. F. ALL MIGHTY ----------------- Prison Minister

NEED A BIBLE?
If you would like a Bible, please put your name, ID number, and address on the back of our prayer card at the service.

WHEN: <u>SUNDAYS</u>   WHERE: <u>CHAPEL</u>   TIME: <u>9 O'clock</u>

"God has plans to prosper you and provide for you, ... and to give you hope." (Jer. 29:11)

On behalf of our prison ministry family at SMBC, we welcome all to attend our service to worship our Lord Jesus Christ in love and fellowship. Amen.

Note. It is always good to go through the jail or prison chaplain and get permission to post advertisements and announcements so that all rules of the facility are observed to avoid possible conflicts of interest. All religious and non-religious groups must be respected in this Millennial postmodern culture.

Sample Questionnaire for Volunteers   July 25, 2020

This is a basic questionnaire to use to assess an inmate's (I/M) needs. Of course, hundreds of questions can be asked; however, the point is to set a plan for success with the I/M so they are working on those objectives you both can monitor and check the progress as time moves on.

Ask your I/M(s):

1. How do you feel today? (Address this concern first)
2. What are the things you need help with?
3. Can we write those down and set some target goals?
4. What's needed to accomplish those goals I may look into helping you with?
5. Since the last time we met, what have you done to meet those goals/ objectives?
6. What's your education level?
7. If you don't have a GED, are you enrolled in an education program? If not, why?
8. Since you have a GED or higher education, do you need more such as a technical trade correspondence course for HVAC, Legal Aide, Electrician, other?
9. What's your financial status? Do you need a small J-PAY or monthly E-deposit (i.e. $50) on your prison/ jail trust fund account to sustain you for stamps and such?
10. What's your spiritual status? Do you need a Bible? Other religious items?
11. What's your job at the jail / prison?
12. How are you spending your time?
13. Have you talked to your family? How often? Can I call them?
14. Who else besides me visits you?
15. Do you have a substance abuse problem? If so, how can I help?
16. Do you have a mental health problem? If so, how can I help?
17. Would you like me to send you a birthday card? Holiday cards?
18. How's your health? Do you need *factsheets* from the Internet?
19. What are the best times you can call me on the phone? E-mail?
20. What are the best days and times I can come visit you?
21. Is there anything special I can get you? Sneakers? A TV? Food box?
22. Would you like me to send you pictures or materials from the Internet, such as of your favorite cars? New technology? Current events? Job listings? Baby items?
Parole.
23. When do you come up for parole or "flatten" (end sentence)?
24. What help do you need with your parole?
25. Do you want me to send the parole board an E-mail and a letter?
26. Do you want me to SKYPE or show up at your parole hearing?
27. Did you make a Parole packet to present to the board?

28. Would you like me to go over your verbal and written statement for the board?
29. Do you need a home plan? Job plan?
30. Is there anything more you can tell me about yourself and the crime before I write my letter and/or speak at your hearing so that there are no surprises?
31. I've looked you up on the Internet, and know what "they" say. Is there anything you can tell me that I can better make the case for your release?
32. As for the victims, can you tell me how you are remorseful, and what you've done to make amends?
33. What changes in your life have you made that I can tell the board?
34. Have you been doing anything threatening in the past year to anyone?
Re-entry.
35. Now that you have an "out date" or "flat date" and are getting out, do you need someone to pick you up at the gate?
36. Do you have money for your home plan?
37. Do you have a driver license? A cell phone (burner phone)?
38. Do you need a ride to the VA? Social Security Office, Employment Office?
39. Do you need assistance with clothing, eating utensils, furniture, a car?
40. How can myself or my church/ organization better help you?
41. Do you feel I have done my job as a volunteer helping you stay focused on what you needed and need to do to be successful in society?
42. Is there any church, AA, drug re-hab center, or facility you need transportation to when you are out?
43. Do you need help with preparing a job résumé?
44. Do you have my 24-7 "hotline" number to call for emergency help?
45. Can you think of anything else you need help with to never again come back to prison?
46. Will you keep God focused first in your life and obey Him?

These are just the bare essential issues to discuss with your sponsored or mentored I/M to encourage them to be on – and stay on – the right path to success; it's up to them and God, for you can only lead the person to the "living water." It's up to the other person whether or not they will drink it. You've done your part if you showed you cared with doing meaningful acts of compassion. Remember, many in prison are homeless the minute they step foot outside the jail or prison. What you did -- or did not do -- will have an everlasting impact on that person, the community, and your soul. Pleasing God is just that – saving souls, and if you have, your reward is in heaven as well as on earth.

"Empowerment leads up to success!" – M.F.M.

Accepting Responsibility for your Actions Checklist

One of the most important things you can do for an inmate is to "motivate them" to act. Governor Bill lee of Tennessee said in his 2019 inauguration speech, that "Incentives drive behavior." For an in mate, that means telling them – in "prison speak" to "man up!" or "Woman up!" and start being responsible.

Here's a simple set of things to discuss with your inmate(s) to motivate them and get them thinking of wanting to change. THEY have to change them, not you. Your job is just to guide them.

A typical idiom in prison describing a person who does not want, most prisons say, "You can't fix stupid." That is, when is the person going to learn doing it "their way" is what got them into prison. But doing things the smart, legal, and practical way are the keys to success which begins with obtaining the knowledge to know what to decide, and gaining the wisdom to know when as well.

1. Being true to yourself. In evaluating one's self, one must ask, "Am I dishonest; can I be trusted?" If the inmate has a problem answering this as a positive question then they are in a state of disloyalty. This means they are loyal to no one. This indicates they will betray the trust of anyone. They may steal from family, friends, etc. with no conscience. They blame their family, the police, drugs, their spouses, parents, etc. but never take responsibility for their part or actions.

2. **Basic Needs**. Is your inmate you are sponsoring:
- Getting good sleep at night?
- Eating three meals a day?
- Getting out on the recreation yard to exercise?
- Involved in activities?
- Have any friends? Who? How are they doing?
- Plans out a day?
- Has a prison / jail job?
- Controlling emotions amidst a prison / jail environment?
- Solving problems with Jesus? Rationally?

3. Getting Control of Self. The first step in changing is to admit you are the problem and must do something about it. You are the source, and must search for solutions. Mentors and sponsors are great sources of help to listen to; they are there to help.
Counseling is for not just people who are weak, but also for strong people who seek out their advice all the time. That's why they are successful because they gather the

resources from other people of what works. They work smarter, not harder. This starts with being honest with the self. Nothing more, nothing less.

4. **Learn To Adapt**. No matter what the condition or circumstance brought you to prison, you are in prison or jail and have to adapt. When you want to change you are learning to adapt. When you get out of prison or jail you are learning to adapt. People adapt all the time to their environments. Learn to accept criticism, not for just yourself but the people around you whom you need to respect. They will respect you if you are respectful as in the "Golden Rule." Your attitude and behavior on the way you have an outlook on life and the relationships around you are all representative of your character. Your character is made up of essentially your attributes – what you and how you respond to others and situations. These attributes then describe your character.

Bad character traits to shed are:

- Getting disciplinary write ups
- Lying
- Cheating
- Stealing from my friends
- Lying around in the cell all day
- Hustling instead of a real job
- Sleeping all day
- Having no spiritual (prayer) time
- Not taking care of yourself (e.g. eating right, exercising, etc.)
- Treating your cellee and others in considerately
- Not offering help to others in need
- Misjudging others quickly
- Solving your problems with violence
- Procrastinating
- others

If this sounds like you (your inmate), then have some character work to do, especially to prove to the parole board they are "responsible" and "changed."

5. **Relationships**. Repairing them is important; the one with your sponsor / mentor/ family is important. Having a support group is "being real," today, because you will be in contact with people wherever you go. If you broke lives, made victims, and were dishonest with them, expecting "absolute forgiveness" for some for what you did could be an uphill battle. However, when people see you make an honest strive to take responsibility, changed, and are a better person, their tendency IS to forgive you, even if you don't think you deserve it. Be humble, and never expect forgiveness, as it is a blessing to get it by the grace of God. You didn't earn it, but rather it is a gift from Him. And when you do receive it (mercy), you better be thankful those people are now looking at you to keep it that way.

6. **Setting the Goals**. In order to stay positive, and to ensure that you stay on the right track, you have to formulate a strategy -- like in business – to be successful. Short term and long term goals are the way to be a successful and make your goals and objective come true. (Realistic goals, that is.) A simple action plan, below will help you get started. You can modify it as your goals change. Remember, hard work pays off. Everything in life is not all "happy gum drops." Life is what you make of it.

(You can get a lot of information from your jail or prison Re-Entry office, such as resource guidebooks to help all pre-release inmates with many re-entry issues.)

Sample Action Plan for I/M's Release Success

Main Idea	Goals	Steps	Resources that help	Projected completion
Legal	Contact parole officer	Check detainer 2. Call PO	Counselor/ IPO; halfway house	Prior to release
Housing	Arrive at Halfway House	Set up ride Back up - bus	Sponsor, Family, friend	1st hour of release
Health	Attend post Release for Benefits, programs	Halfway House pick up; VA	Halfway House; mentor	Prior to release
Family	Arrange for Family to Meet at Halfway HS	Notify when released	Self Cell phone	Prior to release
I.D.s	Obtain	Get Birth Certificate; VA.Govt Cards	Re-Entry; Half-way HS VA	Prior to Release; 2nd Day (VA)
Job(s)	Find Job	Have e-resume' Net work Internet	self	3rd day Of release
Additional Education Needs	Enroll in Truck drive school	Go to Career Center	On-line funding	90 days After release
Finance	Overhaul plan	Determine Needs For banking	Self/ Friend	Day of release
Transportation	Get vehicle	Save cash/ Bus / van Insurance	Self/ friends	30 days After release

Leisure / Friends	Keep Only Good ones	Make time	self	Begin day released

Goal Setting and Negotiating

"If you fail to plan, you plan to fail." –Anonymous

1. Team goals should be precise and match the overall goals of my company
2. You can still meet goals as a team even if half the members aren't contributing
3. Teamwork requires constant negotiation

Step One: Define your main goal.

This is done with a mission statement. Then, set goals to achieve that mission. A good goal has to be specific, measurable, realistic, achievable, cost effective (i.e. not time-consuming), and KEEP IT SIMPLE.

Example: Fundraising for charities. Clearly stated, now list the goals to reach it.

Step Two: Involve the whole team

A strong team means everyone has a part in helping to reach the goal. By empowering your members with tasks, they become involved and produce more having a purpose and because they are emotionally tied to the team's goal. As a leader of team leader, being responsible for your part is paramount to keeping the focus on the goal of the members.

Step Three: Break the goal into objectives

Once the main goal is clear, the task of setting objective [goals] is next to reach the main goal. Dividing the labor amongst team members ensures no team member is overloaded or being under-utilized.

Step Four: Negotiations

Constant assessment is needed to see the goal is being measured correctly, and that the objectives are met. When negotiating with team members to assess the status of each member's task, generally asking them to state an outline of what they have done during the time they have been working will usually require the member to give an explanation of what they have accomplished. Encouraging opinions and recommendations is necessary, as well as giving feedback and notice to those doing a good job meeting or exceeding goals set. Winning arguments is not productive. What is productive is when members work together towards a common goal focusing on the problem not the person and how the team can solve issues perhaps one team member or team group needs assistance with. Fear of failure, pride, failure to listen, selfishness, fear of responsibility, jealousy, racism, sexism, etc. are all negative factors which are counter-productive in the work place becoming barriers to team negotiations. Problems should be anticipated, resolved as they are found, and the goals met. Those doing their "own thing" take away from the team's goal because they are not sticking with the agreed upon process the team has approved for reaching the set main goal of the company [mission].

Step Five: Implementing the plan

This is the final result—putting it all together for the plan to work. The idea, vision, or mission statement become reality, and the team is responsible for accomplishing the tasks to make it happen by working together in a cohesive group and environment using resources of people, technology, space, intellect , and negotiation to produce the final product or resulting goal.

Temperance: How We Respond to People Matters

By M. F. Maraschiello, MCE (2019)

Col. 4: 5-6 'Walk in wisdom toward them that are without, redeeming the time. Let your speech be always with grace, seasoned with salt, that ye may know ye ought to answer every man.

How do you respond? Like Jesus, yourself, or like someone else? Are you sensitive? Blunt? Vulgar? A "wise guy?"
"Thou shalt not murder."

Michael Maraschiello

Jesus used one primary teaching tool when speaking to others – <u>parables</u>. Stories to inspire people to change and come around to His thinking in common ways people could understand on ***their*** level.

Do we "go there," challenge people/ Put them on the defensive? Make them feel comfortable? There are times that is just, such as Jesus and the money changers in the temple. He was making a point.

Seen the acronym, THINK: Thoughtful, Helpful, Inspiring, Necessary, Kind

Do you tell lies? Break hearts? Is what you say productive? Peaceful solution, avoid confrontations, build up, tear down walls, healing, not resentful, forgiving, merciful, prudent, not belittling, not make others laughed at?

An old saying parents and teachers had was,
"If you don't have anything nice to say, don't _____."

Do people avoid you because of what you say or how you act? Do you walk like the "coffee zombies" who come out of their cells every morning with a "I need a wake-up shot" before you can talk to people and visa versa?
Do you greet people with a brick in the face or a balloon? Spew poison? Explode? Or do you have composure?

So how can you be temperate? Make and keep friends? Show your enemies Jesus lives inside of you?
1. Do what Jesus said, which is often tough: Be slow to anger, for starters. (Joel 2:13; Jonah 4:2: James 3)   Understand that people sometimes say the wrong things or make mistakes. Are you perfect? Always right? You never made a mistake, have you? What size foot is your mouth?
2. Listen and observe before just blurting something out. Don't put salt into the wound. (Col. 4: 5-6)
3. Respond with wisdom, kindness, grace, and prudence – what is inspiring, helpful, APPROPRIATE (It is okay to make jokes and stuff, especially in light of situations out of our control.)
4. Keep your voice level, defuse a potential situation. Make people at ease like Jesus did in the boat. (Mat. 8: 23-27)
5. A BIG ONE – LISTEN, and be hospitable, caring, concerned. People feel better when they know you are paying attention. Be considerate.
6. Lastly, and most important, just be you, be real, and LOVE. Treat others the way they would want to be treated. If your brother or sister is hurting, and in pain, you should be able to see that and show compassion. What they really need is your help when they are yelling in distress. That's why Jesus said to offer the other cheek because you are giving God the glory when you take the cross or the sin – the pain of others. That's laying down your life for your brother when you become in touch with them and show your humanity and bear one another's hardships and help them with what they are lacking in. (John 1: 1-13) When you show Jesus in you, people will recognize a Christian is speaking to them?

So the next time someone opens their mouth and out comers the Frankenstein Monster, take a second to analyze what's going on and respond appropriately. Are they in trouble?

TIP: When confronted, imagine yourself in a Job Interview. Don't you want to say the right things and get your point across to get the job – the desired goal? You don't argue with the interviewer, do you? No, you keep your head in the game and say what you think are the best things that can help your position which is "wisdom in action." (Col. 4: 5-6)

> **Takeaway:** How you speak and act reflects your character, establishes your reputation, and either attracts or pushes away people. Jesus was lied on and falsely labeled many things; they didn't know him and LEARN about what he was talking about. Have you been misunderstood? God knows what is in your heart. And if your heart is like Jesus', show it, because that is the way to salvation. (Rom. 10: 9-10) Like Jesus, he met haters too, but he dealt with them HIS way, not the world's. Jesus showed love of life, respected the person, and had love of neighbor in mind.
>
> *"Help me say the right things."*

"Plans to prosper you and give you hope." – Jer. 29:11

Michael Maraschiello

Chapter 7

Making the Commitment to Change a Life In COVID America

Alternatives to Visiting Prisoners during Covid Lockdowns

Imagine you are at the church, and you see empty pews, dust gather on artifacts, and birds flying near the ceiling like in some eerie Alfred Hitchcock horror movie. Now, imagine inmates in prison or jail living in a single cell with no one visiting them for months to bid them any warm comfort, prayer, or spiritual well-being "face-to-face."

Since the COVID pandemic of 2020, churches, schools, jails, military barracks, colleges, and prisons have literally shutdown normal visitation for volunteers, family, clergy – everyone not employed by these facilities, including some places even forbidding attorneys from seeing their clients (inmates). For prison ministry volunteers, this is a heart-emptying blow to the *mission,* because without seeing or going to the jails and prisons, how do we carry out what Christ wants us to do for the *least ones*?

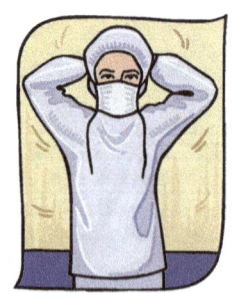

CREATIVE ALTERNATIVES TO CONTACT VISITS

Take these tried and true adages,

"If you first don't succeed, try, try, again." And, *"Where there's a will, there is a way."*

Looking back a century ago at the Spanish Flu pandemic of 1917 in America, we can safely say what the medical experts did to communicate with patients is separate people from contact with each other. Hospitals and other institutions created safe "partitions" of cloth to separate people. Those that were sick or infected never came in contact with visitors, but rather stayed behind a cloth bed sheet-like barrier to keep germs from passing back and forth. That's really all they did, and – today – what really only needs to take place: a simple barrier.

Please don't get me wrong; I am not a medical doctor, nor the spokesperson for the Center of Disease Control (CDC). I do have *refugee processing* training from the U.S. 82nd Airborne Division and experience doing it with the 1st Armored Division during the 1991 Gulf War. I was also quarantined in 2008 while in prison for Mycoplasma Incognitus Tuberculosis I got from that war. I spent twenty-eight days in a negative airflow "isolation room" with no contact with anyone unless in a personal protective equipment (PPE) suit and mask. What struck me as odd was the CDC doctor – a foreign-born medical doctor whom I will call "Dr. G" – visited me with no mask and PPE.

Where's the logic? Why didn't she put PPE on? Wasn't she afraid to get particles I was expelling from my lungs?

 The staff at the *special needs* facility for prisoners took no chances; however, as time went on, and my lab results were showing signs to be less worried about getting what I had, eventually they wore less PPE until they wore none at all.

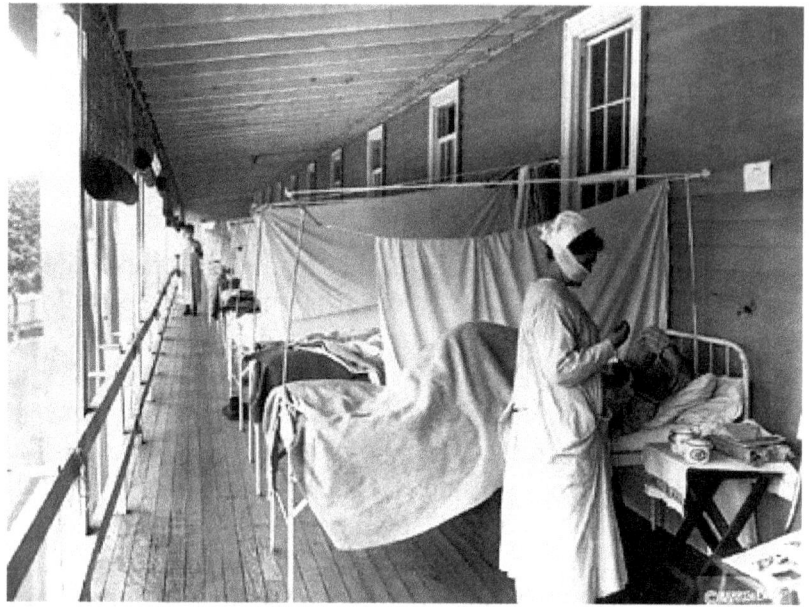
Walter Reed Army Hospital during 1918-19 epidemic.
(photo by Harris & Ewing/Corbis)

So, what's the point?

Depending on what the disease is (e.g. COVID or Flu's), "visitation" calls for the basics – the same as the Spanish Flu: Separation, masks, fresh air, and most importantly to employ disinfectants.

One-Hundred percent COVID Proof: Non-contact rooms.

So, how can prisons and jails get visitation started again or do it "smarter," not "harder?"

The best example of non-contact visitation to be done I personally experienced was at the Montgomery County Jail in Clarksville, Tennessee. They had four (4) visitation rooms with separate entrances to the building having no contact with jail staff or inmates. Visitors saw their inmate through plexi-glass and used the telephone. No air moved between visitor and prisoner -- a "win - win" situation of 100% non-contact.

Visitation **does not** have to stop if these rooms exist because there is a solid barrier between visitor(s) and the inmate who communicate via telephone. Bleach-water, of course, is sprayed on these surfaces after each person leaves, both inmate side and visitor side, so there is a less possibly of getting any germs.

At the *special needs* facility where I was quarantined, the staff put multiple plastic baggies over the telephone so we did not have to touch it with out bare hands. Latex gloves could be used as well, with each new visitor or inmate, and the baggie peeled off the phone so no germs are breathed off the surface of the previous baggie.

This type of visitation, above, any CDC medical person could approve, regardless if every visitor showed proof of being "pre-tested" and negative for COVID-19.

COVID TESTS ARE NOT 100% ASSURANCE.

Common sense says that if I tested "negative" today, for a test I took three days ago, but today came in contact with a person in an elevator who was exposed or a "carrier" of the COVID virus, and now it is passed to me, I am representative of a person who is "positive" with a "negative" test because I contracted the virus after my test was done.

FACT: There is no way that a visitor can pass COVID through plexi-glass barrier or via a telephone to an inmate or visa versa.

So, the odds of an inmate getting the virus from a visitor at the prison or jail visitation room, as in the above jail non-contact room example where there is a 100% barrier, are astronomical. The only way a visitor could get the virus is from another visitor, theoretically, if the room was not disinfected before the next visitor goes in for a visit.

Ergo, with proper disinfecting protocols, non-contact visitation can be done to continue mentoring and sponsoring inmates on their

paths to successful rehabilitation and re-entry back to society. Prisons and jails should not be stopping such visits, especially when their purpose is <u>directly</u> proportional to an inmate's preparation for success when going up for parole and/or released. [1]

A Typical Visit during COVID – Non-contact rooms.

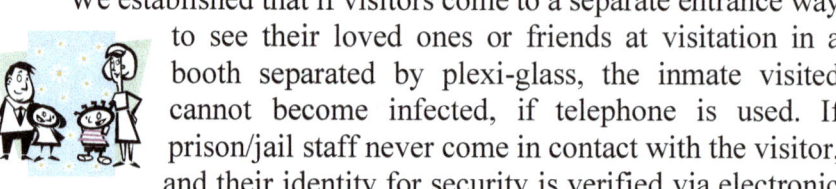

We established that if visitors come to a separate entrance way to see their loved ones or friends at visitation in a booth separated by plexi-glass, the inmate visited cannot become infected, if telephone is used. If prison/jail staff never come in contact with the visitor, and their identity for security is verified via electronic view camera that they are authorized to visit the inmate, and they passed through a metal detector not carrying unauthorized contraband, then security is met as well. Cameras in each room can monitor the visit and even further enhance security. This, then, is the solution, especially for sponsors and mentors to continue the contact and visitation for mentoring and assisting prisoners for their rehabilitation and well-being.

Bottom Line: Adapt /Overcome, because ministry work does not stop. Jesus still visited lepers and the sick with sores to bring hope to such people in need.

Here are some other ways, below, to continue your volunteer work even if the jail or prison won't allow contact or non-contact visitation:

1. Contact the Chaplain. Get his ideas on things that can be done to bring you and your inmate(s) together.
2. Begin a writing ministry to send letters every other week.
3. Get approval to send in CD's and CD ROMs that continue your educational objectives for your ministry so that inmates can listen to them.
4. See if you can do a webcam video for the chaplain to arrange small separated groups in the prison/jail chapel or gym for inmates to watch.
5. See if the prison will allow tablets to be downloaded from your church ministry website or app.

6. Schedule a speakerphone service where inmates can meet with social distance in a classroom, gym, or chapel and the prison/jail speaker systems are used for all to hear.
7. Co-ordinate with your local PBS or AM radio station to broadcast a ministry prison spiritual educational half hour or one-hour program of instruction.
8. Set-up Skype with a smart TV or whiteboard (e-board).
9. Go to www.podium.com and set up some speakers to give classes.
10. Create study guides or instructional booklets and tracts to mail to inmates who can return them to you for feedback.
11. Last, but not least, give a phone number to your inmates and set up a time each week or semi-monthly to talk to them. Continue your work in the most beneficial ways unique to your inmate in their environment (i.e. jail or prison) that is impacted with new procedures and policies affected by COVID.

The New Cost of Visitation – or not.

Prison and jail administrations already have had guards factored in for visitation before COVID, so there should be no complaints for sponsors and mentors to be allowed to do their work which is a vital part of social justice. Further, there should be no complaints to allow inmate family members and friends to have contact with their inmate(s) whom qualify for contact visits, especially when the inmate and their family/friend(s) have no money for their "phone account" to communicate or write letters.

Let's look at the *Realville* budget for a moment, now that COVID is here. Virus protection protocols and extra funds needed for budgeting the emergency staff is now deemed "essential," eliminating the guards – and their budgeted money – once earmarked for visitation staff, is all but gone diverted to offset COVID. Prisons and jails applying for State and Federal COVID emergency funding are reimbursed for their protocols that meet the emergency funding criteria.

Thus, the halting of visitation is really not a matter of funding because the money for the COVID protocols is now budgeted. What is really taking place is that jails and prisons are not implementing any changes to make visitation happen as it could – and should! This reluctance to take any pragmatic steps to make visitation happen again, can – over time – develop into a justifiable reason to not have any contact visitation in the future. This would result in a further decline and breakdown in the human aspect of rehabilitation that comes with family restoration and *restorative justice* effects from mentors and sponsors directly visiting prisons, and denying necessary social and spiritual programs that have been successful at helping the *corrections* goal of a safer public by helping ensure inmates are "corrected" while in prison and ready for release. Inmates without access to these volunteers critical to the *corrections* mission are therefore greater at risk and have a <u>higher</u> rate of recidivism when released because they were inadequately assisted before release, and therefore systematically denied a meaningful benefit they enjoyed from effective prison ministry.

"What's in your state' bank treasury?"

So, the presupposition, here, that "breaking the bank" of the budget is somehow what visitation will do if brought back, is nonsense. Rather, one can postulate that visitation – in the long run –

helps reduce recidivism because those people that primarily visit the prison are volunteers for teaching the additional classes, courses, and programs designed to uplift and better inmates. Everything from *Alcoholics Anonymous* (AA) to *Men of Valor* -- programs designed to change the way a person behaves – is a needed part of the social justice, criminal, and restorative system to orient men and women who fell down to pick their lives up and do better. Denying these additional steps to a system that has a poor track record by itself already, is clearly is a recipe for disaster now and down the road unless action is quickly taken.

WHAT SHOULD BE DONE?

Jails and prisons that do not have contact visitation rooms need to take some of their money earmarked for "COVID RELIEF" and make at least four to ten visitation rooms for visitors to come in and have non-contact.

This is how you do it in America – you build the rooms!

They also need to set-up times and places for inmates to meet in the chapels or class rooms to give spacing enough for inmates to sit with social distance, so that they can listen to a speaker via electronic device or in person that is electronically connected "video visits" for both family members.

in a room either or visually or both for volunteer(s) and

In short, as time goes by, those prisoners denied sponsors and mentors will have longer prison sentences. Why? Because – and I know from experience when they come for legal advice after they "botched" their parole hearings from having no mentor or sponsor and not knowing what to say or do at the hearing -- they are all bitter because they feel let down not having had anyone – including family – visit them and help them get ready for the most important day a prisoner has for his or her chance at freedom. It is pitiful how "the system" funds and prepares victims for the parole hearing via state law; however, the inmates are not. Inmates without mentors often have "stage fright" not knowing what to say that possibly could have given the board the information it was searching for to vote for the prisoner's freedom. This results in bitter inmates with longer sentences who are still in need of mentors and sponsors to help guide them to be responsible adults. If it sounds like a situation that a sponsor is parent telling their kids how to "grow up," that's almost exactly what the majority in prison go through, because most are young and came from homes with poor instruction to be responsible adults and citizens only to fall into trouble with the law. And sponsors and mentors are *experienced* adults – good role models.

Wherefore, visitation *is* a part of the process of rehabilitation to stop the cycle of recidivism, especially when the majority of the visitors are volunteers. During the week, volunteers come in with educational and character building skills and knowledge that young men and women need to model. Something *corrections* does not offer, as any prisoner or even a good corrections officer worth their word will tell you.

Takeaway: Tell the civic and church leaders in your area to demand your state recognize the need for visitation to be a continuous necessity for rehabilitation and restorative justice. Laws should reflect each offender facility have mandatory non-contact visitation rooms to ensure visitation never stops, especially for family members, mentors, and sponsors who are the "backbone" to a prisoner's support group, and part of the key to a prisoner's successful re-entry into society.

Elected Officials Need to Learn from their mistakes and do better correcting Mental, Spiritual, Legal, and Emotional health of prisoners

Where are the social services, religious services, legal services, and other services previous to COV prisoners had?

In her article, "State Corrections Systems Get Failing Grade in Response to COV," Emily Widra says that the most tragic consequence of state inaction were evident in the number of COV deaths behind bars, the report says ... high death indicates systemic failures. As of June 22, 2020, over 570 incarcerated people & over 50 correctional staff have died as a direct result of infection from COVas of today, states have largely failed.

The Prison Policy Initiative (PPI) says the overwhelming majority of states failed to take basic steps that might have saved the lives of hundreds of incarcerated individuals and staff ... no state earned a grade higher than "D," with the majority given an "F" or at most "F^+". Prisons & jails have been the sites of the biggest clusters of COV infections, rivaled only by nursing homes ... failure to act continues to put everyone's health & life at risk – not only incarcerated people & facility staff, but the general public as well, " the report says. "All states failed to implement a cohesive system-wide response," it was further added.

Widra further adds that since the first signs of the outbreak in March, public health advocates have pointed out that the nature of correctional institutions, with hundreds of inmates crowded together in small spaces, increases the odds of spreading the disease.

Only the physical disease is being addressed. FACT: Only Tennessee, W. Virginia, Michigan, Massachusetts, & Vermont did implement detection & isolation protocols to combat spread of the virus. As far as anyone can tell, they do not have any "virtual visit rooms" or kiosks for prisoners to visit, discuss their legal issues with their attorneys, or have visual contact with their mentors and sponsors of various support groups let alone even come out of their cells to get to a phone or put a letter in the mailbox which might be picked up in a reasonable amount of time, depending if the jail or prison is afraid to read the COV through the postal service as at some Tennessee prisons.

The Need for Criminal Justice Reform is here. COVID-19 showed prisoners, especially the elderly, are getting screwed

COV (Covid Virus) has ravaged the nation's prisons. Score of inmates are dead. More are sick. Some 72 federal inmates & one member of the corrections staff have died from the disease, according to the most recent Federal Bureau of prisons (BOP) data. Another 1,956 inmates & 176 BOP staff have tested positive. Even Attorney General William Barr supports the release of inmates, especially older ones at risk, to curb any large death rate. Many vulnerable inmates pose no risk to society. That has led to reform advocates, academics & lawyers to ask why officials in America's states to make more use of compassionate release & home confinement even after the pandemic passes, especially if crime doesn't rise as a result and cash-strapped states want the biggest bang for their public safety bucks?

"The sky's not going to fall," said Kevin Ring, of Families Against Mandatory Minimums (FAMM). "Prisoners are old and sick people too," he added. [3]

Meanwhile, changing economic shifts for calls for de-funding police – criminal initiatives – in favor of social initiatives are getting all the attention, especially to curb the ridiculous population of prisoners in jails and prisons across the nation which are the highest in the world for an advanced society supposedly "compassionate" about people. Yet, American's prisoners still feel trapped in prison, especially in states with parole boards that keep the "cash crop" (prisoners) locked up to draw more tax dollars into the prison industrial complex industry that has a revolving door because it does not treat the underlying issues of meaningful corrections and post-re-entry problems unequipped and uneducated prisoners have when they leave the prison system penniless and with no drivers license to even get to a job interview or have a roof over their head to sleep when they flatten their sentences. A common story heard over and over again as recidivists keep coming back to prison for the "Same Ole Same Ole."

"No state is going to want to build a new prison now," said Douglas Berman, an Ohio State University law professor. "Economics really force the issue. The pandemic has really focused people's attention onto what is really important." [4]

Berman emphasizes, "Re-entry is really going to be more difficult because money will now be diverted from programs in states due to state correction budget cuts. Prison medical treatment, outreach programs, classes, etc. for prisoners trying to leave prison or when they leave prison will be drastically cut from state budget funds once earmarked for re-education and re-entry." [5]

> How am i supposed to make life choices when i still use my fingers to count and sing the whole alphabet to see what letter comes next?

In short, Americans need to begin to see prisoners as a part of society. Long sentences eat away at tax money and budgets for more important things. . An ideology of seeing prisoners as human beings must be fostered, and changes to state systems and the advocating of less incarceration will be better for society in the long run, than to make one segment/ category of society (prisoners) pay at both ends of the "justice and health" stick.

Special Consideration for helping Sex Offenders, Drug Addicts, the Mentally Ill, Gang Members, and the Elderly and Physically-Challenged Inmates

Probably the most difficult situation for a volunteer is to find out that their inmate they are trying to help falls into one of these six toughest categories of inmates.

Let's face it folks, *spiritual* help is one thing. But unless you are 'Dr. Oz" or "Dr. Phil," or "Dr. Ruth" -- and you probably are not – trying to help any of these inmate's will take an extraordinary type person with patience and a heart of compassion. I'm not writing an expose' on psychology, but when it comes to social justice and spiritual love, some people draw a "line in the sand," like the criminal justice system which is only concerned about public safety.

That leaves these type of inmates to be abused, ignored, and receive little or no care even when we have federal programs and laws such as the *Americans with Disability Act* that is supposed to protect people from abuse.

Your job.

As stated many times in this book, every inmate is unique. Your focus is on assessing a plan for your inmate you can work with, or set one up with a team 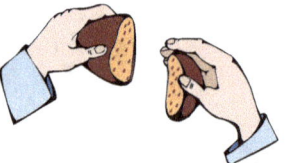 approach. There are no "supermen" and "super-women" who have all the answers; you can only do what you can. However, be aware of some of the things with each of these categories of inmates. Again, once you work your way past the stereotypes and learn more about that inmate's history (i.e. from him, the Internet, about their charges, etc.) you can start the "life recovery" process with your advice and/or assistance that allows that person to improve their situation and begin to rise in their life-style and condition.

Here are just a few simple things to be aware of with each of *these* people – and they are people -- who need care.

The Sex Offender

Without going into all the types of crimes, this is considered the worst over murder in society today, especially rape of a child. These inmates will usually have some type of monitoring device if ordered by the court when released; some for the rest of their lives. They will be recorded on a database, tracked by cell phone, and every person has access on the Internet to see these locations where the offenders are in their community. They can't even drive within 500 feet of a school, and may only be allowed to shop at supermarkets and retail stores approved by their parole officers. When out, they have the hardest time finding jobs and a place to stay because no one wants the "liability" – especially insurance companies – for them. While they are in prison, they may be raped, verbally abused, and often robbed and beaten because they are "fair game" to the sub-culture of the prison for *sanctioned* abuse. (Often this abuse is condoned by prison and jail officials.) These prisoner's mail is routinely read for child porn or other evidence which may lead to other [sex] crimes (e.g. rapes) which are unsolved. Often these prisoners try to be the best disciplined inmates expecting parole; however, parole for sex crimes is almost never granted. People, such as volunteers and clergy trying to help sex offenders, are often the most scorned for trying to help "animals ... scum" who – as most prisoners view them – deserve to be raped, castrated and killed because they raped a defenseless child or 'baby" deserving no quarter. (Often society sees them this way as well, as movements like *Me Too* go after priests, Hollywood stars, tycoons, judges, the Boy Scouts, etc. in an all-out search to bring anyone suspected of a sex crime to justice.) Make sure when you are talking to these inmates and assisting them you don't get "sucked into" bringing contraband "porn" in or your conversations are always about sex. Little "signals," liker those, will jump right out for you to point out to them their conduct needs to be focused on the goals and honestly worked on. NEVER be "used" by an inmate or lie to the parole board for them because that leads to possible trouble where you can lose your "gate pass" to enter the prison or worse – your reputation. Most prisons in most state require you to go through the federal PREA class (Prison Rape Eradication Act) before allowing you to come in. Some sex offenders are homosexual or bi-sexual, and may have several sex offenses while in jail or prison for rape or sexual misconduct. If they "changed," then their pattern of behavior should indicate so. That's what God wants and you want to see taking hold – change, with the new person in front of you guiding to a better life on your compass.

(See also *"Lenny's Story"* in **Elderly**, later in this chapter.)

The Drug Addict

This inmate usually has had a drug problem long before coming to jail or prison. However, in the age of drones and other high-tech ways to introduce contraband into the jail or prison, these people should be in an AA or other type substance abuse program on a regular basis before they leave prison and some after-care as well when they get back on the street. It does not matter what type of drug(s) they used and what for, because they have a physical addiction . It is powerful on the brain, and the first thing the brain tells them to turn to for depression or anxiety to "escape" what situation they are in which they can't socially or mentally handle is drugs. Illegal drugs today are so potent that a pinhead of *Fentanyl* is 40 times more powerful than Methamphetamine and kills brains cells by the thousands in seconds. Some inmates have sold all they own for drugs, robbed family, done prostitution, and destroyed their lives and others for the sake of getting high. Not to mention that they destroyed their gums, teeth, skin, liver, and other organs in the body making a 30 year old look like a 65 year old in some cases, especially the loss of weight. Worse, their immune system is degraded, and many acquired *AIDS* and *Hepatitis C* from sharing dirty needles and unprotected sex. Some of these inmates did drugs to kids and may or may not still be doing drugs. One way to check is to smell the inmate's breath and look at their fingernails for yellow stains. Also, rapid movement and sweating can be signs of withdrawal, and "coming down." Many of these with drug problems have a "history" (Juvenile record, burglary, theft) of which some have taken to violence with assault or murder to obtain drugs. These inmates need to be in programs and have programs or AA on the street to continue to "stay sober." Alcohol destroys the liver and leads to DUI now, just as being impaired by drugs. Often having the right "friends" and support group is needed for these people because often they don't trust themselves, as some have told me. Volunteers need to be real careful about loaning them large sums of money when they are released from prison because sometimes when it is at that level, the money *is* for drugs. Again, "trust" is what these people have broken time and time again due to their "disease." Their conscience only God knows; however, the proof of their heart is in their actions. And if they were fired from work, kicked out of their halfway house, and have no money, the odds are they are headed to the "dope man" to "score at hit" to take away their woes of life they believe God nor anyone can it help them with. Helping them with will power is good; however, they need a "higher power" (e.g. Christ) to give them hope and a future which they need to see is not found in a pill, bottle, or needle.

The Mentally Ill

I hope you volunteers treat everyone with dignity and respect, especially the mentally ill, as this group was my first professional choice of occupation as a Special Needs Teacher.

Once you see your inmate or inmates, you may start to discover some are on medications – "Meds" – which they take for anxiety or anger control issues. These prisoners often are either slow and lethargic or hyperactive as with Obsessive Compulsive Disorder (OCD) always talking and jumping from subject to subject. Some have Post-Traumatic Stress Disorder (PTSD) having suffered traumatic situations they just mentally acquired psycho-somatic or other forms of mental problems that they have not coped well with whatever the traumatic incident was in their life. For example, several inmates over the years told me about being raped in prison. Others told me they were molested as a child, abused, neglected, or abandoned by their parents. One man I knew was in a car accident and can't read. Another if not on his medications began to see hallucinations. One of my old roommates ("cellee") who writes me now from another prison, said he was only given medication for thirty day. When he left the prison, his OCD caused him to burst out and assault a man at a shelter resulting in his arrest. Again, unless you are a trained social worker or doctor of psychiatry, your job is not to be their doctor but their mentor or sponsor. Helping them get their special "needs" from health groups and clinics on the street are places you can direct them too. A lot of times it is a matter of the inmate simply having his medical files sent to the clinic which then provides for what they need. Mood swings, sweats, shouting vulgarities, and changes in attitude are often signs of anxiety levels going wrong. Just asking your inmate how they feel can give you the information about where their anxiety "is at" by the way they respond. Don't be discouraged; it's part of prison ministry, as the environment is one of "high pressure." You just have to have your observation skills and continue to work with your sponsoree as they have to live with their mental illness you may now be aware of. It's how you chose to deal with it that is the hard part.

The Elderly and Physically-Challenged Inmate

Are you so old you can't even walk to the prison? Need a mobility scooter or cane? What about a walker or CPAP machine to breath with? How about simple cataract surgery or a tooth filling? Worse, how about waiting a year for a biopsy, then finding out it is benign and spread so much that you have less than six months to live?

Imagine a prison where every common sense device, above, mentioned, is considered a weapon and prisoners are not allowed them. Does that sound *painful,* when these people are denied these at the jail or even at some prisons?

Some inmates a volunteer may come to want to help are going to be old and close to being ready for the geriatric ward. Their family may all be dead or abandoned them, they may have bloody sores, blemishes, and have to be on a ventilator or breathing device while sitting there talking to you.

Can you stomach that? To look at them like Jesus looked at Lepers back in his day? [6] Give them "eye contact" while a tube is stuck in their nose, or their urine drain bag is leaking on them and they adjust it? (I've seen that at the visitation gallery.)

Volunteers need to be ready for "life's problems," especially at this time of COVID-19 social distancing and exaggerated fear of germs. Germs are everywhere; however, in a prison, the elderly are getting slow, tired, can't hear well, need medications, and some will be coming out of prison to nothing but social security IF they qualify. Many have had heart attacks before age 60 due to the stress, poor food, and lack of reasonable medical care, as some states only provide "treatment." (Note: A real common "treatment' of prisoners for their medical needs is to issue pain relievers like Motrin, Aspirin, and Tylenol to inmates with stomach pains. After some time, the inmate collapses and is sent to the outside hospital, where the inmate finds out what really major illnesses they have such as: ulcers, appendix, kidney failure, hernias', or other bowel problems like cancer. (I know – I was one of those inmates with a heart attack and a hernia!)) Those fortunate enough to have good sponsors to find them assistance when the inmate is released are "angels," I believe, in God's eyes because they are trying to ease a person with little time left to have some decency of care before death.

Lenny's Story. Take the case of Lenny Catalano, 74, who died in prison with cancer in May of 2020 – among *other* things. His pathetic sponsor – I'll keep the name anonymous – for twelve years until July of 2019, only twice mailed Lenny a letter, and never once purchased a gift for Lenny who was going blind, had cancer, and was indigent. I confronted Lenny's sponsor and "chewed him out" for not caring more for Lenny. Four weeks later, that sponsor had a stroke, and was never seen from again leaving Lenny devastated.

What was he doing for Lenny anyway?

By now, the cancer was spreading and Lenny was falling down and had memory lapses. Somehow, another sponsor showed up for Lenny. This time myself and my current cellee, Dean, insisted Lenny be less prideful and tell the sponsor what he needed. Lenny got a little better treatment this time, and was being given food in the VG, not just sitting with his sponsor in front of the chapel -- as with his predecessor -- who just brought Lenny some "company."

Unfortunately, up until Lenny's death, when COVID hit and the visitation stopped at the prison for all outside volunteers, Lenny never got one letter nor was he even given a phone number to call his sponsor. Another blow for a man who was ill, but did not know how seriously ill he was. He fell down and was taken to the outside hospital. Word got back to us that he was cut open for his heart, and cancer was ravaged throughout his chest cavity. This, we were told, meant he had only a few days to live. He fell into a coma, and was dead four days later.

Lenny was a "sex offender" -- a guy who I personally lived with for five years; he was a barber hairstylist. As a legal aide in the law library, I have to treat everyone equally; I don't discriminate. The same with my Christian faith, as I am to love all people, even my enemies and the people "society" says are bad.

Can you tell who is *bad* and who is not?

Lenny's family abandoned him when he came to prison in 2003; his "church" visited him one time and stopped after he pled guilty. He was shocked by that, because he was generous to that church donating as much as $500 a month, sometimes, because Lenny was making good money. He had no prior record – nothing, not even a parking ticket until this one incident – being accused of rape of a child. In Tennessee, that can be anything (e.g. a Q-Tip in a nostril), as the definition of *"penetration"* is:

"Introducing anything into the human body orifice for sexual gratification." [7]

So, like most men never before in their life in conflict with the law, Lenny – like many others – was threatened by this attorney with the typical *"You'll get 100 years at trial unless you plead guilty"* argument. And like so many men after they realize they made a mistake and were probably guilty of something less, they would come to myself or other legal aides for review of their case. Yet, the "system" is really tuff to get one back out of prison, as the law pretty well says once you signed for your plea, you "bought it." And like Lenny, when they ask why their lawyer lied or persuaded them to plead guilty without even doing investigative work or hiring expert doctors as witnesses or to look at autopsy mistakes, I tell them that is it because most lawyers – as in sex offense cases -- do not want to be known as "defenders of child rapists" for fear of losing their business due to social media publicity attacks. That's the bottom line from experience.

A perfect example of this trend with child molesters or "chomoes," is with another cellee of mine, James P. Hyde. He had the typical lawyer described, above, and was taken advantage of at age 62 because he was illiterate back in 2000. He didn't get a fair trial for his alleged "rape" of his mentally-ill 16-year old daughter. [8] NO where from the evidence I saw did Mr. Hyde ever have his clothes off, expose himself, -- nothing. And his wife at the time of the trial was allegedly having an affair, supposedly, with a law enforcement officer close to the case.

Yet, when one is accused of a sex offense, the first *"world reaction"* is to believe the gossip, fake news, or the accuser. And in several other cases I have seen, such as in *Maseenberg v. Massenberg*,[4] -- of which I am personally familiar with -- a deceitful wife wanting a divorce coerced her then teenage daughter to lie and say her father molested her. Years later, when the daughter turned eighteen years of age, she testified her mother coerced her, and he was fully exonerated.

My point is, medically, some inmates have real illnesses for a volunteer to be concerned with. Whether they are a convicted sex offender or not, they still deserve humane treatment, care, and God's love. And for years – including in the military – I've seen cases of soldiers being falsely accused by their wives wanting divorces taking the "easy way out" for custody and service member benefits. This works almost every time to the ignorant soldier's "chain-of-command," and for eager police and Department of Child Services social workers to get in on the "take down," and make a great headline capturing the evil child molester everyone in society loves to hate. Sometimes, such a plan of falsely accusing a husband, father, or boyfriend backfires. The man can't take the pressure anymore and goes berserk, killing the accuser (wife or mother of the child). The humiliation and loss of that man's life having been ruined due to job loss, financial ruin, and all social media shunning him as dirt is just too much, so the man feels his life is over -- hopeless.

Regardless of a person's crime, if you are a true Christian, you are to forgive that man – or woman, and care for them. The sex offender has it the hardest because he or she is under 24 hour monitoring most likely when they get out. They are told they can't be trusted, may have to take oral castration medication, or even a vasectomy operation. Even their Internet is monitored when they get out of prison to check for "kiddy porn" and the like. Difficult topics with this type of inmate in volunteer work, especially when you have to get up in front of the parole board and they ask you the big questions:

**"Why do you want to support a man (or woman) who raped a child?"
Don't you believe that they are mentally ill?**

Gang Members

This last segment of the toughest types of people to do volunteer work with is not so bad at all. Many of these "boys and girls" were from environments where they did not have good or any role models for father and mothers, especially the boys. So they "clichéd up" in the "hood," "barrio," "hollow," or anywhere U.S.A. "neighborhood" and formed a group or alliance of people – usually circle of friends they wanted to be accepted in -- to have an identity and purpose.

Common sense is needed here. (And you don't have to have a Ph.D. in psychology to know this stuff. In America, we have seen "gangs" growing up since we played in our neighborhoods, watched "Little Rascals" re-runs on the TV, seen gangs on cowboy movies (cattle rustlers), and Hollywood and the media glorify gangs in movies and in Rap videos to make this *sub-culture* attractive to sell stuff. The problem is, the violence of the gang "life style" glorified and made popular in sub-cultures, has become increasingly destructive to families, neighborhoods, and now in major America cities with senseless unnecessary shootings in the streets.

Jumping In – Jumping Out. In 1998, I saw one gang's way of getting folks to join at a prison I'll never forget. They told the "recruit" he'd "better join or else." The next day on the recreation yard, seven to ten "dudes" (I'll keep the gang anonymous) surrounded this one recruit and started punching him in the head. (I remember his look, plainly, because they broke his glasses.) If I stepped in and tried to help, I would surely not be writing this book today, because that guy took a blow to the head from a concrete block crushing his skull. I found out he was evacuated, and never came back to the prison. They told him to "check in or else," and he refused. ("Check in" means to go to the prison administration and have your self put in "Protective Custody," (PC), where all the "Check ins" go to hide because they can't live in the open population for fear of being killed, raped, or robbed, or some other fate.) Many who do "jump in" to a gang – that is join it, avoid such a fate; however, may have to prove their "worth" by doing some deed their *lieutenant* tells them to do. This deed can be to stab someone, go pick up a gun or cell phone, or maybe blackmail some inmate or extort commissary for the gang so they can enjoy a big meal courtesy of those that "contributed." Jumping out is a totally different story. Usually this involves a member getting their face stomped. (That is, having the "daylights" beaten out of you.) This can be very bad sometimes, and may even include checking in or moving to another prison. (I've seen both.)

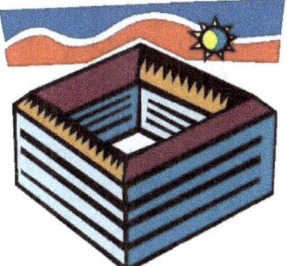

So, how do you, Mr. or Miss. Volunteer, help someone who is a gang member or ex-ganger member?

As the theme is all throughout this book repeats, it's simple – show Christ's love that you care! Give your inmate you have decided to help the care with the work towards them leaving the gang so they can become successful law-abiding citizens. The need to be working on all the same stuff as others to get ready for re-entry. However, they have to be more careful to avoid disciplinary infractions and finding a way to step out of the gang, even if it means going to another prison.

FACT. No matter what prison you go to, there is always someone there from the same gang with a cell phone; you can't hide. That goes for rival gangs too, because if you "dissed" (disrespected) a gang or did something to violate "gang code," the other gang knows too.

The bottom line is, most gang members need a role model – period. Some gang leaders I know are actually pretty good guys, and I am glad they stay true to their "colors" and abide by their loyalty standards. That is, when one of their members gets out of line, they take care to see that rule breaker is "schooled" (disciplined) to stop whatever it is that is bringing heat down on the gang. So, when dealing with the individual gang member or ex-gang member, consider yourself as the new role model offering an _alternative_ to the gang lifestyle.

Are you talented enough to show your sponsoree that making an honest living is the right  way to go? That your faith in God gives you the daily strength and protection, not the gang? That standing up for yourself, wisely, is respectable – not "weak." That – and I've seen it work – you can still be able to live in the open population if what you do – as an non-gang member – benefits the gang. (I've seen it with arts-n-crafts guys who make the gang special items and the gang appreciates the good work – and it pays well!) Most former gang members I know are able to see that, eventually, noting the gang _lifestyle_ leads right back to prison; and they don't want to come back. It also leads to the "grave yard," as one gang member told me.

Nevertheless, you represent the biggest gang in the world – Christ's! Tell them you know what it's like to be in a group that makes you feel wanted, special, have a purpose – loved. And they can be in the same gang with Jesus too if they just believe. It's a "cliché up that's a 'step up," I say to some considering jumping out.

Whatever the inmate's status is, you have their ear, and they are looking to you for life-changing advice. Whether you are helping sex offenders, drug addicts, mentally ill persons, elderly, physically-challenged, or gang members you are acting as Christ's "ambassador" to help save this person's soul, their condition, and provide hope for a brighter tomorrow. No one said it is easy, especially in a prison environment; it's not. Above all, keep it "real," because you are not Superman or Superwoman. You are not God, which is why you have to call on **_His_** power. But you do represent a Super God, with Jesus Christ, and you can tell people about him and show them "Him", by your words and actions. And if you do that, then you are doing effective prison ministry.

Chapter 8

Parole and Re-Entry: Dragging the Sponsoree Out of Prison / Jail

> *"They were hungry and thirsty; their life was ebbing away. In their distress they cried to the LORD, who rescued them in their peril, guided them by a direct path so they reached a city to live in." – (Psalms 107 5-7 (NAB))*

<u>RESTORATIVE JUSTICE</u> – THE *NEW* FOCUS IN AMERICA.

Let me begin by saying churches or other community support organizations including government-supported initiatives need to realize prisoners **are** coming back to their neighborhoods. And not necessarily to their churches, especially if those churches *failed* to support them while they were incarcerated or upon release.

Would you blame them after years of captivity, oppression, and broken promises?

Benjamin Franklin got it right on prisons during the forming of America's first prison system. What was right, then, is needed today. That is: to get restorative justice *on fire* in people's hearts to generate more volunteers for sponsorship which shows *agape* love – "unconditional love" to a prisoner. THIS is the goal:

Restore the prisoner to the community, not release a social and financial cripple.

This form of justice is not new. Benjamin Franklin said,

"A prisoner not out of prison as soon as possible and behind the plow is a drain on the community." (paraphrasing)

Benjamin Franklin, (1775) Encyclopedia Britannica

Franklin saw the effects of poverty and degradation of prisoners and what it does to ruin the family, the farm, and the communities having spent years in France observing the cruel ways the corrupt governments and laws prevented "ex-prisoners" from getting back on their feet. Franklin then took what he saw to make progressive changes in America and championed the argument for the application of beneficial laws, policies, and procedures to treat and/or help ***correct*** prisoners so they get back on their feet – quickly, and kept their farms, family, and children from destructive social vice and decay. Franklin – just as today's modern-thinkers -- argued the other side of punishment which is for the education assistance, job training, and social training prisoners need to be successful members of the community again once released.

Change needed now. The trends in society, today, to get away from the old *retributive justice* (e.g. lock up, warehouse, release, and re-capture) are being adopted, quickly, by more progressive states like Pennsylvania. "Myth-busting" facts about prisoners, tips for volunteers and churches to better assist prisoners by sponsoring them or mentoring them, and what restorative justice does to give hope to the prisoners for success and society – in return – gets a reformed person back from prison rather than a socially-crippled person with bitterness and lack of ability to get a job and be productive.

> **Does that sound like "Jesus?"** Dumping prisoners on the street to fail? Or, black-mailing old prisoners to raise $800 for a half-way house, otherwise they won't be given parole? (How can a prisoner make that on a prison wage of 17¢ per hour?) Is that mercy? Compassionate? Moral?

FACT: God chose two prisoners to be with him at the end of His life. Not kings or disciples, but convicts.

Restorative & Social Justice

> "WE HAVE A *LEGAL* SYSTEM, NOT A JUSTICE SYSTEM."

– A brief exposition.

As seen in 2019 with *federal* legislation reducing the punishment for some *non-violent* crimes with the release of long-sentenced prisoners receiving *clemency* from President Trump's "Second Chance Initiative" and some *state* governors examining state laws to, perhaps, *mirror* the new "atmosphere" of [considering] <u>reducing</u> the number of incarcerated in American state penal facilities (e.g. Cyntoia Brown), we have to historically examine *restorative* justice in brief context to the trends and values shifting in America.

> The great Russian author, Fiodor Dostoyevsky wrote, "If you want to see how advanced a society is, look at the way it treats its prisoners." (*Crime and Punishment*) Dostoyevsky advocated for reforms for the welfare of all – including offenders who one day get out of prison.

First, the United States has over 2.4 million men and women currently behind bars -- the ***highest*** prisoner-to-population statistic (ratio) of people locked up for long periods of time compared to other countries in the *civilized* world. (U.S. Bureau of Prisons and United Nations report, 2018). For over 3 decades *tough on crime* laws and *truth in sentencing* laws have put out the "drag net" primarily on drug offenders at an alarming rate in conjunction

with "3-strikes your out" laws ("Mandatory Minimums") -- the reason(s) for long periods of incarceration such as in the federal sentencing guidelines which could force a judge to send people to prison for 20 years to "life" for even simple drug possession depending on how the law(s) were written at the time. (For Tennessee offenders - "enhancing factors" can do the same.) Looking back in retrospect, these laws now appear in today's progressive society as **out-dated**, **abusive**, **racist**, and **non-reflective** of the values and weight the general population now feels should be placed on such offenses given long-term punishments and the consequences financially, psychologically, and morally they have on the long-time sentenced offender.

Second, *crime* is not only a social and economic problem but also a <u>community</u> and <u>family</u> problem. If "the time" doesn't fit "the crime," then something must be done to **correct** these obsolete law(s) and fix them so that justice *is* served for the victim, society, <u>and</u> the offender and his or her community and family which the offender is going back to.

Ergo, *restorative* justice instead of <u>*retributive*</u> justice is becoming the *hallmark* call for advocates and social reformers to make legislators take note to enact new ***just*** sentencing structures and/or eliminate questionable parole boards, see that appropriate effective corrections is facilitated, and that the lives of the people involved have an opportunity to get on with their lives by giving the offender a chance to recover in prison and as soon as possible be paroled which is the solution to overcrowding. Simply dumping masses of undisciplined "non-violent" offenders back into society in *worse* or no better condition than when they first entered prison doesn't solve the problem. Nor does holding old prisoners in prison for decades who are ready for release solely on the basis they committed a "violent crime". Just because their crime was labeled "violent" does not mean -- after time in prison -- the person hasn't changed. This FALSEHOOD or MISCONCEPTION is now shifting. People, churches, and other organizations on the outside are starting to see that parole boards are NOT evaluating prisoners on WHO THEY ARE, but rather what they did, in spite of one of the criteria for release which is "readiness" for successful release back into society. Obviously to the "reasonable man" a prisoner who has done their time set by the judge and has an outstanding prison record of behavior, discipline and education achievements, support group, job plan, home plan, etc. is ready for parole.

> *"Incentives <u>drive</u> behavior." – Gov. Bill Lee on Prison Reform*

What is Restorative Justice?

<u>Restorative</u> justice is putting emphasis not only on repairing the damage to the victim and society, but also to repairing and helping fix the life of the offender as well to help them make corrections to their lives while in prison – and after prison, if necessary (e.g. chronic care for Bi-polar disorder, drug rehab prevention, etc.) and giving them what they need to become self-sufficient and productive in society again. It begins with EFFECTIVE assistance from government and other groups that foster the prisoner's economic and social ability to function successfully when they return to their community. It is giving HOPE to inmates to have a future when they have **INCENTIVES** to eagerly do the right things and make the changes to their lives especially when "freedom" is an obtainable goal and a reality – the 'number one" incentive. It is uniting family members with their brother, sister, father, son, and daughter or mother that restorative justice provides them an opportunity to be together again within a supportive family and/or support group. It is giving *merit* to people at the parole board for their accomplishments in changing their lives such as being: Honorably-discharged veterans (which shows community service and sacrifice), education degrees, an outstanding disciplinary behavior record, having a support group visit them to ensure their transition back to society is successful, and that they are adjudged on **who they are** – and ready for release.

– What is NOT Restorative Justice?

Restorative justice is NOT warehousing prisoners for decades to degrade them and make them so physically and mentally pathetic. It isn't watching older crime-labeled "violent" offenders rot in prison as other crime-labeled "non-violent" offenders go in and out the revolving door of prison un-prepared for release because they have no incentive to change versus the "violent-labeled" offender who is adjudged at the parole board as "violent" for a crime that occurred 30 years ago even if that person is no-longer violent with an outstanding prison record. It is not releasing old people out of prison with just a check for $70 dollars, no driver's license, and no place to stay. It is not making prisoners take un-warranted classes they don't need to make parole when they are told they are *never* making parole but have to "flatten" their sentence because their crime was labeled "violent," yet they have not done a violent thing in all the years they have been locked up getting no credit for their *excellent* non-violent behavior while in prison following all the rules. It is not making a recently released offender who has no job and no place to stay pay outrageous court costs and fines after 20 or 30 years and they are too old to work. It is not the STRIKE FORCE going into a parolee's homes at 2 O'clock in the morning trashing their apartment throwing them to the ground and abusing them because they are a *sex offender* and making a sport out of harassing them in hopes of finding anything to [parole] "violate" them. It is not adjudging a prisoner at the parole board solely on his crime, what the victim says, and ignoring the corrective changes the prisoner has made while in prison that society and the legislature believe deserves credit. It is not keeping old prisoners locked out who have excellent disciplinary records and the courts set the sentencing "release dates" but the parole board is holding them past those dates when the prisoner is ready for release.

As you know, *parole is a privilege, and not a right.* So, preparing for parole or "flattening" your sentence has a lot to do with *you*, the offender. What you do to prepare yourself for release in a manner to restore you to a functioning free-world person has an enormous impact on how the parole board perceives your sustainability once released. Your ability to obtain employment, to provide for your needs, and the after-care you may require (i.e. counseling, drug-relapse assistance, etc.) depends on how you plan and quickly acquire a *support network* and knowledge of how to "thrive" in the free-world as a law-abiding citizen expected to live appropriately and comply with the terms of your parole. As explained in **Part I**, *"Restorative Justice"* is giving you the strengths and skills to become self-sufficient when released. EFFECTIVE restoration to re-enter society begins within the confines of the prison to _correct_ your "behaviors" (character) before you are released so you avoid those mistakes of the past and don't end up back on the police blotter and in prison again.

SO, HOW DO I GET RESTORED?

Nothing is written in stone. Today's offenders have man opportunities in prison to make changes in their lives to better themselves with, of course, seeking a better education. GED, college courses, or vocational classes (i.e. woodshop, masonry, electrical, computers, barbering, HVAC, etc.) all provide for self-improvement.

As Gov. Lee said, "Incentives drive behavior." As the governor knows, better educational assistance for prisoners like more colleges, PELL grants, etc. assist prisoners to get higher educations so there is a **_less_** likelihood of recidivism as statistics have shown. Individuals such as family members and friends can help prisoners with financial assistance to obtain correspondence courses to foster skills and knowledge to make the inmate economically viable upon release to be hired in today's modern workforce. Every certificate earned while in prison is a "plus" to add to one's repertoire of skills and accomplishments for a resume' to take to the board and streets to show your transformation and readiness for employment.

LET'S FACE A MAJOR FACT: UNLESS AN INMATE HAS $4,000 COMING RIGHT OUT OF PRISON, HE OR SHE HAS NO PLACE TO STAY, NO TRANSPORTATION, NO JOB, AND NO DRIVER LICENSE UNLESS THEY HAVE A FAMILY OR SPONSOR[SHIP] HELPING ASSIST THE INMATE LEAVING PRISON.

First, every inmate is a "human being" with a dignity that should be respected even though they wear a label of "ex-felon". People make mistakes everyday, but don't wear this label unless so deemed by the law and courts. Most people want to be treated with respect and have the same basic goals and values as most people. People – adults – usually want a decent place to stay, a car to get around to work and back, to eat decent food, and to live somewhat comfortably and not in squallier. If a released inmate has no home, transportation, food stamps, cell phone, etc. they are doomed to fail. These things cost money, and the majority of released inmates struggle if they don't have a family member, sponsor, friend, or half-way house to go to, or need money to get a place on their own, temporarily, so they can begin the process of *re-entry*. Re-entry that is supposed to start at the prison with filling out the papers for SSI (if needed), obtaining half-way house acceptance, food stamps, VA enrollment, job resume', and even driver license manual copy to take the test upon release. ALL these an inmate should be addressing before release of which the parole board may want to also know HOW an inmate intends to support him or herself and go about getting these tasks done.

SPONSORS. An inmate can't have enough mentors and sponsors. They can be family, friends, or even groups from generous organizations or churches such as: MEN OF VALOR, TPOM, TAKE ONE, or others who "adopt" inmates and wish to partake in prison ministry or volunteer programs or actions designed to "drag" a prisoner out of prison and restore them to the community by providing needs for them while in prison and beyond the walls. The key is "resources" available drive what can be done.

From money and time spent at the prison before they get out, to driving the released inmate to the dentist or job site ALL are the steps in the  right direction for seeing the inmate become self-reliant and capable of living on their own successfully – the number one goal. By actively showing the inmate the right direction to live through love and care, the sponsor creates a *new* energy in their adopted inmate who may – for the first time – have a chance at avoiding falling back to old habits because they have been given more opportunity and resources to sustain living *crime-free* by making better choices given their better environment of support and support group [of people] who are there to assist them in most anything they may need until they can live on their own. Remember, it's good to have mentors to talk to you, but *sponsors* make the big difference in deeds and needs.

Ergo, genuine restoration occurs when sponsorship is staying with the inmate AFTER release, often for a few years, especially with former drug-addicted inmates who need aftercare or have some other disability. Effective sponsorship is treating the inmate with dignity and helping them get started with: secure housing, being linked to finding medical, eye, and dental care, obtaining funds for utilities, helping them get to the motor vehicle driver's test, to the job interview, and maybe for a few trips to the job site until the inmate can afford a car and insurance.

All these tasks are "mountains" to some people, especially penniless inmates coming out of prison with nothing but the clothes on their backs. Even a trip a few times to the GOODWILL or SALVATION ARMY may have to be done to help the recently released inmate to put the basics (clothing, shoes, tableware, a bed, a chair, a table, etc.) into the inmate's new residence.

In closing, my dad used to say, 'If you teach a man to fish, he can feed himself." That's all a person coming out of prison wants – a chance at freedom again and to live right and never go back. But if he is not given the tools to do the job, he or she is destined to fail. Restoring a person *is* JUSTICE, because that person and the way they are treated reflect the society in which he comes from. And if a person has done their time, they deserve a "second chance" and should be given a hand to be picked up, not kicked or kept down. END.

Importance of Showing up and Testifying: "Stage Fright" To Avert Rolling the Dice for Clemency

Have you ever had a loss of words? Been "tongue-tied" or just didn't know how to respond to a significant question that was either embarrassing or really telling the truth you were afraid of getting out or needed to get out but didn't know how?

Imagine a job interview and the boss asks you questions about yourself which are reveling. Many interviewers want to know exactly who you are and want the facts to decide whether your character is genuine and your actions and behaviors to work around people will profit them and their co-workers. Well, it's the same in a parole interview. If the inmate is a "clam" – doesn't say anything, then the member of the board asking the questions has little with which to decide the fate of letting a prisoner go or not. The same with a supporter who comes and just gives "yes or no" responses to questions needing explanations to make the board understand the inmate you are sponsoring is ready for release. However, if the inmate – when it comes time for his or her time to speak is silent – then the reasons for release are limited to what was said or not said by the supporters, protesters, and the "record" of the parole board looking at a computer screen which may have extremely devastating false information about the inmate before them which the board was hoping would be cleaned up by the inmate.

Please remember, it is extremely important for sponsors, mentors, volunteers, and family members to practice with their inmate they are sponsoring how to act and what to say at prison parole hearings. Why? Because many inmates have no idea what to say or are woefully prepared to answer difficult questions.

For example, would you respond to the questions, below, just as impartially as if someone were asking you the time of day?

- Why did you kick the victim eleven times in the head?
- How much blood did the victim lose?
- Do you know how many times the victim was shot?
- Can you explain why you sold drugs to children?
- How come your "charge partner" squealed on you?
- When you exposed yourself in public, were you aroused?

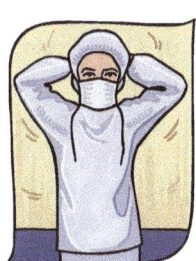

Keep in mind, the parole board, today, is changing due to COVID and contact (social distancing) rules restricting all supporters from speaking in-person at parole hearings for inmates at the board. Protesters can; however, come to the hearings. This deprives the inmate of emotional testimony form the supporters – testimony that is invaluable to persuade the board in favor of release in opposition to the testimony of the protesters. And many inmates ill-prepared are being denied parole because they are not prepared as to what to say at the board and why, like the protesters are who have state-supported victim impact coordinators who "coach" and assist victims as to what to do and say to prevent inmates from making parole. This unfair and unjust practice leaves the inmate to look more heinous or less prepared for parole, and often results in more cases of parole denial. Supporters need to show up at the hearings regardless if they can't speak, render e-mails, and even SKYPE if possible to speak up, especially when their inmate may not know how.

Ergo, if you "bomb" (fail to make a good impression at the board with facts warranting and meriting parole), your odds for clemency are astronomical, unless you can prove almost absolute innocence or some overwhelming mitigating factor on the inmate's behalf. This was emphasized by Beth Schwartzapfel in her article, "How Parole Boards Keep prisoners in the Dark and Behind Bars (And why the Pre-Sentence Report (PSI/PSR) needs to be accurate for parole). Schwartzapfel said that the PSI was one of the most dangerous articles for the parole board to use the label "Seriousness of the Offense" to deny a person parole when the PSI is totally inaccurate as the nature of the crime, history of the inmate going up for parole, prior crimes, propensity for violence, education data, work history, etc. which could all be wrong and prejudice the prisoner at their hearing. She writes:

> "The nature of crime as described in public hearing causes further concern." [1]

Schwartzapfel found in a Stanford university stud that older inmates who had committed the most serious crimes, and served the longest terms, are least likely to commit new crimes upon release. Of 860 murders paroled in California found only five returned to prison with new felonies – and none for murder. This is especially true for old prisoners.

SOME PAROLE / CLEMENCY FACTS.

In Tennessee, for example, since 2011, Governor Bill Haslam has not granted a single pardon until July 2018, when he gave four grants (one commutation and three pardons). [2] Up to January 19, 2019 -- Gov. Haslam's last day in office -- he only had a total of six commutations, 15 pardons, and one exoneration. This did not include, until the day he left office, the full exoneration for Cyntoia Brown, who received a commutation for first-degree murder of a man whom she killed while she was a 16-year old prostitute (juvenile) and received a "life-51-year minimum sentence" for the killing. [3]

Up till then, Gov. Haslam was following in the footsteps of his predecessor, Gov. Phil

Bredesen, who hadn't pardoned anyone until right up to the time of his final days in office. [4] Attorney Benjamin K. Raybin explains that in Tennessee, the governor has exclusive authority to issue "reprieves and pardons." [5] Yet, the Tennessee Board of Paroles – an independent agency – has "gatekeeper" duty to screen all applications for clemency filed by inmates or their attorney(s). More often applications screened by the board's seven members *never* reach it to the level of formal clemency hearing. The alarming fact is that if a hearing is denied by the parole board (gatekeeper) – the same board turning the inmate down at the parole hearing – the application is rejected without ever being seen by the governor. As Raybin says:

> *"This practice may violate the board's statutory "duty ... to make nonbinding recommendations concerning requests for pardons."* [6] *If the board conducts a clemency hearing, the recommendation for either approval or denial is sent to the governor."*

The board does not keep records of how many applications for clemency it denies. However, statistics available to show how absurdly low clemency is done in Tennessee, can be seen by these two sets of charts below which include the current Governor Bill Lee's consideration for Adam Brassell who, in July of 2020, when he received seven votes at his clemency hearing for full exoneration.

Total	Bredesen (2003-11)	Haslam (2011-2019)	Bill Lee (2019- July 2020)
Reviewed by Board	1,411	692	not available
Sent to Governor	29	21	1
Granted Relief	29	21	1 pending

From Tennessee Board of Parole on-line

Governor Lee expressed in his State of the State address on 2/03/2020 addressed several social justice and economic initiatives to protect the public and help inmates such as ***Apprenticeship TN***, which – to a former businessman like Lee – offers incentives for re-entry prisoners to learn job skills and enter the workforce. This includes programs like "Grow Your Own" for local districts to be given grants for needy programs as well as criminal justice reforms to save money. [7] Not just two weeks later, Gov. Lee began to change decades of no early clemency by directing the board of parole to reverse the trend in light of 34 other states that reduced both their imprisonment and crime rates during the same periods as Lee's predecessors. [8] Tamburin notes that 23 recommendations were sent to the governor and state lawmakers to shape lee's legislative priorities which, below, were to be considered to affect criminal and social justice reform:

"•Rewriting the criminal code and sentencing matrix ...
•Changing state rules that keep people in prison ...
•Expanding services for inmates released from incarceration ...
•Reducing prison time for technical parole / probation violators." [9]

These changes do begin to help only if they are meaningful, and release in large numbers occur for especially the older inmates who have been incarcerated for decades, especially the ones labeled as "violent" because that label is misleading, given a person can kill someone out of the heat of passion (e.g. domestic spousal abuse), yet that person harbors no ill-will towards anyone and demonstrates they are no threat by their prison disciplinary record of non-violence.

Ergo, parole is still a subjective determination with the power of decision in people's hands which can be swayed by emotion or false data on a computer or even lies by vigilante protesters out for vengeance blood no matter who's it is. That's why proponents to disband or dissolve the board and replace it with mandatory sentences to eliminate interpretations and prejudice is so called for, as too often the number of errors made at the board denying release are greater than the number of prisoners being set free, as in the statistics of the State of Tennessee and money spent on corrections budgets. [10] Offenders are still being denied at hearings for "seriousness of the offense" – a "catch all" because what offense is not serious? Otherwise the offense would not be listed on the law books as a criminal offense if violated.

Thus, if you look at the chart, below, you can see in fiscal year (FY) 2015-2016, a typical trend of no parole which, now, Gov. Lee is slowly trying to end so that social justice is reached at a pace that is not too offensive to victim's rights groups, politically correct conservative groups, and radicals looking who don't care about the crime rates if released prisoners don't have job when released. [11]

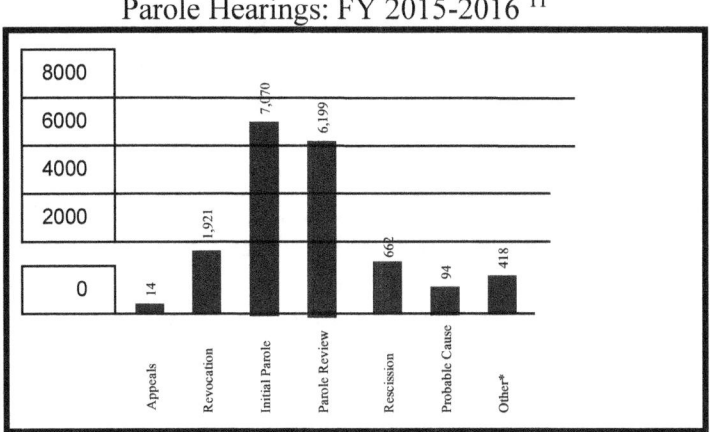

Parole Hearings: FY 2015-2016 [11]

Thus, with these figures, above, one can reasonably see parole controlled by the parole board does not mean clemency is a viable option that is meaningful given the pitifully low number of applications making it to the governor's desk for a reprieve, based on the gate-keeping parole board that society believes is a governor's privilege to appeal too, as was Governor Pontius Pilate the authority to appeal to when Christ seeking justice was wronged. It is a "conflict of interest," that the parole board deny a prisoner parole, then when the prisoner applies for clemency (i.e. commutation, pardon, or exoneration) the board usurps the governor's authority and arbitrarily declines to send the prisoner's appeal to the governor in effect overturning it's earlier rendered decision declining parole. In theory, a governor's "clemency" – on paper, but in reality, a duty usurped by the parole board and not an independent agency to consider clemencies which, in effect, are to overturn parole board denials.

Prison Ministry In Covid America

LABELS HURT and RE-ENTRY HALFWAY HOUSES

Funny, sad, how people stereotype "ex-cons" or "ex-felons" not as "re-entry individuals," but rather as spinoff-titled derogatory names normally associated with pulp-trash Hollywood cop shows on TV or in the movies. Rarely, if any of these shows or in the media do you see people try to help ex-offenders or portray them in a positive light re-deeming their lives and putting them back together after "doing time." Instead, it's all the derogatory stuff with ex-cons hounded by cops and being treated like second-class citizen just below "bum" and, perhaps, even or slightly above a dog. Labels from propaganda that hurt and harm and need to be stopped.

So, what do you know about the major labels, stereotypes, and problems facing inmates to make parole and succeed after release?

One of the biggest challenges is for an inmate to find a place to stay when he or she gets out so they can look for a job – if they are not too old or unable to work.

I came across a book at the prison chaplain's office entitled: "*Beyond Bars*," by Jeffrey I. Ross and Stephen C. Richards who had a chapter titled "Halfway Houses and Work Release Centers." [12] In this book, I found some remarkable coincidences to a lot of what they wrote which I found factual from my experience and from feed back from many over the years who were released from prison. In particular, I was amused they made a reference to an ex-con living in a cardboard box as a place to sleep. For years, I had used as a joke a drawing of a cardboard box as a back-up "Home Plan" to tell the parole board if an inmate didn't have the $1,500 the average halfway house wants before an inmate can go there and get a room to stay. [13] (See Diagram 8.1 -

Home) I also had a back-up "Job Plan" that's always a favorite. [3] (See Diagram 8.2 - Job)

Funny how perceptive *experienced* people can be about things like the cardboard box. Ross and Richards used it as an example of describing an ex-con who is homeless, then showed the compassion a waitress had 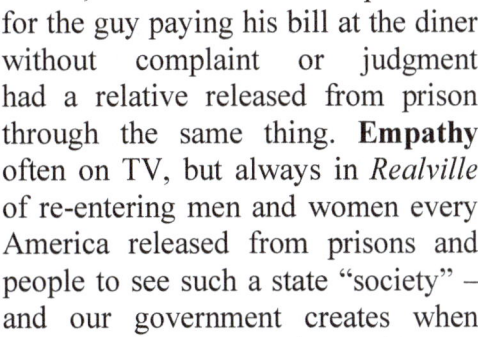 for the guy paying his bill at the diner counter without complaint or judgment because she had a relative released from prison who went through the same thing. **Empathy** displayed, not often on TV, but always in *Realville* for thousands of re-entering men and women every week in America released from prisons and jails. I want people to see such a state "society" – "The System" and our government creates when returning men and women are just "let go" from prison without a driver's license, no money, no job, and no place to stay. Especially true for offenders over the age of 62, like a guy I know who my friend just bought a bicycle for at the pawn shop in Nashville in July after the guy had spent 38 years behind bars. (The Internet wasn't even invented when he was locked up! *Reality*.)

That goes to show you how prisoners are treated. Like Rodney Dangerfield said, "I get no respect!" Prisoners are treated the same way. It's like the "Mark of Cane" in Genesis in the Bible. You can't get rid of it – the label: "ex-con."

Another example is the *"Blue's Brothers"* movie which Ross and Richards mention in their book which is also pretty close to reality which I just described. Dumped out of prison with nothing but what one of the brothers had when he went to prison, it's like time stopped while he was "in the joint." Pathetically not even well-welcomed back into society – a result of *"felonization"* (being treated as a felon for life) --, the older brother picks his younger brother up and they just go to a dumpy apartment only fit for one person. No big meal, no new clothes, not even a bathtub to wash in. No better than when he first went in. That's "The System." And a 40-year old movie still tells it like it is today for some people leaving prison, sadly:

> "You go in with nothing, and you come out with nothing -- no better economically-wise."

    I will say this, to understand more on how to find a good way to help a prisoner who needs a halfway house, *Beyond Bars* is right on the money. For juveniles, adults, from jail or prison, they describe it accurately. From my experience and knowledge of them, halfway houses are an invaluable tool for re-entry prisoners to get a start. There should be hundreds of them in each state. If a person is qualified to be in one (that is if that bed is "paid for" either by the inmate, grant money, by the state, or other), they locate to one where they are "paroling out to." Located in many communities, re-entering inmates can have a "step-down" from prison [life] to free-world. Halfway houses give inmates an opportunity to adjust and gather their thoughts and re-establish themselves into the mainstream especially to learn the technical skills of an electronic age for those who have been "inside" (away) from normal social and economic interaction for decades.

Diagram 8.1 "Home Plan"

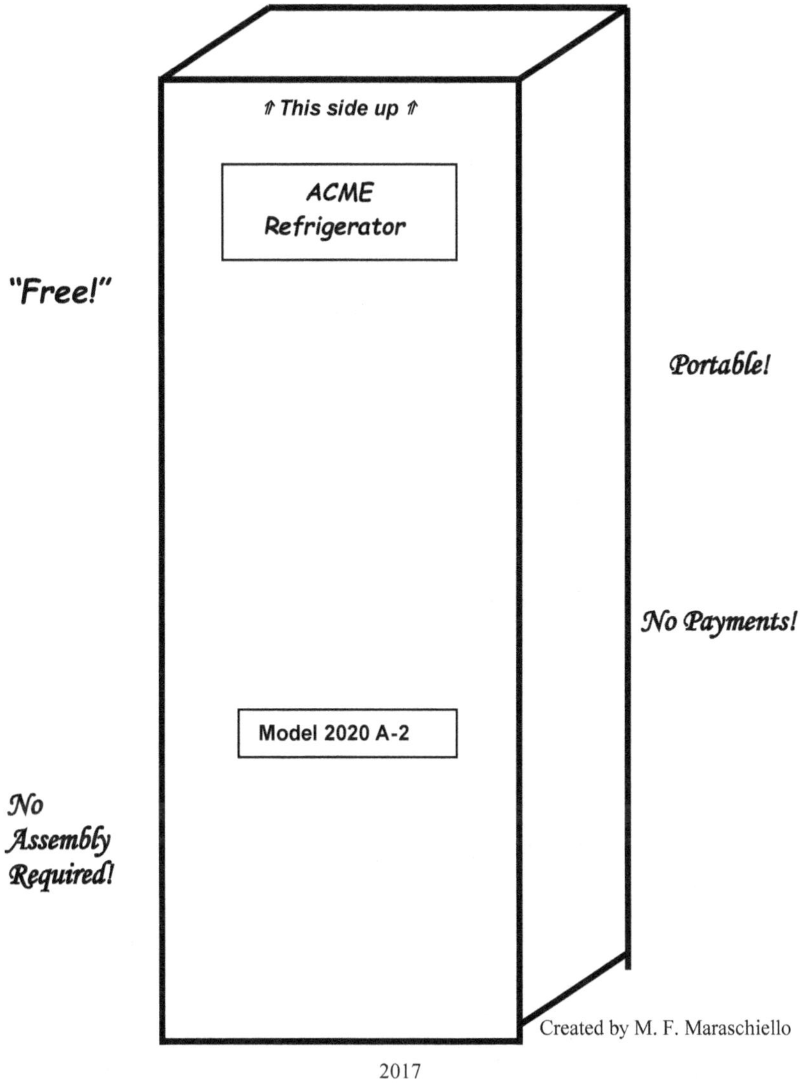

Parole Board Back-up "Home Plan"

The Model 2020 A-2 Box. Obtainable at several different home curbs – is guaranteed to last until the first rain or the wind blows it away. This free box not only provides you the temporary shelter a returning convict can afford, but is mobile as well giving you the added comfort of knowing you can always avoid staying in one location ahead of the police. Easily folds up to carry to the dream location of your choice avoiding those outrageous realtor costs. (Not warranted against dogs or drunks urinating on it.)

Diagram 8.2 "Job Plan"

Created by M. F. Maraschiello 2020

Parole Board Back-up "Job Plan"
An entrepreneur's dream job for self-employment. Selling No. 2 pencils has been a mainstay worldly-celebrated means of employment as far back as the streets of New York, when the first graphite pencil replaced the charcoal stick. Since the 1880's, pencil manufacturers have relied upon thousands of homeless and recently released prisoners for the distribution of pencils to the most needy of business people around the steps of the capitol and business buildings for years. Guaranteed never to fail, No. 2 pencils durability and design give the entrepreneur magnificent ideas with which to peddle these writing instruments for monetary gain and the prestigious reward of a sale closing.

As Ross and Richards explain, often the best halfway houses are run by ex-offenders. ² That is because ex-offender run houses don't put up with "BS" and are the most efficiently run because they can relate to a re-entering convict's situation more effectively, and also not put up with "cons" trying to con them. Staff comprised of former inmates I know are even getting their *masters* and *doctorate* degrees so they can minister as professional counselors as well with local churches and pastoral centers in addition to running or managing the halfway house. Best is that halfway houses are designed to also get prisoners out of prison faster. Imagine an inmate told they "made parole," yet has to save up $1,500 for the first month rent on a prison wage of $58 dollars a months. It can't be done!!! In what, 25.86 years?

That's nuts!

How does that help offenders to be motivated to change? To succeed when out if all his or her money goes for room and board? What about job interview clothes? Medical expenses? A cell phone? Shoes? Teeth?

THE SOLUTION

The bottom line is prison ministries, philanthropists, mentors, sponsors, family members, corrections and legislative persons, etc. need to "think" about what's going on when prisoners are released. There are no "magic wands" or "genie lamps" giving prisoners a driver license, a job, a car, or a place to stay so they can be functioning in society. Spending money to get to the board, then no "after-prison care" is a recipe for disaster. And the **only** defense to thwart recidivism is to equip and empower men and women leaving prison. Even if the states and federal government go back to World War II-style "work camps" with prisoners working their last year in prison on a bridge and road repair crew, imagine how the neighborhoods, streets, roads, and bridges would be today in America. Clean. Every neighborhood a

 green lawn, good roads – all from labor from prisoners on their final journey home people can look at and say, "Hey, there's those road crew guys from the prison!" Not with anger or disdain, but with a smile because they do good work and contribute to society.

Doesn't that work better than a man or woman rotting in a cell with no purpose? No job until he or she scrounges for one when they get out of prison? Bitter because of years of idleness and no good old-fashioned real *Christian* compassion and mercy?

Wake up, America! It's time to make some changes, and it starts with laws on the books to create revenues for funding work programs, not just talking about them. That's why Jesus flipped over the tables in the temple to get the "fakers" out of their, so the real temple worshippers and servants could do their work. That's what is needed to help prisoners – sincere workers  (mentors, sponsors, volunteer retired teachers, ex-cops, ex-lawyers, doctors -- professionals) in prison ministry. Not afraid to turn some tables if it means making a difference in saving just one life of a prisoner who Jesus said had value. (Appendix 3 describes a typical inmate's parole packet that should be prepared and discussed with the volunteer, then sent to the parole board and used by the inmate and volunteer at the parole hearing or appeal to the governor for clemency. You can find sample letters to the parole board in Appendix 4. In Appendix 5, are some re-entry tips, ideas, and facts to help prepare inmates.)

Michael Maraschiello

Chapter 9

Incarcerated Veterans and Their Needs: A National Failure

As a disabled Gulf War combat veteran, I can't find a more sad topic than this, and the failure of nationally-recognized veterans groups not wanting to take a more active stance in helping the over 200,000 veterans currently in prisons and jails, according the to Bureau of Prison Statistics on the internet. Many were and will be homeless, had TBI, PTSD, and drug-addictions. Many came home to cheating spouses and "lost it," having only been in combat just a few weeks with no "transition phase" and did not expect "Jody" was in bed with his or her spouse.

Wherefore, it is important for those volunteers who help veterans to be especially cognizant of the veteran's benefits they can get while in prison and when released. Below is a paper I did in 2018 which was sent to all the major veterans service organizations with absolutely no response from them. Seems – from a "little birdie" – that incarcerated veterans get deliberately "passed over" because they don't get the public support that disabled and homeless veterans get.

What? Incarcerated veterans don't get a "helping hand up" like the homeless?

How many homeless take their money and go by crack?

How many homeless sell their VA checks for drugs?

How many men and women veterans in prison are not worthy of the same help these "groups" claim they help all veterans – except prisoners? That's hypocritical in the eyes of many incarcerated veterans, especially ones with wounds from the wars and the state prison or jail won't give them medical attention nor take them to the VA for FREE health care they earned with their blood!

So, read this carefully and understand that veterans – like other human beings – deserve a "thanks" from a grateful nation. Veterans need help, even in prison, when they need the help to get back up just like those in the free world.

IT'S TIME FOR THE TRUTH: "Why Veterans Still Get Left Behind in the Courts, in the Legislatures, and at the Parole Board"- And What Should Be Done About It

By M. F. Maraschiello (Gulf War Veteran) FALL 2018

QUESTION.
What ever happened to the *call* by veterans groups, legislators, and members of the Halls of Justice (court "legal system") claiming to be supportive of veterans activities, rights, and programs to help fix the plight of returning veterans, veterans re-entering the civilian sector, and veterans – Active Duty, Guard, or Reserve – who are in trouble with the law?

BACKGROUND. As expected, many people continue to see the same-ole "cycle" has repeated itself once again. Specifically, after American servicemen and servicewomen put their civilian lives on hold to go [serve in uniform] to fight for our country – usually overseas, only to come back to find out that they get little re-entry adjustment assistance, are held in contempt sometimes by people with unsympathetic and/or un-patriotic eyes and ears even when the veteran has a disability that one cannot see such as Post Traumatic Stress Disorder (PTSD), Traumatic Brain Injury (TBI), or is addicted to some form of medication that does not allow the veteran to function normally. This *ignorance* problem has enormous consequences and is widely apparent shortly after a war begins and long after a war ends as now further discoursed.

THE KNOWLEDGE GAP.
FACT: When all wars start, usually there are numerous un-trained veteran-sensitive staff at Veterans Administration (VA) hospitals, in the legal system, in the legislatures, and on parole boards who cannot recognize and properly make good decisions regarding the veteran because they have no knowledge or experience to the current war's [veterans'] unique problems. ONLY when the

war is in progress or when the VA, legal system, and parole boards "gear up" (hire and/or train) *qualified* staff, can the veteran's overall situation, need, or "case" come into meaningful perspective for proper and just assistance to be rendered to the veteran. This "process" (closing the gap) only gets going when enough calls from people (i.e. family members of veterans, veterans themselves, or representatives of public constituents, veterans advocacy groups, or veterans-related government agencies) shine light on whatever it is that the veterans have a problem with so the issues can be addressed in some appropriate forum for resolution.

It should be noted, that as the war ends, and the number of veterans returning home decreases, the VA facilities, the legal system, and the parole boards lose – over time – those *trained* veteran-sensitive members or staff, thus allowing veterans coming to them for assistance or adjudication to fall victim to an otherwise ignorant and unsympathetic situation whereby they do not receive full and fair assistance, or in the alternative, mitigating and proper representation of their (the veteran's) true condition, status, ability, medical need, or character – for a fair outcome.

FACT: Only 2% of the U.S. population are ever in uniform performing military service.

VETERANS FATE: THEY SUFFER.
FACT: When any veteran's condition, case, character, history, or status is not fully represented and/or investigated, the veteran suffers. Case in point: **PORTER v. McCOLLUM**. [1] In *Porter*, the court held that a defense attorney is *guilty* of Ineffective Assistance of Counsel (IAC) when they fail to investigate the veteran's **military** record which includes: the veteran's mental and physical health records, records of disciplinary actions, records of good service and awards for outstanding or excellent performance, [military] job history, interview fellow service-members to confirm facts, behaviors, or other evidence, and present these records and facts to defense experts and/or the court – which includes the jury – to show the "BIG PICTURE" of the veteran. Many courts of law, before sentencing offenders, prepare what are called **Pre-Sentence Investigation Reports (PSI/PSR).** These reports are supposed to give the court *accurate* facts about the military [veteran] offender; however, they are often completed by poorly-trained probation officers who fail to include favorable and accurate data about veterans.

Usually, the PSI/PSR has very little to none of a veteran's *military files* data included in the PSR/PSI. This leaves the professional **_career_** service-member (veteran) open to flawed and prejudicial information the probation officer compiles from sources sometimes unreliable or prejudicial to the veteran. Much of an Honorably-Discharged veteran's service is just listed on the PSI/PSR as "Served in the military" or "Received a Discharge," which woefully misrepresents the veteran's resume' of often years of achievements and accomplishments. Not listing the service-members earning of: Bronze Stars, Silver Stars, Distinguished Service Crosses, or other medals or citations for gallantry, valor, or outstanding service representing the veteran's upstanding character denies the veteran **_pivotal_** facts as to WHO he or she really is.

Ergo, if done correctly by DAs, defense attorneys and parole boards, for example, obtaining **_complete_** records and facts about the veteran helps the decision-makers to make a more **_accurate and fair_** judgment in providing not only the veteran with proper representation of his or her situation and/ or condition, but gives the body of decision-makers a clear ability to make their just decision based on the veteran's complete service record which society – as deemed by the U.S. Supreme Court – demands to be considered because -- in the "big picture" -- it truly helps to represent the veteran more fully and accurately. If a decision-making body is **_void_** of sufficient records that should be at the decision-maker's forum, the decision-makers are apt to make fatal errors of judgment because – as the U.S. Supreme Court said in **_Porter_**, the veteran's FULL military records are to be available. [2] Otherwise the veteran suffers a fatal prejudice of being adjudged without all the significant material evidence and vital facts that give reasoning and mitigation, perhaps, to a veteran's case so the veteran receives a fair trial by *due process*.

TYPICAL *MAL-LEGAL* SCENARIO FOR A VETERAN.

Consider this often reoccurring scenario: A 21-year old combat veteran who is on Active Duty, in the National Guard, or in the Reserves comes back to his home or duty station in the USA after a one-year front-line tour in Afghanistan, Africa, or Syria. He served honorably in the combat zone, sometimes under hostile conditions, and did his duty meriting promotion and a reputation for being an "all-around good soldier." Yet, he has some PTSD "re-adjustment" problems upon return. He went out partying, smoked some marijuana -- for the first time -- to "deal" with his stress, and ended up falling asleep next to a minor at a crackhouse, only to be arrested on *felony* child abuse and *misdemeanor* drug possession charges the next morning in a raid.

THE PROBLEM: Mistreatment & Misrepresentation. How *should* this veteran's case, in the above scenario, be handled? Should the military take over the situation and get the veteran treatment, and the veteran receive some extra duty, reprimand, or probation period? Should an overzealous district attorney (DA) throw the book at the veteran and call the veteran a "crackhead" or "menace to society" -- like one DA did, in court with a *bogus* PSI/PSR filled with falsehoods -- just to prejudice the veteran and push hard for a conviction and stiffer penalty? Should the veteran be sent to a **Veterans Drug Court?** (Assuming a Veterans Drug Court is in the jurisdiction.) Should the court and/or the defense lawyer for the veteran order an evaluation and drug tests (e.g. mental health, drug screen, etc.) and get the records of the veteran to give the court sufficient relevant material information about the veteran to better help the court [decision-making body] decide what is the appropriate next step? (e.g. Drug Re-habilitation Program) Should the soldier's *chain-of-command* (military leadership supervisors) come to the court to give testimony or give affidavits as to the soldier's *honorable* conduct while the veteran was in uniform? Or – <u>retributively</u> speaking, again -- should the veteran be labeled and *lumped in* with typical "crackheads" who are often jobless, never served in the military, never did community service, less educated, less disciplined, less responsible, and often have an extensive *track record* or "history" (reputation) as a prior drug user or drug addict? Or, even worse, should the DA and others who are not sympathetic to any "law-breakers" or veterans, characterize and stereotype the veteran as a trained "blood-thirsty Vietnam baby-killer dope smoker pothead," who has no conscience to break the law, is narcissistic, a sex offender giving drugs to a minor, no remorse, no conscience for making victims, and has no ability to follow rules, especially ones for rehabilitation, probation, or parole?

RESTORATIVE* JUSTICE QUESTIONS:** First, is restorative justice present for a veteran to receive a conviction or appropriate and fair sentence when overzealous DAs – like in the above scenarios -- deliberately only present all the *negative* and inflammatory accusations and assertions that can be said about the veteran? Second, is restorative justice present for a veteran to receive a conviction or appropriate and fair sentence when ineffective defense lawyers or un-trained probation officers – like in the above scenarios -- deliberately only present all the *negative* and inflammatory accusations and assertions that can be said about the veteran? And third, who is going to stand up for the veterans to see that they are represented in a more factual and positive light to receive restorative justice, especially when they served their country *honorably* and often meritoriously -- which is supposed to ***count for something?

Disgracefully and sadly, the plight of the *incarcerated* veteran still exists today. Nine (9%) percent of the U.S. prison population is comprised of veterans, according to the U.S. Bureau of Prison's statistics (2016). Many still going back to the Vietnam War, and many who were **Honorably** discharged or deserved a discharge "upgrade" based on mitigating circumstances the military didn't care to investigate or defense lawyers failed to present favorable evidence to counter overzealous DAs who lusted for convictions and harsh sentences. FALSE information, poor investigations, lack of witnesses from the service-member's unit, and lack of *exculpatory* evidence ***favorable*** to the veteran always seems to plague the veteran when in conflict with the legal system. And all too often the press and/or law enforcement focus entirely on the negative aspect of the veteran's alleged criminal "act," damage to the victim(s), or purported story surrounding the case – no matter if it "fake news." The result is pressure via e-mails, tweets, and public outcry for what is now called "politicized-justice," meaning no matter if the alleged crime was done by the veteran or not, the story in the "news" is presumed to be the factual truth regardless of what the veteran can prove or say in his or her own defense. (After all, who wants to help or support an **alleged** or **convicted** "baby killer sex offender crackhead," even if they are an honorably-discharged and/or a once heroic veteran?)

Wherefore, the veteran – as in the scenarios above -- being judged without his or her FULL military records and accurate facts, can be erroneously and ***morally*** wronged with often devastating consequences.

AMERICA'S *LEGAL SYSTEM* DOESN'T CARE.

Decades ago, especially veterans of America's "Greatest Generation" (World War II), veterans received "credit" for their service and sacrifice. Many a veteran who distinguished themselves in uniform and on the battlefields were categorized as: un-selfish, self-sacrificing, patriotic, humanitarian, responsible, learned, capable of achievement, trustworthy, disciplined, and other character-rich and meritorious descriptions. Many veterans were caring leaders who protected their fellow veterans by doing their duty as supervisors and kept other "vets" from loss of life or limb at great risk to their own life. Sadly, most of today's parole boards, judges, and DAs have no respect for the service and sacrifice veterans have done; they frankly **_don't care_**, and haven't for decades about a veteran's "service" and "character." ONLY the crime (conviction), the victim, and the punishment are the sole "focus" of the legal system. Some DAs and some parole board members categorize and stereotype veterans right in with the crackheads and violent career criminal-stereotypes, often twisting or "spinning" the veteran's *service* records and job skills against the veteran by misrepresenting the veteran's **"training."** Good soldiers with *longer* periods of service are labeled as especially-skilled or especially-trained *planners* or "leaders" who plot and execute their "cool and calculated cold-blooded crimes," as the DAs and the media love to say for dramatic effect to make the accused or guilty appear more heinous, mentally deranged, or psychopathic. Further, career service-members are labeled as "trained killers" who show no remorse and mercy. These deliberate exaggerations inflame the public, juries, courts, victims, and others into believing the veteran's crime(s) are more serious or "heinous" especially since we *were* trained to kill and use "violence" as a solution to problems - what all service-members are trained to do, in combat or other situations. (**FACT:** It's never brought up – for political reasons -- that a returning war vet never receives *adequate* "violence **step-down** training" to *de-program* violence as a choice of options to solve problems.) Some veterans went through life and death situations of enormous stress while serving. Each veteran has unique experiences which need to be considered by those sitting in judgment of the veteran; however, that is often not the case, and the veteran is misunderstood and/or improperly treated. Thus, the "vet" receives unfair judgments and excessive punishments in most cases.

    Parole Board Errors. Some boards – if not fully aware of the veteran's true military record and/or case -- could wind up *erroneously* denying parole to a worthy veteran deserving parole based with one or both of the following prejudices: (1) The board only hearing or reading the inflammatory and often exaggerated remarks by the DA and/or or the court [judges] and victim rights groups about the crime, as previously discussed, above. (In other words, *deliberate* arbitrary and capricious conduct of choosing not to consider and/or include anything favorable (i.e. the veteran's service record of achievements and awards, civilian achievements, or other favorable conduct or meritorious character evidence) about the veteran that merits a **_high degree_** of reasonably moral and ethical *positive* facts to grant the veteran parole.); (2) The board shows no interest in giving credit or "recognition" to the veteran for their **_sacrifices_** made for our country, especially if that veteran had participated in wars saving lives, was in numerous protective missions of people of other countries, provided humanitarian relief, gave medical aid, or gave relocation assistance helping in construction projects for the benefit of children and families.

TAKEAWAY REALITY CHECK QUESTIONS:
WHY do parole boards let out 25-year old high-school dropout "crackheads" on meth, who still steal and rob – even in prison -- to support a drug addiction only to appear on the six o'clock TV news police report a month after release on parole? YET, the board won't release *honorably-discharged* "old-timer" first-time offender *military* veterans who are disciplined, and make up the **top one (1%)** of the ***most model*** of prisoners meriting morally-grounded release by society's standards?

Case in Point1: WHY does a crackhead get paroled over a 66-year old **Vietnam War Vet** who had a job in the *free-world for 30 years*, but lost it to one (1) crime? The crackhead had no discipline, and will be right back in prison. As for the Vietnam Vet, he – has: a high-school diploma and a military service record showing 6 (2) tours in Vietnam, earning two and a Bronze Star for Valor dragging a wounded soldier to safety under machinegun fire. The veteran is over two (2) decades in prison, is changed his life, has been a has family, community leaders, and support, and has numerous  still in prison -- some college, a years in with two Purple Hearts, enemy disciplined, spent remorseful, Chaplain's Aide, prison staff certificates and awards for being a *model* prisoner who mentors and leads other inmates in a personal growth program, versus the crackhead who just wants to go back to the streets to – most likely – sell dope, again, and "pimp ho's." (Used with permission. Crim. Ct. of Appeals, Case No. M2000-00369-CCA-r3-PC, *Rhodes v. State* (Whiteville, TN) July 27, 2000).

SAD FACT: The parole board did not ask one question about this veteran's honorable military service ☹

> **QUESTIONS.**
>
> •Is that justice for this veteran, above, in prison? To get no consideration for his honorable service?
>
> •What did the crackhead ever do for his country? For his community? To better himself or others?
>
> •And WHY is the veteran still in prison?

THE TRUE PICTURE OF PRISON –"REAL VILLE".

It is simple – **economics** and "job security." Prisoners make money for others. Prisoners have to be housed, guarded, and fed; that costs money and creates jobs. As with the scenario of the aforementioned un-disciplined "crackhead," he is in the **highest** statistic category group to be a "re-peat offender" to commit a crime and go back to prison. Thus, the crackhead *feeds* the "Criminal Legal System." (You can't say *Justice System* anymore because that presumes no error [in justice].) Prisoners equate to an economic synonym to mean "profits" to private companies and governments who house, transport, feed, and provide medical, maintenance, and other "services" connected with the prison complexes. It's an "industrial complex," *per se*, with "revolving doors" deliberately designed that way. Basically put, the "system" knows these un-disciplined, un-skilled, and anti-social prisoners will be returning. And they do, as you only have to turn on your television to see them reported as "*ex-felons*" who violated probation or parole. However, it is the veteran who suffers the most because they are deliberately passed over for parole because they "keep the peace," by **off-setting** violence and un-skilled prison staffs and un-skilled inmates to "run" (operate) the prisons as now further discoursed.

The Prison Industrial Complex *Favors* Veterans: Here's how it works.

First, the majority of good *rehabilitated* prisoners – which includes veterans -- **are** the <u>most zealous</u> and hard-working of all categories of prisoners. Most are "*minimum*-security inmates" who have high school or college educations and possess computer and literacy skills comprising all the "high-tech" (technical) or administrative jobs (i.e. clerks, computer operators, HVAC, legal advisors, electricians, etc.) in the prisons to help the staff **run** the prison "incident-free" (safely) and efficiently. Second, older **minimum-security level non-violent** prisoner [veterans] don't "make waves," and keep the *violence statistics numbers* and *riotous situation reports* low because they are never the trouble-makers in the prison. Anyone with common sense knows that if the prisons were filled with the most violent and un-disciplined of criminals that no one would want to be a correctional officer or guard and work at that prison.

TEACHABLE MOMENT: THE PREJUDICIAL "VIOLENT OFFENDER MYTH - CARD."

Everyone knows that murder, rape, robbery, etc. – crimes against persons -- are "violent" offenses, *per se,* even though there are **degrees** of crimes and often extenuating or mitigating circumstances which, usually, never get the visibility like the "title crime." Unfortunately, in the fallout of the legal system's process, prejudice attaches to a "convict" when people begin defining a person's *daily* and *yearly* conduct and character [behavior] by just the one (1) crime. This misleads and often prejudices the offender with harmful consequences, especially when that "label" is pinned on them for their entire life no matter if the offender has turned their life around 180 degrees and has never broken the law since then.

FACT: No where in America has anyone ever met a "24-7" murderer and robber, who runs around all day and every day murdering and robbing people as their typical behavior and character or "profile." It's absurd!

Unfortunately, the Legal System, the media, victim rights groups, psychological services, and, of course, parole boards like to use time and time again the "offense" conduct as the **sole** identifying fact that embodies a prisoner's description or character. In other words, it doesn't matter if a person got into a bar-room fight – for the first time, and killed someone. For the rest of their life, they will be labeled a "murderer" or "killer," with the hash tag additional applicable labels or adjectives such as: heinous, violent, malicious, crazed, felonious, remorseless, vile, contemptuous, and other such **negative** words to "demonize" or portray the offender as a continuously infinite killer.

You heard the old saying the DAs, judges, and vigilante groups used to say, "Once a criminal, always a criminal." The same illogic applies today, where hate-filled people like to say offenders – who committed a violent act decades ago – are still violent because "criminals can't change – they're criminals." That is to say, these illogical people don't believe people – including prisoners – can change because they broke the law, and will always be and act like criminals for the rest of their lives.

Thus, in the discourse of this paper, in some circumstances, a prisoner – who hasn't been violent, ever, except for the offense [date] for which he was convicted and sent to prison – could be prejudiced by the playing of the *violent offender card* to say his or her offense was "serious," even though the violent offense was decades earlier and the inmate is and has been a non-violent inmate ever since the offense which is totally unrepresentative of the inmate's current level of conduct and character.

Simply put, the inmate is **re-judged**, and is denied parole on the offense of the past, rather than on the inmate's current and more accurate status as they currently are in the present day.

"An advanced (merciful) society is known by the way it treats its prisoners." – Dostoyevsky (Crime & Punishment)

Thus, old-timer veterans kept in prison hoping to make parole some day are <u>routinely</u> denied their freedom, and left to rot and age, undeservedly because the system -- through deliberate indifference -- passes them over for parole knowing the veteran is "good for the business of running the prison."

> **COMMENT/ THOUGHT:** Besides, WHO is going to work at a prison if it is violent where you can get hurt?

Case in Point 2: <u>Murdock v. TN Bd. of Paroles</u>. [3] In Murdock, Dr. Murdock – an Honorably-discharged Vietnam veteran -- first-time offender, and "disciplinary-free" prisoner for over 10 years. He had family supporters, took every conceivable and mandated "corrections" class (i.e. Victim Impact, Anger Management, Substance Abuse, religious classes, etc.) that the prison system said he "needed to make parole." Yet, in spite of all his preparation, education, non-violent rule-abiding character and reputation as a model prisoner, he was denied parole the first time for "Seriousness of the Offense," and 3 years later, told he is never getting parole, and would have to "flatten" his whole sentence. To his amazement and to many, the insanity of the parole board not releasing him was present,

when the board **<u>granted</u>** parole to an *medium*-security level offender with the **<u>same</u>** charge as Dr. Murdock. The insanity of the man being released is that the man was a career criminal with over ten (10) felonies, had a record of using drugs and other prison disciplinary violations, had no education, took no self-improvement classes, served years in prison over 3 decades, and had killed a man serving time for Manslaughter. (Used with permission. Civil Case No. 3:12-CV-1244, *Murdock v. Patsy Bruce, et al.*, (Nashville, TN) March 7, 2016). [3]

How is that fair that Dr. Murdock, above, didn't get parole? It's not.

FACT: Only about **10%** of veterans ever return to prison, as compared to 60% of *non-veterans who* return to prison as repeat offenders. Veterans are at the TOP of the list of the *most disciplined* of prisoners.

Summary of How Veterans are used to offset prison violence Statistics:

To off-set "prison violence," veterans are *more likely* to be passed over for parole and kept in prison longer because:
• They are the least violent • They are the most disciplined • They are the ***least likely*** to re-offend • They are more likely to follow instructions • They fill a cell that would otherwise go to a *violent* younger offender, making prison more safe to work at and recruit prison correctional officers if the cells are filled with less violent prisoners (e.g. veterans).

So, if you balance the prison population by keeping in old veterans, you make the prisons safer and thus the business [of corrections] becomes more profitable and lucrative. (A "good deal" for the prison profiteers who, essentially, use veterans as *slaves* or slave labor, based on tendentious financial motivations by those who profit off the backs of America's veterans of which most were or are "wounded warriors" (disabled veterans.) And WHERE are the veterans groups coming to the prisons to help ex-felon veterans who are having a tough time GETTING THEIR FREEDOM, only to transition into today's "electronic society" without the internet skills and *re-entry* assistance that they need?

FACT: The <u>VETERANS ADMINISTRATION (VA)</u> falls short in many states when it comes to *incarcerated* veterans receiving healthcare for service-connected disabilities. Many VA hospitals don't

evaluate properly eligible service members even before trial when the veteran has a right to produce evidence of their medical and/or psychological disability which may have impacted upon the alleged crime they are accused of. Further, jails and prison "health care" horror stories give testimony, that veterans are not receiving adequate care they deserve, especially from qualified VA staff more appropriate and better for the veteran who earned those benefits, of which, now, are "meaningless," if the prisons and VAs won't transport the incarcerated veteran because they simply don't want to and won't fund for it. The incarcerated veterans are not forgotten, they are just simply <u>ignored.</u> VAs "talk" about helping veterans in prison; however, it is just *lip service* "hash-tagging," because the VA does not want to pay money for helping vets in prison, the same way – and excuse – "for security reasons" – the prisons don't want to transport prisoners to the VA even though some prisons do.

Ergo, this is the **<u>Plight of the Incarcerated Veteran</u>**: He or she is ignored and abandoned by our governments – state and federal, while the socially-fallen veteran either awaiting trial or incarcerated, gets left behind. Instead of helping "pick up" the fallen socially-wounded and legally-handicapped veteran trapped in the criminal legal system, the veteran – without a voice – is left to the broken penal system and the corrections industrial complex. Denied medical treatment for service-connected disabilities, denied <u>equal opportunity</u> for parole, growing old and becoming embittered, crippled economically (job wise) due to later-year release, the veteran goes back into society un-empowered and set-up for failure.

<u>The *Moral* Questions for Decision-makers to Act:</u>

1. Is this how *American* society wants and expects veterans to be treated? That "crackheads" should get *priority* for release over the best-disciplined and parole-ready veterans who served honorably?

2. Why are our state, local, and federal government legislators avoiding their duty to properly

investigate, fix, and protect the *least* of the category of veterans when it comes to the legal systems, prisons, and parole?

3. WHO is going to "step up" and enact or improve meaningful laws that will help America's 200,000 (+/-) veterans in jails and in prisons who fell down, and now, need help to "getting up and out" of the American's broken prison system?

4. And, again, how is it that America's aging veterans get no credit for their SERVICE in court and at the parole boards, regardless if they did a violent crime or not, yet the repeat offender non-violent or violent *non-veteran* "crackhead" – gets all the grace and mercy for parole?

"Act now, and correct this travesty of justice.
Give veterans the credit where credit is due."
- M.F.M.

What Should Veterans Advocacy Groups, Organizations, The VA, and Legislators Do To Correct This Travesty of Justice For America's Veterans?

1. LEGISLATE THAT THE PAROLE BOARD MUST HAVE **MANDATORY** INCLUSION OF A VETERAN'S SERVICE RECORDS AT THE PAROLE BOARD

2. LEGISLATE THAT THE PAROLE BOARD MUST GIVE MANDATORY CREDIT FOR PAROLE RELEASE TO VETERANS WITH *HONORABLE* DISCHARGES
3. LEGISLATE AND FUND FOR TRANSPORT OF VETERANS FROM PRISONS TO THE VA HOSPITALS FOR THEIR SERVICE-CONNECTED DISABILITIES (PTSD, TBI, other)
4. LEGISLATE AND FUND FOR VETERANS COURTS IN ALL JURISDICTIONS
5. LEGISLATE AND FUND FOR VETERANS COURTS TO INCLUDE *FELONY* OFFENSES
6. LEGISLATE AND FUND FOR VETERANS CELL BLOCKS IN ALL PRISONS
7. LEGISLATE THAT DA'S, DEFENSE LAWYERS, AND JUDGES ARE REQUIRED TO INCLUDE IN PSI/PSR REPORTS A VETERANS FULL SERVICE RECORD
8. VETERANS GROUPS SHOULD ESTABLISH AND FUND FOR SPONSORSHIP AND MENTORSHIP PROGRAMS WHEREBY EVERY VETERAN IN JAIL OR PRISON HAS SOMEONE TO ASSIST THEM TO PREPARE THEM TO MAKE "LIFE CHANGES," PREPARE FOR PAROLE, AND PREPARE FOR SUCCESS IN RE-ENTERING SOCIETY THROUGH RESTORATIVE JUSTICE.
9. LEGISLATE THAT THE PAROLE BOARD ALLOWS THE PAROLE CANDIDATE TO CHALLENGE ANY STATEMENTS BY PROTESTERS TO CLARIFY OR EVIDENCE ANY FACT OR PREJUDICE SO THERE IS NO MISUNDERSTANDING ON THE PART OF THE BOARD.
10. LEGISLATE THAT THE PAROLE BOARD MUST ESTABLISH A **STANDARDS OF CRITERIA LIST** FOR PRISONERS AND THEIR MENTORS TO SEE SO THAT THE PRISONER CAN MEET THESE OBJECTIVE STANDARDS TO MAKE PAROLE. **(SEE SAMPLE PAROLE CRITERIA NEXT PAGE)**
11. **OR, ABOLISH THE PAROLE BOARD** AND GO TO MANDATORY RELEASE ELIGIBILITY DATES **(RED)** LIKE MANY OTHER STATES TO SAVE MONEY, REDUCE AGING PRISON POPULATION, OVERCROWDING, AND ELIMINATE *RETALIATORY* RETRIBUTIVE PAROLE BOARDS

Michael Maraschiello

SAMPLE PAROLE BOARD CRITERIA LIST FOR PRISONERS TO MERIT PAROLE

Meritorious acts and achievements meriting parole:

1. Distinguished themselves through rehabilitation
2. Distinguished themselves through contributions to society
3. Distinguished themselves through contributions to the community
4. Distinguished themselves through personal growth programs
5. Distinguished themselves through obtaining higher education of a college degree
6. Distinguished themselves through mentorship of others (i.e. inmates, youth, etc.)
7. Served as a mentor and leader to other inmates
8. Earned the respect and support of both prison officials and numerous community leaders and organizations
9. Personifies Model Inmate

Other information or acts meriting parole:

1. Served large (extended) number of years in prison
2. Less culpable than others for the same crime
3. Over age 70 (Federal criteria)
4. Held jobs that attested to clemency candidate's character and community/ society contributions
5. **Military Service – Honorable**
6. Accepted responsibility for the crime, speaking out about *reforming* one's self
7. Awards, certificates, etc. for distinction
8. Letters of character
9. Transformed – "changed" -- self into a new person
10. Medical Condition (e.g. terminal illness, blind, amputee, etc.)
11. "Release will help further these individuals' positive influence on their communities and the lives of their fellow Tennesseans." – Gov. Bill Haslam (Tenn. July 26, 2018) Addressing his four clemency choices

NOTE ON ABOLISHING THE PAROLE BOARD.
Parole boards are **prone** to errors, prejudice, and fatal retaliatory vendettas and influences normally unfair and unjust, particularly when the boards are not "open to the public," and – in some states – anyone can send a "hate-

letter" or **hate-speech** e-mail protesting any inmate for any reason, regardless if the information is FALSE. Current laws in some states prohibit the parole candidate from even knowing they have been protested, and boards don't check for "fake news." Thus, inmates are denied the right to even morally defend themselves against otherwise prejudicial lies or misinformation tendentiously designed to prevent the inmate from making parole. Ergo, this is why *mandatory* release dates (RED) are needed to eliminate any harm to the offender, protect both offender and victims, and give fairness and justice all cases. **By removing the board, you remove all chances for impropriety, errors, and save millions of tax-payer dollars which can be used for restorative and re-entry programs to better inmates for greater empowered success.**

Disclaimer: This document is used to *inform* those applicable as to the plight of the incarcerated veteran for the purpose of improving the standards which affect the legal system, parole boards, and society which includes our veterans who have sacrificed so much. The information, above, is verifiable upon request.

Remember to: *"Sponsor an incarcerated veteran and change their world by giving them hope."* – M.F.M.

Distributive Justice.

We need society to hear our cries for help, and make some noise in the Halls of Justice to change the laws and bring changes to our courts and parole boards that provide for our veterans – *misdemeanor* and *felons* alike. Society must give justice to our group (veterans) it says it wants to help, but has not done so effectively. A *veteran* is a veteran – period! And some of vets suffered the ultimate indignity of having their government turn their backs on them, resulting in suicide, drug addiction, and poverty, to say the least.

Remember, all gave some, but some gave all.

MICHAEL MARASCHIELLO

Epilogue

The "Pay off" (Victory) with Christ-centered Dividends for Spiritual, Social, and Restorative Justice

Levels of Prison Ministry

"People are sent to prison *as* punishment, not sent to prison *to be* punished." – M.F.M.

Uncommon among religious groups and churches across American is the calling for strongly-devout people to deliver the Word of God to the sick, the homeless, the destitute, and last and least the errants (prisoners) who are in juvenile detention centers, in jails, in prisons, correctional facilities, half-way houses, or any other place of mass incarceration. Generally, the intention of such devout volunteers is to save souls and /or recruit people who are marginalized by society to seek a faith [in God]. However, today's society demands expanding volunteership in prison ministry work to focus on **_reclaiming_** prisoners through mentorship and sponsorship as we shall further discuss.

In the "Four (4) Levels of Prison Ministry," we take a look at not only does each category reflect what level of service(s) are done by churches and / or their volunteers, but these levels also serve to reflect all church or religious centers with the range in which a church and /or its representative volunteers – "ambassadors" – can better serve the community especially helping persons to become healthy both spiritually and otherwise as explained further throughout this section and guidebook.

WHAT IS GOING TO HELP?

By meaningful involvement from the community of churches and their affiliate organizations, putting forth positive efforts through ministry volunteership, sponsors,

mentors, etc. who contribute their time and resources to go out to the prisons to help awake the *"spiritually dead"* and heal the *"socially sick"* (errants), invaluable knowledge and experience is gained to be taken back to the churches and communities to tell the people about what **_really_** goes on at prisons and in prison ministry [work.] It is absolutely necessary for church and community leaders to spread the truth about prison ministry involvement and participation and break down the myths and prejudices Satan and his minions use to cast a negative shadow stereotype on every prisoner or what goes on and what prison ministry work involves and the positive results or "fruits" that come about from it.

FRUITS OF MEANINGFUL MENTORSHIP & SPONSORSHIP

The prisoner:

1) Is no-longer or less criminally-minded having guidance and a purpose with a mentor to change.
2) Is better focused on God in a relationship with a mentor of strong faith.
3) Has taken more responsibility for their crime(s) and life failures to strive to be more mature.
4) Has hope and trust rekindled because the mentor is physically present which shows involvement.
5) Becomes more loving and humbled due to the love, kindness, compassion, and mercy shown.
6) Obtains more self-improvement and greater self-esteem especially with additional education.
7) Lives a little better life while in prison with the mentor's assistance concerning advice, financial needs, diet recommendations, stress management, etc. through social interaction.
8) Is less likely to turn to crime or break laws because the sponsor has committed themselves to further find assistance for the I/M when released eliminating crime as an option or choice.
9) Is more likely to succeed finding and holding a job, finding a place to live, and maintaining their family having a sponsor guiding them as needed to become confidently independent.
10) Is less likely to turn to drugs in a crisis knowing that the I/M can contact his or her sponsor or others in the I/M's support group which the sponsor helps the I/M establish.
11) Anything else that helps in the re-entry and reclaiming or "regeneration" process of I/M.

FACT. THE _AVERAGE_ PERSON FEARS GOING TO A PRISON OR MEETING A "CONVICT" AND BELIEVES MOST OF WHAT PRISON IS LIKE FROM TV AND THE MOVIES, DEPICTING ALL PRISONERS AS ILLITERATE CRAZED PEOPLE WHO RAPE, LIE, AND ARE FOREVER "CRIMINALLY MASTERMINDED," TO INCLUDE BELIEVING THE TYPICAL PRISON MINISTRY WORKER IS WEAK AND FIGHTING A LOST CAUSE TO GET INMATES TO BELIEVE IN GOD. WHAT THE AVERAGE CHURCHGOER DOESN'T KNOW, IS THAT "EX-FELONS" MIGHT EVEN BE SITTING RIGHT NEXT TO THEM IN CHURCH WITHOUT THEM EVER KNOWING IT.

WHAT DOES AN *EX-FELON* LOOK LIKE?

You don't have to search far, today, to find that the average American household has someone locked up behind bars, or knows someone close who is or was in jail at sometime. "Crime" or crimes today are more easily committed whether deliberate or not than years ago, such as it is a misdemeanor in some states to leave your car running to warm it up while you run back in the house to get ready for work. Nowadays, there are so many laws and ways to get a fine or ticket that it is impossible not to have contact with someone who is or will be in trouble with the law.

QUESTION. So, if you went to prison today, who is coming to see you? Who comes to see those people who don't have family to come and minister, feed, cloth, or support them? WHO?

Fight or flight. The average person goes through the *Fight or Flight Syndrome* when a person they know closely is arrested or charged with a crime and is sent to jail or prison. This even applies to family members who claim to "have your back," which – as they say in prison – "You know who your friends and family are when you come to prison." This phrase basically describes the worst feeling a prisoner gets, and that is <u>abandonment</u> by his family, friends, or even church for support. Cutoff from family, friends, and – if a weak faith – cut off or discouraged from God, someone has to "step up" and take action before the inmate falls to Satan's angels who lurk the prisons and jails to prey upon the lowly-hearted prisoner – especially the first-time offender – who is raped, beaten, lied to, and robbed when they come into the world's or "state's" prison system, which has always been a breeding ground for bitterness, lose of hope, loss of the will to live, and death, if there is no ***meaningful*** intervention.

QUERY TEACHING POINTS

QUESTION:
So, what is the number one reason why people don't want to help someone in trouble with the law or in jail or prison?
Easy! They are afraid something bad is going to happen to them – like "Big Brother Government" arrest them if they get involved with a person in trouble with the law. This reaction results primarily because they are ignorant of what to do to help someone in jail or in prison and they don't want to take the risk of sometimes the imaginary or exaggerated consequences brought on by <u>human nature</u>.

QUESTION:
How many times has a person who claims to have faith, and then when that person is challenged, they collapse like jelly for not knowing what to say or how to respond? (Someone once said, "If you don't stand for something, you'll fall for anything.")

QUESTION:
WHO stands up for the prisoner – someone who went astray, got caught, and is now trapped in a prison [system] that degrades prisoners, is anti-god, does little to help prisoners prepare for parole or release back to the community, and embitters the prisoners with no mercy, no forgiveness, no respect, and little hope?

QUESTION:
How do you see prisoners? What's your general opinion of them? Are they garbage? Non-redeemable? All Guilty? Or, do you see them as someone's father, mother, sister, brother, son, or daughter – as one of god's children?

Ask yourself:

● Do you judge others? If so, would you help a prisoner who stole a loaf of bread to feed his family? Or should that thief get twenty (20) years like any other common criminal?

WHO IS A MENTOR OR SPONSOR? WHAT CAN THEY DO, *REALLY?*

We all know that Genesis story in the Bible when God addresses the issue of "Who is my brother's keeper?" situation between Cain and Able. And the New Testament analogy Jesus relates for his disciples to be like shepherds feeding people like shepherds take care of their sheep. These two stories work together to show the level of care those entrusted by God to look over *flocks and others,* namely human beings -- our brothers and sisters.

A. **MENTOR.** As defined in Webster's Unabridged 3rd Addition, a "MENTOR" is defined as a "close trusted and experienced counselor or guide; a teacher, tutor, or coach." In laymen's terms, a mentor is one involved in mentorship of which one person, usually, who is well-educated in a specific area or field who possesses a substantial knowledge and experience to help guide a lesser experienced or less knowledgeable person to learn and develop the necessary skills to be successful.

B. **SPONSOR.** As defined in Webster's Unabridged 3rd Addition, a "SPONSOR" is defined as "one who without request intervenes in behalf of another; one who assumes responsibility for some other person; one who assumes responsibility for someone who is delinquent; one who presents and supports something." In laymen's terms, a sponsor is one who adopts (takes on) a person to do or complete a certain task and is willing to advocate and do the necessary work to assist that person or persons to complete the task or tasks assigned.

Michael Maraschiello

CHARACTER REQUIRED:
ONLY THE STRONG NEED APPLY

WHAT CHARACTER TRAITS DOES A SPONSOR OR MENTOR NEED?

A Mentor or Sponsor is:

1) **Not a Quitter, loyal and committed**. They are fearless and don't retreat from failure at the first sign of trouble in their relationship or dealings with the prison or I/M. Satan is trying to kill everything good, so the mentor / sponsor must be prepared for things that arise and must diligently investigate the situation or set-back to look for solutions or changes before ending ministry support for an I/M deciding on which course of action.

2) **Dedicated to God or moral cause**. They have a rich faith and desire to help the I/M. They pray with the I/M and inspire the I/M to give hope and promise of a better life and future.

3) **A person of valor**. They lead a righteous life that is prudent and an example for others to follow to be successful in all things.

4) **Humble.** They don't look upon the I/M in a "we – they" manner that is degrading or putting down the I/M because of their poverty, illiteracy, ignorance of things, a weak faith, their appearance, or any other weakness that causes harm to an I/M's self-esteem which the sponsor or mentor is supposed to uplift.

5) **Empathetic** – Compassionate. _Altruism_ is at the apex of a sponsor's sincere genuine desire to uplift someone's condition, status, or state. A sponsor loves to help others expecting no pay or reward except to see the I/M prosper and improve their life.

6) **Pragmatic, Real, Optimist**. A sponsor acts from the present giving real-time advice and projects forward thinking guidance teaching I/Ms to make realistic plans to achieve obtainable positive goals and make the necessary changes to achieve those goals by working smartly not hard.

● ●

So, what ever level of prison ministry one chooses to check out, get involved with, or serve with, doing something is not what is needed. What is needed is doing the right level of ministry which is the one you can and should do that God has put on your conscience and heart. Jesus taught to give your "all" as He did in service to others, especially to the least ones in society of which the "least of the least" are prisoners. Joining a ministry where prisoner's lives are easily influenced by _free-world_ volunteers and giving them false hope or token "hash-tag" support for self-serving purposes, as did the Sadducees and Pharisees to be seen in public and in the temple as "champions of the people," will just crush the faith a prisoner has not only in God, but in the faith of future ministry volunteers if one's intentions are not sincere.

THE TAKEAWAY

In conclusion, if you are serious about helping prisoners to be successful, god-fearing, and make it back in society, tell your congregations and members in your hall, mosque, church, or other gathering places the TRUTH about prisons and that prisoners are worth the effort to be reclaimed. Invite discussions, seminars, talks, and information trips to your local jails and or churches. Don't settle on bringing one "ex-con" to a church for a  *testimony* to fill you in or read a book on prison reform -- that's the easy way out! Experience the ministry yourself and get down to those prisoners and TALK to them. Like any other area of study or group, the more you get involved, the more knowledge you have to make informed decisions, especially as to what IMPACT you can personally make to helping the prison ministry achieve their goal(s) and your personal goal(s) as well as, perhaps, as a sponsor or mentor.

Always remember, the people leaving your church and / or your community today for "The Big House," will be back at your church and community in the future. And having them come back to your community in bad or worse shape than when they went to prison is not only a *drain* or problem, but a tragedy that could have been prevented. As the old cliché' goes, **"An ounce of prevention is worth a pound of cure."** This readily can be applied to *young* undisciplined I/Ms – mostly ones with "non-violent" offenses -- coming out of prison in such a state of poverty, hunger, and ill-skilled that no wonder they end up back in trouble [as ironically compared to meritorious I/M "old timers" who the parole board won't let go because the old timers won't be coming back to prison]. Sponsorship and mentorship no matter what **type** of I/M is sponsored, has a greater chance for changing their life and success in prison and for release. Ministers have the power to choose the level of ministry they wish to bring to a prison and / or prisoners, whether it is preaching the word of God or literally "***dragging***" the I/M out of prison through sponsorship and advocate at the parole board and/ or in court because the [prison] system is inherently flawed keeping older "reformed" I/Ms in, and not helping them prepare and be ready for release.

 God's "least of the least" – the prisoners – really need people who care to help them one way or another. God is looking for a 'Few Good Men and Women" to take up their cross and fight for a prisoner, just as Jesus did while literally hanging and dying on His cross as a part of His ministry work. Now that's real sponsorship – [Jesus] advocating for mankind! End.

> "I'm blessed to have a God and a family that forgives me for my mistakes, I'm also grateful for my sponsor who lifted me up to be with my family again."

Sponsors and Mentors need to use education and work release programs, not warehousing to change prisoners.

In her article, "How Norway is Teaching America to make its prisons more Humane,: Laura Paddison writes, "It's like Disney World compared to our [U.S.] prisons," said Donna Virgilio Mattia, a parole agent of Pennsylvania's SCI Chester, a medium-security state prison just outside Philadelphia that houses 1,270 men. [1] She, along with 13 other officers & administrators from SCI Chester & six researchers have come to Norway to learn from the country widely considered to have the best correctional system in the world. Recidivism rates in Norway are among the world's lowest. She added that around 20% of those released from prison are arrested within 2 years. In the U.S., about 68% of released prisoners were arrested within 3 years. The gap between the 2 countries narrows significantly when you look only at re-incarceration (and ignore arrests). Norway's rate is 25%, compared with 28.8% in the U.S. But there's another important statistic to take into account: The percentage of the total population each country puts behind bars. While America jails 665 of every 100,000 residents, Norway's rate is less than a tenth of that – just 63 of every 100,000.

"For an officer [U.S.] it was a culture shock. I'd never really looked at my job as an opportunity to change somebody's (a prisoner's) life," said Matthew Tompkins, U.S. Correctional Officer working at Ringerike Prison, Norway. "They (Norway's correctional officers) are serving their community and society…changing prisoners."

WANTED: VOLUNTEERS! Mass Incarceration/ People of Color

More about fixing America's broken prison system and making social justice better is covered in another article by Neil Barsky titled "How to Fix Our Prisons. [2] Barsky advocates the push for the public to see what's going on inside prisons, and calls for a broad national effort to recruit volunteers to educate & counsel the incarcerated. "What's happened over the years inside prisons has not changed at all since Donald Trump's First Step Act of 2019," Barsky says. "What's needed is the public should see first hand the conditions within the walls, meet men and women who reside in our prisons, look them in the eye, shake their hands and teach them skills they can use once they are released. After all, 90% of them will end up back among us (the free-world society) ... yes, some prisoners already have programs that allow outsiders inside the walls for teaching and counseling."

"To change the system, of mass incarceration, a diverse group of criminal justice experts should be assembled – including corrections & law enforcement officials, former inmates & their families, defense attorneys, judges & inmate advocates – to develop a national program to create paths for trained volunteers & professionals to work inside prisons." Michelle Alexander, author of *'The New Jim Crow: Mass Incarceration in the Age of Colorblindness"* said that mass incarceration created a "racial caste system" that has disproportionately punished a generation of young usually male, people of color."

The *Vera Project* in and article entitled "EXAMINING PRISONS TODAY," mentions that "Life in America's prisons is dismal, and the brunt of these dismal conditions falls overwhelmingly  on people of color and those who are socially & economically disadvantaged, the result of their systematic & historic economic & social exclusion from mainstream – predominantly white – American society." [3] Once in prison, their ties to that mainstream society are severed – often irreversibly – through prolonged separation from family & community. While behind bars, incarcerated people are subjected to degrading treatment, inhumane conditions, & abusive interactions – all of which result in substantial social, behavioral, & cognitive trauma that handicap them in their efforts to reintegrate into society upon release. In short, prison thwarts their chances for successful & fulfilling life. The [non]value of mass incarceration.

In Tennessee, under the premise – or guise – of "protecting the public," a late 2019 report released by the Criminal Justice Investment Task Force (CJITF) on the state of Tennessee's prison (corrections) criminal justice system. Though this book is not a condemnation of Tennessee's handling of the mass incarceration problem in America, it does point out some of the statistics from the four CJITF subcommittees to reveal that Tennessee is sentencing individuals to prison for longer periods of time and reducing the number of those it releases on parole, while at the same time, the state's recidivism and violent crime rates remain high. [4]

One alarming trend the report uncovered is that despite a growing prison population and increasing corrections budget, Tennessee's recidivism rate remains high. [5] Not only that, it's prison population grew 12% over the past decade, driven by a growth in time served due to increasing sentence lengths and decreasing parole releases. More alarming, is Tennessee's re-arrest rate of parolee's for *technical violations* in FY2018 increased. [6]

Sadly, as Tennessee's prisons population increases and crime rates rise, Tennessee continues to waste its taxpayer dollars in supposedly more effective and less costly evidence-based strategies to reduce recidivism, address gaps in victims' services, and improve public safety to no avail. Meanwhile, the programs (i.e. education incentives) that could use the taxpayer funds to make drastic results in the recidivism rate problem, get earmarked elsewhere (e.g. *Public safety* is "code" for more bullets, tasers, and security items like vests, vans, new "tactical" gear, etc. – anything but to directly benefit prisoners).

Governor Lee of Tennessee said, **"Incentives drive behavior."** And everyone – especially prisoners – agree. Yet, where are the incentives, like "early release" for exceptional behavior and educational transformation?

An ***education*** and a ***job*** are <u>what prisoners want</u>, so they can make the transition from prison to free-world. You don't need a Vanderbilt 2-year psychological study to find that out, then another 2 years to test the theory. Plenty of existing data shows this is reliable to make changes to Tennessee's laws to help prisoners and give tax dollars back to the state for other uses like better education for our children and not building new prisons.

Yet, education budget just for GED and only a few vocational jobs around the state don't give prisoners competitive electronic or technical skills for a prisoner to be able to get even a starting re-entry job and medical treatment leaving prison, especially when the state corrections budget only gives education programs a token amount while money is earmarked for "public safety" – security. [7]

Parole numbers in Tennessee continue to baffle many. The Board of Parole revealed 40% of the 15,840 inmates granted parole or 6,308 people from FY2015 to FY2019 did not in fact leave custody on parole but "flattened" – expired their sentences – meaning they got no parole. [8]

One such inmate, Dr. Marshall H. Murdock, PhD, an 67-year old honorably-discharged Vietnam veteran, successful businessman, and ***first-time offender*** who pled guilty to attempted first-degree murder and was sentenced to 20 years @ 30% eligibility for parole, and with an impeccably perfect prison record was denied parole arbitrarily and capriciously. [9] A legal aide, with a deaf wife, he did every thing humanly possible in prison to have a chance at parole earning all good time and taking every education program in the state. Yet, instead of being given parole – which he expected as being told and agreed upon by the judge at his plea bargain, the parole board nevertheless chose to ignore his transformation, age, and other mitigating information and told him to "flatten," meaning no parole at all. This, while at the same time going up, another inmate for the same offense received parole, and that inmate had a terrible prison record, was doing drugs in the prison, had only a GED, had no good job history, was not a veteran, and – had a conviction for "homicide." More fascinating, Murdock was a *minimum*-classed security inmate, and the other man the parole board let go was a *medium-classed* inmate more likely to re-offend and be a recidivist.

What's wrong with this picture?

Why did the parole board let a guy that is more likely to re-offend go, but not the prisoner who was proven a low risk and totally qualified to be released having gotten all the "incentives?"

This is why there is bitterness and mistrust among prisoners, justice advocates, and families of inmates today. They see loved ones in prison get further degraded and crippled by horrible decisions un-called for by the board that does not use a "merit system" but a whimsical subjective personal "score card" the board can re-invent as it pleases to give any reason why a prisoner should not be released. Prisoners, like Dr. Murdock, who – for 55+ years was "crime free" and then made a big mistake and broke the law for the first time, gets smashed at the board, while a career felon gets to go free for the same offense.

Where's the justice?

That's why the legislative branch needs to get in gear and start looking at how liberal they made the policies giving the parole boar absolute power to deny parole for anyone for anything.

Who has more power, the Parole Board or the legislators?

Bad laws affect prisoners in all sorts of ways, which means they affect families, victims, and the public. Victims have to "re-open" wounds every time there is a parole hearing. Errors with parole board members voting this way and that way and never see the same evidence, per se, to vote consistently, as I've seen prisoners Board members one year vote "yes," only the next year to vote "No."

265

What did the board member see this year that turned his vote from a yes to a no? And the prisoner had no disciplinary infraction since last year. (Simply mind-boggling.)

So, for mentors and sponsors assisting prisoners preparing for the board, understand that errors always occur with board members because they are human too. That's why eliminating the RED "Release Eligibility Date" and changing it to a "Release Effective Date" will eliminate the problem. When prisoners who earn their "good time" (incentive) get to that date, and they are "drug-free" and have a job skill and no disciplinary record for one year, then they are released and on parole. This is the cost-saving way and gives prisoners the incentives they need to change.

So, in short, the CJITF did come out with the right assessment, which is that researchers have concluded that tailoring supervision conditions to an individual's criminogenic needs and responsivity factors in critical to changing behavior and reducing re-offending. [10]

However, as Gov. Lee said, there won't be any changes in behavior unless there are incentives. Most experts would agree. And as long as Tennessee's corrections goal or *mission* remains public safety minus education, the status quo will remain in place with taxpayers, inmates, inmate's families, victims, and society paying an even greater price unless the laws are changed.

> "The measure of a failure is that everyone fails. The difference is we all fail in life. But going to prison maintains the failure in a *twilight zone* vacuum. And when set free, we're right back where we left off if no opportunity or incentives to change." -MFM

Michael Maraschiello

SOME RECOMMENDATIONS TO GOVERNOR'S TASK FORCE ON PRISON REFORM AND RESTORATIVE JUSTICE (January 2020)

1. Offenders are first <u>human beings</u>. They comprise two classes: 1) Those that are *career* criminals, and 2) Those that made a mistake(s) and are now <u>changed</u>
2. ALL offenders, above, need *correction*.
3. Not all "correction" works. (i.e. drug programs, un-necessary programs, and long-term confinement) Each offender has specific needs and the "system" should provide for those needs to get the offender corrected and out of prison as soon as possible so they are able to: (a) No-longer drain the taxpayer of money (b) Contribute back to society (c) Help stabilize their family (i.e. if they are a parent or spouse) (d) Have new or refined skill sets for immediate employment upon release
4. No inmate should have to be "passed over" for parole for "seriousness of the offense" when they have demonstrated they are no-longer a threat, have a good disciplinary record, are capable of surviving and/ or thriving when released either with a job or other income plan, free of drugs and alcohol addiction, and given an opportunity to prove their ready so inmates NEEDING incarceration can occupy a cell.
5. Ergo, eliminate the parole board and save money and gives compassion to the victims who do not have to stay in perpetual victimhood but can transition to becoming "survivors" and heal. (Not every person can heal; we are all different. Nor can people be made to forgive offenders. The "system" is NEVER FAIR, because sometimes the victim can't be pleased and wants revenge keeping parole-ready inmates in for longer periods of time that is necessary, especially when the inmate is old, now law-abiding, and no threat.
6. That "Parole Violators" not come back to prison for simple stuff, but rather as punishment: (1) Go to parole violators camp for 2 weeks, or (2) pay a fine, or (3) do community service work. Coming back to prison for missing an appointment or phone call with the parole officer is a waste of money and harmful to the parolee's family and job
7. When denied parole, and you receive 1 to 2 votes, that it should remain till the next hearing if in your favor, as long as there are no "discriminators" to lose them such as a disciplinary write up or a new conviction.
8. Programs in prison need to be CHANGED to fit the times. When an inmate comes within a year of release eligibility, the State should have a Tennessee Department of Transportation Motor Vehicle Exam for the prisoner. Then, every six (6) months, a vehicle brought to the prison for **ready-for-release parolees** or people flattening their sentences to take the driver's test.

SENDING "EX-OFFENDERS" out of prison with a driver's license provides them with a better chance for securing a job, providing for their needs to be self-sustaining with their support group or family, and give them a head start to avoiding recidivism. Or, those eligible for release within one (1) year should be given a FURLOUGH to take the driver ROAD TEST.

9. Every inmate in prison within two (2) years should have a "SPONSOR." The sponsor is NOT a mentor. A mentor just talks and guides a person – that's not what prisoners need. A sponsor helps them while in prison as a mentor but also is INVOLVED in their life, helps the inmate develop and learn a skill or education either correspondence or other for job readiness upon release, helps them out financially with making sure the inmate has money on their account for toiletries, shoes, and the phone to stay in contact with their family and/or the sponsor. A sponsor is one who is going to be with the "ex-offender" after they get out of prison to check up on them, help them get a place to stay, help them get "re-adjusted" to society in a support group, church, or organization that fosters success. THAT STARTS WHILE IN PRISON.

10. "INCENTIVES DRIVE BEHAVIOR." Inmates ready for parole want to work outside the gate. ALL inmates within one (1) year of getting out, including first-degree murder with "life" sentences past their RED DATES should be able to work for a crew outside the fence and MAKE MONEY. The average "working man" wants a job, even in prison. Jobs need to pay better, and more of them. This helps inmates avoid borrowing money and getting into trouble. PRISON WAGES NEED TO BE INCREASED. A inmate today makes 17¢ -- 1984 wage. The average prisoner who does not work a high-paying TRICOR prison job leaves prison with NO MONEY – a "recipe for disaster." Every person leaving prison should have at least $1000 voucher – if qualify – for housing. They should have their food stamps, housing voucher and an increased in "gate money" for the first month when departing.

11. JOB INTERVIEWS. Those leaving prison and needing to job interview should get a JOB INTERVIEW FURLOUGH. A sponsor picks them up, takes them to the interview, and then brings them back.

12. Drugs and alcohol. There is no "cure-all." But the alternatives to drugs lay in PEER COUNSELING. Many inmates do drugs to "escape" because of depression and stress, not always to "get high."

13. More programs for our military veterans. Years of lies telling veterans their service means nothing is a disgrace. Further, the VA and TDOC are playing "games' as each blames the other for not transporting our veterans who have VA hospital care for FREE but can't go because the VA and TDOC argue over who is going to pay for the transportation. The VA does with 'courtesy vans, " so the TDOC should just provide a guard. A VETERANS

PRISON should be established because veterans comprise 90% of the SKILLED TDOC jobs in prison and are among the most disciplined ready to correct themselves and be released

14. Bring back PELL GRANTS. Go on-line: getting a college degree especially a MASTERS is 'ZERO" recidivism.
15. Young offenders 18 to 21 years old need MANDATORY "mentors" so they don't fall to vice and gangs in prison. There are plenty of older prisoners who are college graduates or ex-counselors who can be their mentors.

These are just a few suggestions. Bring back AUTO-MECHANIC SHOP, HVAC, AND MORE TO GIVE SKILLS THAT BUILD LIVES, foster success, and get the community of supporters to sponsor all inmates getting out to thrive.

FIVE (5) THINGS TO TELL YOUR GOVERNOR ABOUT <u>PRISON REFORM</u> TO SAVE MONEY AND MAKE THE SYSTEM SAFER/FAIR.

1. **RE-INSTATE THE PRISON OVERSIGHT COMMITTEE.** This ensures budgetary compliance and human rights are not violated, specifically with the Parole Board usurping judicial authority to implement policies and procedures contrary to legislative meaning whereby they are draconian and punitive only rather than fostering restorative justice to be fair not only to victims but to giving parole-ready "ex-violent" offenders parole release rather than for them to meet their FULL expiration date or long-term incarceration years after they have changed .
2. **DISBAND THE PAROLE BOARD.** Second-guessing and "re-trying" prisoners extends the hardship for victims and does not foster restorative justice when the board has a "re-trial" of offenders and arbitrarily and capriciously ignores the merits of the prisoners who changed their lives in favor of retaliatory reasons and "policies" re-labeling offenders to keep them in prison longer.
3. **CHANGE THE RED DATE (RELEASE ELIGIBILITY DATE) TO "RELEASE *EFFECTIVE* Date.** This pushes qualified prisoners out of the prisons because the RED date is the date set by the Tennessee Legislature assuming a person has "changed" or been "corrected" (reformed) by then. A prisoner's disciplinary record clearly shows that if they are non-violent and have an outstanding record that they merit release.

4. **CONSIDER FIRST-TIME VIOLENT OFFENDER CASES TO BE EVALUATED AS "EX-VIOLENT OFFENDERS".** People over time CHANGE. Many prisoners convicted on so-called "violent offenses" are not violent for the rest of their lives. For example, a spousal killing. Then, the offender is sent to prison and NEVER commits another violent act. Yet, when they are up for parole they are labeled ""violent" for an offense 20 years ago, rather than their CURRENT or representative "character behavior" pattern which is NON-VIOLENT. These offenders are ready to leave prison but for the label "violent offender." That needs to be changed to "ex-violent offender," a GOAL or INCENTIVE for the offender to strive for and receive parole.
5. **RAISE INMATE PAY. There has not been an increase in inmate pay since 1984,** when the price of a U.S. postage stamp was 17¢. Now it is 55¢. **SAFETY WILL INCREASE. With money in an inmates hand,** they do not have to sell drugs, prostitute themselves, rob, steal, rape, or burglarize in prison making the environment safer. The prices of commissary food have gone up so much the average physically-working inmate cannot live on the little amount of non-nutritional food available most of the timer that is one level above dog food. (You doubt it – come sample it. No school kid would eat it.)

Simply put, the governor needs to use a "New Broom" to "Sweep Clean" the system so it is fair and just. Prisoners are human beings too. The great literary writer, Dostoyevsky wrote, "If you want to know how advanced a society is, look at the way it treats its prisoners." (From his book: *CRIME AND PUNISHMENT*)

Prisoners made mistakes, and need the incentives to change, then the HOPE to get out soon so they are not too old and feeble – drained and embittered by a government that exploits them. A prisoners leaving prison should have the opportunity to be confident they have some hope and faith in the State of Tennessee to not only be fair but responsible for some assistance re-entering the past-paced society they have been away from for so long. The Tennessee Department of Correction, for example, just dumping an "ex-felon" at the bust stop with a $70 check does not ensure successful re-entry, safety for the community, nor the welfare of the former prisoner now too old or un-skilled to make a living, especially with court costs and fines saddled upon his or her back. That's no life to look forward to when getting out – hopelessness and poverty.

ARTICLE ON SOCIAL JUSTICE ABOLITION (2020) PUBLISHED IN *THE MAXIMUM TIMES*

"Abolition in Today's Prison Reform"
— by M. F. Maraschiello (Legal Aide)

The first thing most people in America today think of when they hear talk about "abolition," is *slavery* and the *abolitionists* prior to and during the American Civil War. As the son of an Italian-African American father who taught Black History at the U. S. Army's Warrant Officer School at Ft. Rucker, Alabama in the 1960's and 70's, and lived in *French* Algeria (North Africa), a memory pops into my mind of one of Harriet Tubman's "Underground Railway" stations on the Niagara River at Buffalo, NY my father took me to in 1979. He took me in the tunnel that led to the river at the shortest point between the United States and Canada. I envisioned what it was like to *experience* such an epic struggle, as runaway slaves were ferried to freedom by those championing the cause of abolition and civil rights.

Hence, I learned the goal of "abolition" was to <u>abolish</u> (do away with wholly - *Webster*) the enslavement of Africans and African-Americans. (SEE: Emancipation Proclamation and the *Battle of Antietam,* 1862, after which President Lincoln officially issued it on Jan. 1, 1863.)

Today, the *modern* abolitionist is concerned with the abolishment of **<u>oppressive</u>** [penal system] human rights violations, harsh conditions, un-just laws, and practices which have exacerbated the "mass incarceration" rate of America's citizens and illegal aliens of all races and creeds in the now infamous realm of the **Prison Industrial Complex (PIC).**

What is the Prison Industrial Complex? The PIC is a *system* that uses policing, surveillance, and imprisonment to address social problems, control people, and maintain oppressive [penal] structures while also making it hard to change given it is *profit-driven* over the value of human lives (i.e. prisoners, inmates, offenders, errants, etc.). The PIC has only been growing over the last century in America, to where it is now one of the largest economic budgets in some states costing taxpayers billions each year to maintain. State and Federal *criminal justice* "systems" employ thousands of support staff and guards who provide everything from supplying food to prisons, transportation, medical care, court and legal operations, drug rehabilitation centers, half-way housing, probation and parole, maintenance, construction, commissary, phone monopolies, and other associated *corrections* "markets." It is a tough job that has to be done with the <u>goal</u> centering on public safety. However, it comes with a price when the corrections systems turn *industrial.* "Bureaucracy-creep" can invite corruption and infect the operations of corrections to become focused with profits rather than the priority of humane *social welfare* justice system laws and practices which are designed to better society's lawbreakers and foster an offender's ability to change. The result of the PIC is then a slow decay of offenders relationships with their families, a mockery of justice for the victims, lower wages for corrections employees, mass incarceration, and creates new or worse offenders when they are released or kept in prison until they are too old and without hope and a future.

What is the Goal of PIC Abolition? The goal of abolition [modern] is to **break down** the *false* paradigms in society we have about just "locking people up," and start doing smart **alternatives** to mass incarceration with doing corrections *smarter,* not harder.

MECHANISMS TO REDUCE AND/OR ELIMINATE THE PIC IN FAVOR OF ALTERNATIVES
1. Transformative Justice upfront at representation and sentencing
2. Restorative Justice by abolishing Parole Boards for mandatory Truth in Sentencing
3. Meaningful Job Training while incarcerated and after-prison employment
4. Affordable housing or housing plans
5. Effective Treatment For Substance Abuse and Mental Illness (In-prison/ Jail and after-care)

"God knows when the best time is to work miracles at the right time in the lives of his children."
–M.L.K.

It's a fact: People commit crimes and some need locking up. But by educating and holding accountable the public and legislators to build up strong and healthy relationships within our communities without fear or repercussions from the influences of those who are *non-progressive*, we can realistically deal with today's modern criminal justice system needs. Specifically, starting with prioritizing financial investments at the beginning of a person's "entry" into the criminal justice system for better and meaningful effective representation. This has always been proven to save money so that resources are not wasted on appeals, facilities with outrageous costs for services, ridiculous legal fees and costs for housing at jails and/or detention centers (i.e. when a parole or probation violation is present), and other up-front costs such as the human toll of parents separated from their children. Tax disparity is also of concern with the waste of revenue being spent more on imprisonment over prevention, imprisonment over re-habilitation, imprisonment over Truth in Sentencing, and parole boards in some states holding people longer than their Release Eligibility Date (RED) when the prisoner is overdue and ready for release.

The *Bottom line* is, people who go to prison are still people from **your** community – they're just in "time out" -- for "grown ups," or like a car in an auto race taking a pit stop to re-fuel and get back in the race as soon as possible. But it takes a **TEAM** (community and government(s)) to manage the team properly to maximize and economize the effort to ensure public safety, justice, and re-entry. Errants correct themselves when *positive* steps are available to them and taken advantage of, with the reward being given for their achievements. Many *corrections workers* are sincerely concerned about helping people reintegrate into society. Common sense says if a person wants to better themselves they need to take advantage of the programs offered to make parole, re-entry, and get a job. Punishment is being sent to prison for a crime. Prisoners are not supposed to be sent to prison to be punished. However, while out of *normal* society living in jail or the prison, they are supposed to be given the **tools** to change and better themselves. If offenders choose to become bitter or disenfranchised it is on them. 'The cause" in abolition today is to **fix** the broken system(s) where they need fixing. Families suffer when their loved ones are separated from them for too long, and the emotional ties broken seem never to be able to be mended. Even some victims feel cheated when they don't see their offenders change but rather get worse. Sometimes even suffering more when they see offenders suffering more for their crimes due to excessive periods of imprisonment.

Simply put, relying on prisons and punishment for profit to solve our problems and using *mass* incarceration as a means of generating and creating profit and employment, only has reduced America's citizens into being labeled and treated as "cattle" or as a economic *commodity* to be devalued by consumers in the PIC for no other benefit but to those who profit from it. That is why the abolishment for the PIC is a must, in favor of meaningful effective corrections beneficial for all.

<u>COMMON SENSE?</u> It only stands to reason that going to prison **should** be a time and place for a person to get back on their feet (i.e. get off drugs, get an education, get a job skill, etc.), not just become stagnant, embittered, and waste away.) And if the government [prisons and jails] <u>**create**</u> a person's capability or incapability while they are in jail or prison, then the state and federal governments are also responsible for when the offender gets out to have programs to help them <u>**stay out**</u> which is <u>**cheaper**</u> than incarceration.

Studies have shown that states with more prisons and prisoners <u>do not</u> have *lower* crime rates. What the PIC actually does is make already marginalized groups less safe. Violent drug addicts come in, they don't obey the rules or change their behavior because of the prison system's lack of INCENTIVES, as the money for profit goes to the profiteers, not for the programs that are effective in curbing *anti-social* behavior and fostering discipline [reasons] for offenders to *want* to change.

Coming from a diverse family that still has living relatives in Italy where my family emigrated from, I have great respect for African-Americans and all peoples. I've lived in Europe and traveled the world from Asia to Europe and from the east coast of America to the west coast, from Canada to trips to Mexico from living in Waco, Texas. The majority of people everywhere just want to live and be free. That's why abolishing the PIC in favor of good effective meaningful corrections, should be the goal of all "Americans" because freedom is *a right* – for all people, and our leaders should safeguard corrections systems with oversight, fairness, and justice in addition to security. Quoting Dostoevsky, "A society is known by the way it treats its prisoners." We must be vigilant that our leaders make good choices for laws and policies for *smart* "cost-effective" **quality** prison reform to be realistic and pragmatic, not doing prison "on-the-cheap" by putting profit before people. After all, where would the tax money come from if we lock people up for long periods of time? Who'd pay them? When is enough taxes ever enough? When is enough prisons for people who make mistakes and deserve a second chance. "Incentives drive behavior," is the call from Governor Lee. Corrections *is* necessary; however, it should be done right. People can change with a safe and efficient system that fosters change. And prisoners ready for release should be kicked out of prison at the earliest eligible date to save money and create space for those who need the "time out."

In closing, both Martin Luther King and Benjamin Franklin were advocates for short prison sentences because people are what make up society and the nation. And they believed prisoners were not productive for the society or their families if castigated to prisons that don't produce the "fruits" of a changed man ready to become productive for the society as quickly as possible. Words echoed in one of Franklin's quotes: "A man in prison not behind his plow is not producing for his family and community." Dr. King and Franklin were both God-fearing and understood why offenders should be returned soon to their families and farms. They saw people as human beings who had ***value*** to produce, love, and had a God-given right to be free, especially from oppression.

For more on abolition, check out: www.criticalresistance.org, www.usprisonculture.com , www.prisonploicy.org , www.projectsouth.org , www.survivedandpunished.org , www.nonewjails.nyc

(About the author: Maraschiello is currently in a Ph. D. program with I.C.C.S. college and has degrees in Sociology, Psychology, and a Masters degree in Christian Education. He studied law and did his first field work for his college thesis on "Probation and the Parole Board" with the Erie County Probation Department and at Attica State Prison, New York, before becoming a Special Needs Teacher in 1984.)

Notes

1. Genesis 4:3-5
2. Beyond Bars: "Rejoining Society After Prison," Jeffrey Ross, Ph.D., and Stephen Richards, Ph.D., Alpha Books (New York: Penguin Random House LLC, 2009).

Prologue

1. *Crime and Punishment,* Fyodor Dostoyevsky, (1866) as *Prestupleniye i nakazaniye.* Dostoyevsky's first masterpiece, the novel is a psychological analysis of the poor student Raskolnikov, whose theory that humanitarian ends justify evil means leads him to murder a St. Petersburg pawnbroker. The act produces nightmarish guilt in Raskolnikov. The narrative's feverish, compelling tone follows the twists and turns of Raskolnikov's emotions and elaborates his struggle with his conscience and his mounting sense of horror as he wanders the city's hot, crowded streets. In prison, Raskolnikov comes to the realization that happiness cannot be achieved by a reasoned plan of existence but must be earned by suffering. The novel's status as a masterpiece is chiefly a result of its narrative intensity and its moving depiction of the recovery of a diseased spirit. **Fyodor M. Dostoyevsky** (b. 1821 – d. 1881) Russian novelist and short-story writer whose psychological penetration into the darkest recesses of the human heart, together with his unsurpassed moments of illumination, had an immense influence on 20th-century fiction. Dostoyevsky is usually regarded as one of the finest novelists who ever lived. Literary modernism, existentialism, and various schools of psychology, theology, and literary criticism have been profoundly shaped by his ideas. His works are often called prophetic because he so accurately predicted how Russia's revolutionaries would behave if they came to power. In his time he was also renowned for his activity as a journalist. Dostoyevsky is best known for his novella *Notes from the Underground* and for four long novels, *Crime and Punishment, The Idiot, The Possessed* (also and more accurately known as *The Demons* and *The Devils*), and *The Brothers Karamazov.* Each of these works is famous for its psychological profundity, and, indeed, Dostoyevsky is commonly regarded as one of the greatest psychologists in the history of literature. He specialized in the analysis of pathological states of mind that lead to insanity, murder, and suicide and in the exploration of the emotions of humiliation, self-destruction, tyrannical domination, and murderous rage. These major works are also renowned as great "novels

of ideas" that treat timeless and timely issues in philosophy and politics. Psychology and philosophy are closely linked in Dostoyevsky's portrayals of intellectuals, who "feel ideas" in the depths of their souls. Finally, these novels broke new ground with their experiments in literary form. (Encyclopedia Britannica, 2014)

Chapter 1: Setting up a Prison Ministry that's real

1. Dr. Mario E. Rivera, *Facing Unresolved Conflicts: Theotherapy - God's Healing*, (Rivera, 1992), 123.
2. Abdullah Yusuf Ali, *The Meaning of the Illustrious Qur'an*, Saeed International, (New York, 2011)
3. Howard Zehr, *Changing Lenses: Restorative Justice for Our Times*, (Herald Press, Virginia, 2005), 129.
4. Ibid., 131.
5. Ibid., 134, (drawn from Perry B. Yoder's book: *Shalom: The Bible's Word for Salvation, Justice, and Peace* (Newton, KS: Faith & Life Press, 1987).
6. Ibid., 135.
7. Perry B. Yoder: *Shalom: The Bible's Word for Salvation, Justice, and Peace* (Newton, KS: Faith & Life Press, 1987), 21.
8. Zehr, *Changing Lenses*, 136.
9. Rev. Jeffrey K. Krehbiel, *Reflective with Scripture on Community Organizing*, (2017)
10. John 8: 11 ("Go and sin no more.")
11. Erwin Lutzer, *Pastor to Pastor: Tackling the Problems of Ministry*, (Kregel Publications, 1998), 94.
12. Ibid. 95.13.
13. Ibid., Lutzer, 95.
14. Ibid.
15. Ibid.
16. John L. Allen, *The Future Church: How Ten Trends are Revolutionizing the Catholic Church*, Jr., (New York, Image, 2009).
17. Survey, random, M. F. Maraschiello (2020), See Appendix 2.
18. Allen, *The Future Church*, 155-160.
19. Ibid., 160.
20. Ibid.
21. Ibid.
22. Ibid., 161.
23. Chris Hodges, M.M., *The Daniel Dilemma*, (Nelson Books, Nashville, 2017), 201-205.
24. Holman Bible Dictionary, Holman Bible Publishers (1991)
25. Ibid., 363
26. Ibid., 364
27. Ibid., 365

28. Ibid., 366
29. Ibid.
30. Ibid.
31. Ibid.
32. Ibid., 367
33. Ibid., 1414
34. COMMUNITY ORGANIZING, Encyclopedia Britannica (2014)
35. Ibid.

Chapter 2: Finding Volunteers to "talk and walk" (Not just feeding the animals at the zoo)

1. New American Bible, CCD, New York (1970)
2. Webster's Third New International Dictionary (New York, 1961)
3. Matthew 19:26.
4. Entrepreneurial Financing: Fundamentals of Financial Planning and Management for Small Business, M.J. Alhabeeb, PhD (Wiley & Sons, Inc.) p411-412 (2015)
5. Let's Talk: A Catholic Ministry to Prisoners, Paulist Evangelization Ministries, DC (Jan/Feb/Mar 2020), Excerpts from Tell the Prisoners I pray for Them, by Pope Francis, Copyright © 2016 by Liberia Editrice Vaticana. (Jan/Feb/Mar 2020)
6. Ibid., Let's Talk: A Catholic Ministry to Prisoners: Article: "Sent on Mission!", by Anthony Bosnick
7. Ibid., Anthony Bosnick

Chapter 3: Breaking down the Fear of Prisons

1. Counter Culture: Following Christ in an Anti-Christian Age, David Platt, (Tyndale House Publishers, Inc.)(2017)
2. Ibid., 249
3. Luke, On Mercy: The Good Samaritan (10: 30-37); On Hate: (6:22)
4. Pew Research Center, national survey conducted March 19 – April 19, 2014, N=2, 439, as part of their American Trends panel.
5. Entrepreneurial Financing: Fundamentals of Financial Planning and Management for Small Business, M.J. Alhabeeb, PhD (Wiley & Sons, Inc.) p376-377 (2015)
6. Ibid. p377
7. Ibid. p378
8. Ibid. p416
9. Ibid.
10. Ibid.

11. CHARGED: The New Movement to Tranform American Prosecution and End Mass Incarceration, by Emily Bazelon, Random House (2019)
12. (p. xxviii)
13. See. <u>Rodriguez v. Providence Community Corrections, Inc.</u>, 155 F.Supp.3d 758 (M.D. Tenn 2015); 191 F.Supp.3d 758 (M.D. Tenn 2016)

Chapter 4: Building up Prisoners for Success

1. Merriam-Webster Dictionary, (®Encyclopedia Britannica, Inc.) Ultimate Reference Suite (2014)
2. America at the Crossroads: Explosive Trends shaping America's Future and What You Can Do About It, George Barna, Baker Books, MI (2016)
3. Ibid.
4. John Lehrer, "Which Traits Predict Success? (The Importance of Grit)," *Wired*, March 14, 2011, <u>http://www.wired.com/2011/</u> <u>03/what-is-success-true-grit/</u>; "Gallup: The Six College Experiences Linked to Lifelong Success," Education Advisory Board, April 9, 2015, <u>https://www.eab.com/daily-briefing/2015 /04 /09gallup-life-success-linked-to-6-college-experiences</u>.
5. Accenture, "Accenture Research Finds Most professionals Believe They Can 'Have It All,'" news release, March 1, 2013
6. Ibid.
7. Based on a national survey conducted by Ipsos, for Strayer University, N=2,00, in 2014; Smith, "How Americans Define Success."
8. A College Education for Prisoners Reduces Recidivism: Prison Education Reduces Likelihood of Reoffending", Signal Group, Elizabeth Northrup (2017)
9. Ibid.
10. Article: "A truly just system must do more than protect the rights of the innocent; it must also respect the humanity of the guilty," from "Who Belongs in Prison?," Adam Gopnik (The New Yorker, 2019) Journal of Prisoners on Prisons, Justin Piché, PhD, Department of Criminology of Ottawa Canada (2019)
11. Caroline Wolf Harlow, *Education and Correctional Populations, Bureau of Justice Statistics Special Report* (Washington, DC: U.S. Dept. of Justice, Office of Justice Programs (2003)
12. Ibid.

Chapter 5: Leadership

1. Franklin Delano Roosevelt, (b. 1/30/1882 d. 4/12/1945), 32nd U.S. President (from his first inauguration speech, March 4, 1933).

2. D. A. Carson, PhD, *The Cross and Christian Ministry: Leadership Lessons from 1 Corinthians*, Baker Publishing Group, 2018), 108.
3. Ibid., 109-110.
4. Ibid., 92.
5. Ibid., 100.
6. Ibid., 105.
7. Ibid., 105, 113.
8. Ibid., 82.
9. Ibid., 122, 123-126, 129.
10. Ibid., 109.
11. Ibid., 116.
12. Ibid., 62.
13. Ibid., 29-30.
14. Ibid., 113.
15. Ibid., 113, 115.
16. Ibid., 122.
17. Ibid., 129.
18. Ibid., 149.
19. Ibid., 108.
20. Rom. 3:10, 23; 5:12; 6:23; 10:9-13 (King James Version)
21. Tammy Richmond and Dave Powers, "*Business Fundamentals for the Rehabilitation Professional,*" 2nd ed., SLACK Incorporated, 2009, 2.

Chapter 6: The 4 Levels of Prison Ministry (The Four Types of Sponsors)

1. Herald of His Coming, Gospel Revivals, Inc. (Indiana) Quoted from Article: *The Real Presence of Jesus*, Issue: May/June 2020
2. Ibid.
3. Ibid.
4. COMMUNITY ORGANIZING, Encyclopedia Britannica (2014)
5. Ibid.

13. Book: Taking Sides: Clashing Views on Education Issues, Glenn L. Koonce (2014)
14. Ibid.
15. Book: Critical Issues in Education, Eugene F. Provenzo, Jr., (2006)
16. Encyclopedia Britannica, W.E.B. Du Bois, (2014)
17. Ibid.
18. Plessy v. Ferguson, 163 U.S. 537, 16 S.Ct.1138, 41L.Ed.256 (1896)
19. Ibid.

Chapter 7: Making the Commitment to Change a Life in COVID America

1. Other flu's in the United States of America included: The Asian Flu of 1957 (150,00 deaths); the Hong Kong Flue of 1968 (100,000 deaths). Note: NONE of these flu's never shut down the country as during the COVID pandemic of 2020. (Source: America's Voice News Report, The *AV Channel*, August 14, 2020.)
2. Emily Widra & Dylan Hayre, "State Corrections systems Get Failing Grade in Response to COV," Crime Report Staff (August 2020)
3. Will the Pandemic Be the "Tipping Point" for Justice Reform?, Jordan S. Rubin, Bloomberg Law (June 2020)
4. Ibid.
5. Ibid.

6. Matthew 8: 2-4.
7. Blacks Law Dictionary (11th ed. 2019), from *WestlawNext*. ©2020 Thomas Reuters.
8. *James P. Hyde v. Carlton*, 2003 WL 21766620 (Tenn., July 31, 2003) *WestlawNext*. ©2020 Thomas Reuters.
9. *Massenberg vs. Massenberg,* ------, ------, (1986, N.C.)(Expunged due to exoneration of army officer Major Massenberg.)

Chapter 8: Parole and Re-Entry: Dragging the Sponsoree Out of Prison / Jail

1. Beth Schwartzapfel, "How Parole Boards Keep prisoners in the Dark and Behind Bars (And why the Pre-Sentence Report (PSI/PSR) needs to be accurate for parole)," *The Marshall Project*, March 2017.
2. *Haslam Grants Executive Clemency to Four Tennesseans*, July 26, 2018, https://www.tn.gov/governor/news/2018/7/26/haslam-grants-executive-clemency-to-four-tennesseans.html.
3. *Cyntoia Brown Clemency*, Internet (Google, 2/9/2019).
4. Benjamin K. Raybin, *"Pardon me: How Executive Clemency Works in Tennessee [And How It Doesn't]," Tennessee Bar Journal* (August 2016).
5. Tenn.Const.Art III, Sec. 6. This power is codified at Tenn. Code. Ann. (TCA) § 40-27-101, et. seq.
6. T.C.A. § 40-28-104(a)(10).
7. *Gov. Bill Lee Delivers 2020 State of the State Address*, February 3, 2020, https://www.tn.gov/governor/news/2020/2/3/gov--bill-lee-delivers-2020-state-of-the-state-address.html.

8. Adam Tamburin, "Lee Loosens Clemency Conditions," *The Tennessean* (Nashville), January 21, 2020.
9. Adam Tamburin, "Gov. Lee Group Backs Rewriting Sentencing Laws," *The Tennessean* (Nashville), December 20, 2019.
10. Appropriations Budget of the Tennessee Department of Correction for FY 2020 (Total Title III-7: $ 1,049,982,200.00); of that the amount spent on Probation and Parole Field Supervision: $ 91,831,200.00) WestlawNext, https://nextcorrectional.westlawcom/Document/ I667DA3307B0A1E9B270F8E5843847... (9/25/2019)
11. Chart from: Tennessee Board of Parole (BOP) Annual Report. (Note: in FY 2015-16 the BOP conducted 16,378 hearings.), (2017) p. 6.
12. BEYOND BARS, Jeffrey I. Ross, PhD and Stephen C. Richards, PhD, Penguin Random House LLC (2009), Chapter 4.
13. Ibid, Ch. 4.

Chapter 9: Incarcerated Veterans and their Needs: A National Failure

1. <u>Porter vs. McCollum</u>, 130 S.Ct. 447, Supreme Court of the United States, (Nov. 30, 2009).
2. Ibid.
3. Murdock vs. Patsy Bruce, et al. (Tennessee Board of Paroles), Civil Case No. 3:12-CV-1244 (Nashville, TN) March 7, 2016.

EPILOGUE: The Victory: Relationships that "Pay off" with Christ-centered dividends to last a lifetime

1. How Norway is Teaching America to Make its Prisons more Humane: - The Broken Prison System is in Desperate need of Reform U.S. Prisons are trying to Find Answers Overseas," by Laura Paddison (Internet, 2019)
2. "How to Fix Our Prisons? Let the Public Inside; We need a broad national effort to recruit volunteers to educate & counsel the incarcerated," by Neil Barsky, *New York Times* (2020)
3. "EXAMINING PRISONS TODAY," (Vera Project) (2020)
4. Executive Summary Report, State of Tennessee's Corrections (Prisons) and Criminal Justice System, est. by Gov. Bill Lee, Criminal Justice Investment Task Force (CJITF), Ex. Order No. 6, Chair Brandon Gibson, Senior Advisor, Office of the Governor (2019)
5. Ibid., p. 5
6. Ibid.
7. Ibid., pp. 7-9

8. Ibid., pp. 13
9. <u>Murdock v. Bruce</u> (Bd. of Parole), 2017 WL 1322075;

(See also: *Murdock v. State*, 2011 WL 1844029)
10. Executive Summary Report, State of Tennessee's Corrections (Prisons) and Criminal Justice System, est. by Gov. Bill Lee, Criminal Justice Investment Task Force (CJITF), p. 17

APPENDICES

Appendix 1

Sample Ministry or Organization Mission Statement

Prison Ministry Mission Statement

Our goal through regular volunteer services based on the discipleship model of Jesus Christ, by applying effective sponsorship and mentorship principles that foster positive life-building changes, through personal communication, compassion, ethical rapport, inmate-centered goals, education, and measurable outcomes is to meet inmate's spiritual and particular needs for finding hope, faith, and character for successful transition back into the community."

Social Justice Mission Statement

Our goal through regular volunteer services based on the models of discipleship and coaching, by applying effective sponsorship and mentorship principles that foster positive life-building changes, through personal communication, compassion, ethical rapport, inmate-centered goals, education, and measurable outcomes is to meet inmate's particular needs for finding hope, purpose, and character for successful transition back into the community."

Prison Ministry In Covid America

Sample book cover for your notes and mission statement

The Happy Go Home Church
Of Middleton, NC

Basic Guidebook
for Prison Ministry
Sponsor's / Mentor's

"Theology"

"Empower"   "Success"

"Attitude"

"I know the plans I have for you... for welfare, and a future of hope." (Jer. 29:11)

"... In prison, and you visited me... what you did for these least ones, you did for me." (Matt. 25: 35, 36, 40)

(N.C. 2020)

Sample Book for Sponsor/Mentor Volunteer

Guidebook
Index

2   Preface --

3   The Four (4) Levels of Prison Ministry and
Relevant Prison Ministry Articles ---

    a) Introduction
    b) "The Four (4) Levels of prison Ministry"
    c) "What Should prison Ministers Do?"
    d) "Things Ministers or Their Church Can Do for Inmates"
    e) "Prison Visitors Extend Hope and Mercy to Those Behind Bars"
       (also known as " "Breaking Myths About Prisoners")
    f) "Retreat at Prison Deepens Faith of Inmates and Volunteers"
    g) "Assaults on Ministers, Mentors, & Sponsors"
    h) "Things Ministers Can Do the Prison System Won't Tell You"

4   Sample Parole Packet for Sponsored Inmates ----------------------------------

    a) Introduction
    b) Sample Parole Packet

5   Parole Sponsor's Preparation Checklist and
                Re-Entry Issues ---

    a) Introduction
    b) Checklists
    c) Re-Entry Issues

Parole: "The Plain Truth" (In a Nutshell);
Policies, Procedures, and Rules Affecting
Prisons and Parole -- **6**

    a) Introduction
    b) Articles
    c) Policies Affecting Prisons and Parole
    d) Procedures Affecting Prisons and Parole
    e) Rules Affecting Prisons and Parole

PREFACE -------------------------------------- 2

**The Four (4) Levels of Prison Ministry
and Relevant Prison Ministry Articles** ------------------------ 3

    a) Introduction
    b) "The Four (4) Levels of Prison Ministry"
    c) "What Should Prison Ministers Do?"
    d) "Things Ministers or Their Church Can Do for Inmates"
    e) "Prison Visitors Extend Hope and Mercy to Those Behind Bars"
          (also known as "Breaking Myths About Prisoners")
    f) "Retreat at Prison Deepens Faith of Inmates and Volunteers"
    g) "Assaults on Ministers, Mentors, & Sponsors"
    h) "Things Ministers Can Do the Prison System Won't Tell You"

**Sample Parole Packet for
Sponsored Inmates** -- **4**

a) Introduction
    b) Sample Parole Packet

**Parole Sponsor's Preparation
Checklist and Re-Entry Issues** -- 5

    a) Introduction
        b) Checklists
        d) Re-Entry Issues

**Policies, Procedures, and Rules
 Affecting Prison and Parole** -- **6**

    a) Introduction
        b) Articles
        c) Policies Affecting Prisons and Parole
        d) Procedures Affecting Prisons and Parole
        e) Rules Affecting Prisons and Parole

Appendix 2
Results of Prisoners' Computer Literacy Random Survey

Sample Population: 20
Total Sampled: 20
Percent Sampled: 100%
Median Age: 42
Range of Age: Lowest 20 Highest 64

Race: 10 White
7 Black
3 Latino

Sex: All Male

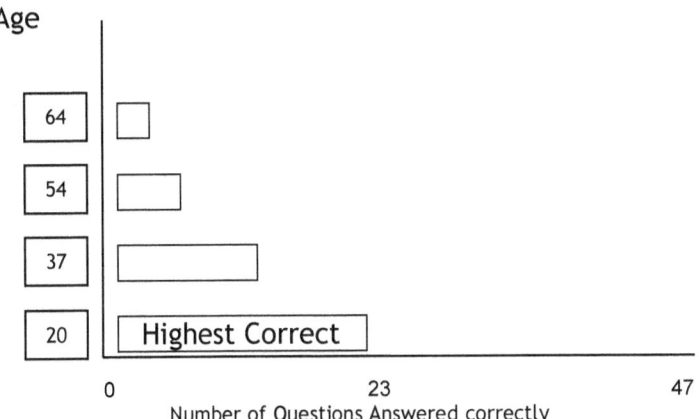

Data

Median (Avg.) Score: 30% Lowest Score: 14% **Highest Score: (21/47) 45%**

Have you ever used: A computer? 10/20 (50%) said Yes
Have you ever used: A Mobile Device? 7/20 (35%) said Yes
Did you own on the street: A computer? 4/20 (20%) said Yes
Did you own on the street: A Mobile Device? 10/20 (50%) said Yes
How do you rate your computer skills: Zero said EXCELLENT
2/20 (10%) said GOOD
3/20 (15%) said OKAY
10/20 (50%) said POOR
5/20 (25%) said NONE

How many days a week <u>can</u> you use a computer? Zero said Daily
1/20 (5%) said 1 to 2 Days
9/20 (45%) said 3 to 7 Days
10/20 (50%) said None
How many times a month <u>do</u> you use a computer? 2/20 (10%) said weekly
3/20 (15%) said 1 -2 wks per mo.
15/20 (75%) said None
Are you able to use a computer often: At the library? 17/20 (85%) said No

At a computer class? 19/20 (95%) said No

Observations / Notes:

Age. The younger the individual tested, the *more* they indicated having computer skills with hand-held mobile devices, computers, tablets, etc. from either experience or some formal instruction or a combination of the two. Whereas the older prisoners showed less aptitude, nor particularly had they ever owned or used such computer devices having either been incarcerated for so long, never taken any formal instruction, or a combination both. (No consideration was taken into account for older inmates who were computer literate having come into the prison system at a later time in life already possessing some adequate computer skills.)

Race. Race had no bearing on this survey. The highest scoring subject was black. The oldest subject, white, did the poorest. The oldest never used a computer, never owned one, nor ever used a mobile device or e-game.

Effect of Release. These basic statistics were not compiled from a comprehensive analysis, however, they indicate a "snap shot" of a problem within the prison population of computer illiteracy for older convicts. Demographics, of course, would vary from prison to prison and state to state depending on programs available, number of computers, and whether or not some prisons allow tablets or have kiosks to familiarize prisoners with the skills they would need when released. Those released from prison without the basic skills would - theoretically - be disadvantaged by virtue of being technologically illiterate as this survey suggests -- a hypothesis which should be considered and appropriately addressed in *corrections* so prisoners leaving the system are capable of at least the computer and Smartphone basics to electronically navigate to post electronic job resume's, pay bills, and other necessary tasks in today's society.

Test subjects for this random survey were not evaluated for English reading comprehension. All tests (raw data) were destroyed for confidentiality after data was collected.)

(Survey conducted by M. F. Maraschiello from Jan. 1 to Jul. 1, 2020)

SURVEY — TEST YOUR KNOWLEDGE OF COMPUTERS

(Survey Designed by M. F. Maraschiello, 2020)

Age: _____ Have you ever used: A computer? Yes ☐ No ☐   A Mobile Device? Yes ☐ No ☐

Did you own on the street: A computer? Yes ☐ No ☐   A Mobile Device? Yes ☐ No ☐

How do you rate your computer skills: EXCELLENT ☐   GOOD ☐   OKAY ☐   POOR ☐   NONE ☐

How many days a week <u>can</u> you use a computer?   Daily ☐   1 to 2 Days? ☐   3 to 7 Days? ☐   None? ☐

How many times a month <u>do</u> you use a computer?   Weekly ☐   1 to 2 weeks per month? ☐   None? ☐

Are you able to use a computer often: At the library? Yes ☐ No ☐   At a computer class? Yes ☐ No ☐

INSTRUCTIONS

Match the term (below) with the correct definition on Page Two by placing the corresponding number from page two in the blank beside each term or abbreviation below. There is only <u>one</u> (1) answer for each term.

_____ App –
_____ Blog –
_____ Browser -
_____ CD-ROM-
_____ DTP- Desktop Publishing Software –
_____ eBook-
_____ E-mail –
_____ Firewall-
_____ Gigabyte (GB)-
_____ HTML – Hypertext Markup Language –
_____ Internet –
_____ Link –
_____ Modem –
_____ OSP- Online Service provider –
_____ Program –
_____ Rubric –
_____ Search Engine –
_____ Software –
_____ Terabyte (TB) –
_____ Title Bar –
_____ VR – Virtual Reality –
_____ Wi-Fi –
_____ Worm –
_____ USB-

_____ Blended Course -
_____ Bluetooth –
_____ CD –
_____ Cracker –
_____ DVD –
_____ eLearning –
_____ Facebook –
_____ File Transfer Protocol (FTP) –
_____ Home Page –
_____ Icon –
_____ Kiosk –
_____ mLearning –
_____ Optical Mouse –
_____ Power Point –
_____ ROM- Read Only Memory –
_____ Search Tool –
_____ SMART Board –
_____ Template –
_____ Text –
_____ Track Ball –
_____ Virus –
_____ Wiki –
_____ URL –

PAGE ONE

PAGE TWO   Match these with the Abbreviation or Term on page One

Prison Ministry In Covid America

1 – Universal Serial Bus – a port that connects up to 127 peripheral devices with one connection

2 – Digital Video Disc   3 – 1 trillion bytes

4 – Communication device that converts analog signals into digital for computers to communicate via telephone lines

5 – A program that interprets HTML and displays Web pages and enable you to link to other Web pages and Web sites (Also called a Web Browser)

6 – (Compact Disc) Holds 650 Megabytes

7 – Optical disc that uses the same laser technology that audio CDs use for recording music

8 – One who tries to access a network illegally; a hacker

9 – Allows you to design, produce, and deliver documents that contain text, graphics, and brilliant colors

10 – Uniform Resource Locator – The address for each Web page on a Web site which consists of a protocol, domain name, and sometimes the path to a specific Web page

11 – Malicious software program that copies itself repeatedly in a computer's memory or on a network using up resources and possibly shutting down the computer or network

12 – Classes held in face-to-face classroom sessions and online course sessions

13 – An interactive white board (IWB) that allows users to process on its large, touch sensitive surface

14 – Uses radio waves to transmit data between two devices

15 – Electronic mail – The transmission of messages and files via a computer network

16 – An electronic version of a printed book readable on a computer

17 – Instruction that utilizes a local network

18 – An online social networking application

19 – Hardware and software used to restrict access to data on a network

20 – an Internet standard that allows you to exchange files with other computers on the Internet

21 – Special codes, called tags, that define the placement and format of text, graphics, video, and sound on a Web page.

22 – A small image that represents a program

23 – A global network of computers that contains information on a multitude of subjects

24 – a collaborative Web site that allows users to create, add to, modify, or delete the Web site content via their Web browser

25 – Short for "Weblog" – an informal Web site consisting of time=-stamped articles, or posts, in a diary or journal format, usually listed in reverse chronological order

26 – The simulation of a real or imagined environment that appears as a three-dimensional (3D) space

27 – A free-standing computer that provides information to the user

28 – Allows users to navigate quickly from one Web page to another

29 – Learning that incorporates use of cost efficient, light weight, portable devices such as smart phones or tablet computers

30 – Has no moving parts. Uses an optical sense light or "eye." (Cordless/ wireless)

31 – Organization that provides access to the internet, as well as members-only features that offer a variety of special services

32 – Software that allows users to make presentations

33 – A series of instructions that tells a computer how to perform the tasks necessary to process data into information

34 – Instructions in storage that does not change in the computer's memory even when turned off

35 – Explicit set of criteria that the student can use to self-evaluate his or her work prior to submission and that a teacher can provide feedback

36 – Enables users to locate information found at Web sites all over the world

37 – A specific type of search tool that finds Web sites

38 – Series of instructions that tells hardware how to perform tasks

39 – A document that contains the formatting necessary for a specific document type

40 – Output of characters that are used to create words, sentences, and paragraphs for all digital media applications

41 – Located at the top of a window, a horizontal space that contains the window's name

42 – A stationary pointing device with a ball mechanism on its top

43 – A potentially damaging computer program

44 – Wireless fidelity – outlines standards for wireless technology

45 – Starting point for a Web site   46 – 1 Billion bytes   47 – A program you can download and use primarily on your mobile device

Michael Maraschiello

Definitions taken from: "Integrating Technology in a Connected World: Teachers Discovering Computers, 7th Edition, B. Shelly, G. Gunter, and R. Gunter, Course Technology, Cengage Learning (2012)

App – A program you can download and use primarily on your mobile device

Blended Course – Classes held in face-to-face classroom sessions and online course sessions

Blog – Short for "Weblog" – an informal Web site consisting of time=-stamped articles, or posts, in a diary or journal format, usually listed in reverse chronological order

Bluetooth – Uses radio waves to transmit data between two devices

Browser – A program that interprets HTML and displays Web pages and enable you to link to other Web pages and Web Sites (Also called a Web Browser)

CD – (Compact Disc) Holds 650 Megabytes

CD-ROM- compact-Disc Read Only – Optical disc that uses the same laser technology that audio CDs use for recording music

Cracker – One who tries to access a network illegally; a hacker

DTP- Desktop Publishing Software – Allows you to design, produce, and deliver documents that contain text, graphics, and brilliant colors

DVD – Digital Video Disc

eBook- An electronic version of a printed book readable on a computer

eLearning – Instruction that utilizes a local network

E-mail – Electronic mail – The transmission of messages and files via a computer network

Facebook – An online social networking application

Firewall- Hardware and software used to restrict access to data on a network

File Transfer Protocol (FTP) – an Internet standard that allows you to exchange files with other computers on the Internet

Gigabyte (GB)- 1 Billion bytes

Home Page – Starting point for a Web site

HTML – Hypertext Markup Language – A set of special codes, called tags that define the placement and format of text, graphics, video, and sound on a Web page.

Icon – A small image that represents a program

Internet – A global net work of computers that contains information on a multitude of subjects

Kiosk – A free-standing computer that provides information to the user

Link – Allows users to navigate quickly from one Web page to another

mLearning – Learning that incorporates the use of cost efficient, light weight, portable devices such as smart phones or tablet computers

Modem – Communication device that converts analog signals into digital for computers to communicate via telephone lines

Optical Mouse – Has no moving parts. Uses an optical sense light or "eye." (Cordless/ wireless)

OSP- Online Service provider – Organization that provides access to the internet, as well as members-only features that offer a variety of special services

Power Point – Soft ware that allows users to make presentations

Program – A series of instructions that tells a computer how to perform the tasks necessary to process data into information

ROM- Read Only Memory – Instructions in storage that does not change in the computer's memory even when turned off

Rubric- An explicit set of criteria that the student can use to self-evaluate his or her work prior to submission and that a teacher can provide feedback

Search Tool – Enables users to locate information found at Web sites all over the world

Search Engine – A specific type of search tool that finds Web sites

SMART Board- An interactive white board (IWB) that allows users to process on its large, touch sensitive surface

Software – Series of instructions that tells hardware how to perform tasks

Template – A document that contains the formatting necessary for a specific document type

Terabyte (TB)- 1 trillion bytes

Text – Output that consists of characters that are used to create words, sentences, and paragraphs for all digital media applications

Title Bar – Located at the top of a window, a horizontal space that contains the window's name

Track Ball- A stationary pointing device with a ball mechanism on its top

VR – Virtual Reality – The simulation of a real or imagined environment that appears as a three-dimensional (3D) space

Prison Ministry In Covid America

Virus – A potentially damaging computer program

Wi-Fi – Wireless fidelity – outlines standards for wireless technology

Wiki- a collaborative Web site that allows users to create, add to, modify, or delete the Web site content via their Web browser

Worm – Malicious software program that copies itself repeatedly in a computer's memory or on a network using up resources and possibly shutting down the computer or network

URL - Uniform Resource Locator – The address for each Web page on a Web site which consists of a protocol, domain name, and sometimes the path to a specific Web page

USB- Universal Serial Bus – a port that connects up to 127 peripheral devices with one connection

Appendix 3
Basic Guide with Typical Inmate's Parole/Release Packet

BASIC INSTRUCTIONS FOR PAROLE PREPARATION

Consider the following:

1. Send an Information Request form to your Institutional parole Officer (IPO) and set up an appointment to review your parole file and provide the IPO with what they need.
2. Fill out sample Presentation Packet from your prison or jail resource center, library, or other source (i.e. sponsor) and begin to assemble your own folder to show the board all your documents, certificates, letters, etc. you feel you need to present to the board and state your reasons for release.
3. STUDY the parole board rules and become familiar with victim's rights, presenting your speakers, set-up your telephone conferencing with your speakers (if non-contact rules are in effect with the board prohibiting your supporters from being there) presenting a supporter DVD, etc. so you are not denied your right to present any evidence/ statement you feel the board should know.
4. Above all, remember it is _your day_ to present yourself. So, be humble, do it well, and be realistic just like it was the most important "job interview" ever.

Address of my parole board where to send my letters of recommendations and for my supporters to send and e-mail theirs is:

_____

_____

Phone: _____

E-mail: _____

A Minister's Guide to the Inmate's Parole Packet

 *A MINISTER'S INTRODUCTION to the IMPORTANCE OF THE PAROLE PACKET*
By M. F. Maraschiello

This section is comprised of a generic format or "packet" of what
information or answers a prisoner may or might send to the parole board for the board's consideration to vote in favor of the prisoner's release.

SPONSOR/MENTOR + I/M + PAROLE PACKET = GREATER CHANCE FOR SUCCESS

As stated in the last section of this guidebook: POLICIES, PROCEDURES, RULES AFFECTING PRISONS AND PAROLE, the most important *earthly* thing to a prisoner is his or her freedom (i.e. parole or release from prison). Ministers who take the next step to become sponsors or mentors often have different approaches and reasons for staying out of or getting involved in a prisoner's *legal business* (i.e. parole) for reasons of a *spiritual* or moral nature. Fear also is a motivator to stay out of a prisoner's parole situation, as compared to an enthusiasm for justice which one may be motivated to see the prisoner gets a full and fair opportunity for parole and release because the prisoner may have been wrongly incarcerated or doing too much time as compared to other prisoners set free or who received *lesser* sentences.

So, whatever the motivation is behind a minister becoming a sponsor or mentor, the opportunity to do a *__greater service__* is presented for a minister to "step up" to *advocate* on behalf of a prisoner.

WHAT'S IN THIS SECTION?

In short, this section deals primarily with what a *sponsor* or *mentor* can do to assist *their* prisoner [whom they sponsor or mentor] with their I/M's parole preparation of which the packet contained in this guidebook can be a component of the overall parole board process.

NOTE: The terms *mentor* and *sponsor* are synonymous in this guidebook as they apply to parole.

PAROLE PACKET GOAL: INFORM THE BOARD WITH ACCURATE DATA

As detailed in the *Maximum Times* Articles "Preparing for the Parole Hearing" Part I: Your Parole File(s) and "Preparing for the Parole Hearing" Part II: The Facts and the Victim(s) (2018), the premise is simple: A prisoner *__must__* establish an *accurate* good record before the parole board commences, ensure the board received the information or "packet" before the hearing, and make sure he or she has their packet with them when they go to the board, as explained in the articles, above.

PAROLE CHECKLIST.

This easy and valuable tool is a great way to keep up with the chronological steps or timeframe in which to help monitor the progress of a sponsored prisoner's life preparing themselves. Everything a prisoner does is important, specifically: completing all required classes, course, or requirements recommended by the parole board, Department of Correction (TDOC), and/or court(s), having a good disciplinary record, a good *Strong R Report* from the prisoner's unit counselor, a good support group of mentors, church people, and family, victim reconciliation, mental health plan, job plan, home plan, and other requirements or applicables (i.e. enrollment in Alcoholics Anonymous (AA) group on the street if inmate (I/M) had a drug problem) which shows the board the I/M has changed their life with positive accomplishments, taken responsibility for their crime, and is humble knowing parole is a privilege and not a right.

SO WHAT CAN A *MINISTER* DO AT THE PAROLE BOARD?

FIRST, remember, the parole board — in practice — *"re-trys"* prisoners, generally, focusing not on the *present state* of the prisoner, but rather on the past crime or "incident(s)" which led the person to prison in the first place. This is where it is absolutely INVALUABLE to have a minister (sponsor / mentor) *advocate* and put a truthful "good face" on the I/M going up for parole by articulating in a charismatic manner the accomplishments and "transformation" the I/M has made in recent years or over their incarceration. Many I/Ms have families, are mothers, fathers, sons, etc., or have no family at all, with sometimes the ONLY person to speak for them is the minister who can make all the difference putting a *human face* on the prisoner instead of the parole board just reading from a computer screen or bunch of documents which hardly ever get looked at. But when a Mentor speaks, the board takes notice, especially if the mentor sought for the I/M to have a FULL and FAIR hearing with facts brought to the parole board's attention, such as from e-mailing or Return-Receipt mailing of the I/M's parole packet being received by all the board members for an I/M's parole hearing.

FACT: HAVING A SPONSOR *INCREASES* THE LIKELIHOOD FOR THE CHANCE FOR PAROLE BECAUSE IT SHOWS THE I/M HAS A SUPPORTER WHO IS INVOLVED, AND – BY STATISTICS – IS LIKELY TO SUCCEED WHEN RELEASED AND NOT BECOME A RECIDIVIST BECAUSE THE SPONSOR IS MENTORING (GUIDING) THE I/M NOT JUST IN PRISON, BUT WILL CONTINUE TO DO SO AFTER THEY ARE RELEASED AS A PART OF THEIR SPONSORSHIP AND COMMITMENT FOR THE I/M TO RE-ENTER SOCIETY AS EQUIPPED AND READY.

OVERALL DECISION: IT'S IN GOD'S HANDS

Let's be absolutely clear: Parole — in Tennessee — is a privilege, and not a right BY MANS STANDARDS. That does not mean an I/M going up for parole is to be prejudiced, given a board with no fairness or opportunity to be heard and evaluated without the facts, and for errors to be ignored. Yet, the way the board sometimes operates is flawed, especially when I/Ms do everything morally, academically, procedurally, and ethically right in the eyes of God — and man (i.e. have no disciplinary write-ups, no mental health issues, no drug problems, served a lot of time, completed all courses, etc.). Yet, as we know, the giving of parole is *subjective* to the parole board's privileged authority by the legislature. Tennessee Law provides also for *Victim Impact Coordinators* in every county's jurisdiction to notify victims and to orchestrate *strategies* (i.e. bus in, make DVD protest videos, sign petitions, send protest letters, etc.) to "protest" (prevent) the parole board from granting release to prisoners even if the I/M is no-longer a threat, the I/M has spent numerous years in prison more than others of the same offense, the I/M has demonstrated great humbleness, a relationship with God and a strong support group, etc.. Though the argument for parole is *Restorative Justice*, the argument against parole is *Retributive Justice*, meaning no parole and to serve the maximum time for all crimes at the highest end of the spectrum. Sadly, as with the flawed Tennessee law, the parole board can receive "fake news" — false information letters, e-mails, or phone messages and other mal-dicta to prejudice the parole-eligible I/M seeking parole by denying him or her access to these fake news documents because they are categorized as "confidential" when received by the parole board and un-viewable by the I/M going up for parole. This denies the I/M any chance to rebut any such "hate-speech" of falsehood designed for the purpose of denying the potential I/M from being granted parole. The worst prejudicial lie, of course, for an I/M going up for parole, is for a fake news letter to accuse the I/M of being a "child molester," which most assuredly would deny any I/M parole.

FACT: THE PAROLE BOARD <u>DOES NOT</u> VERIFY PROTESTER LETTERS FOR THEIR VERACITY.

This is not fair.

So, in conclusion as stated before in other sections of this guide, it is incumbent on the religious church sponsors, mentors, ministers, and leaders to be aware of what may or may not be affecting or at stake with the prisoner(s) they encounter and encourage seeking more than just God for guidance in life. Prisoners only get to <u>see</u> GOD in the *level of care* a church's ministry provides them of which the church minister(s) coming out to the prison(s) as the "ambassador" [of Christ, Buda, Mohamed, etc.). "Drive by" messages, prayer beads, tracts, food, singing, and pats on the back are okay for getting some I/Ms to hear about God, but are not enough for the saved I/M seeking more than "manna" in the form of community volunteers to help I/Ms with needs God's servants are called to provide for the "least ones (i.e. prisoners)." (Matt. 25: 35 -44) And for religious leaders held to higher standards to be taking care of least ones (i.e. prisoners, the sick, hungry, unclothed, widowed, orphans, etc.) it is sinful — according to the Bible -- for leaders to speak of doing such care for these least ones in the community, yet don't act and carry out what they preached to be done, especially when the "least of the least" are prisoners who need the most care based on their treatment of condemnation by our present day society. (Matt. 23: 1-34)

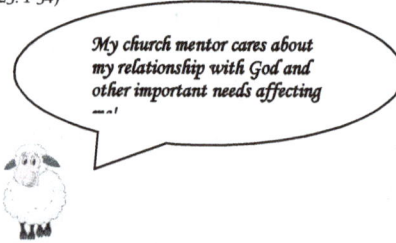

My church mentor cares about my relationship with God and other important needs affecting me!

CAVEAT.

Simply put, the prisoner *knows* his shepherd's heart by the <u>way</u> he or she is cared for. Giving a Bible, Koran, or Torah to a prisoner with no love behind it, is like giving a *toothbrush* to a prisoner who needs a pair of shoes. The "follow up" to any church's success is the care for its community members — all of them. That's why, in Jesus' mission, He went out to the *least ones* to perform miracles just as he went to the synagogues to preach to the self-centered and intellectually sick Pharisees who could not interpret and follow the Scriptures but went with what they <u>believed</u> looked good — like politicians – in view of the public to feed their self-serving agendas.

Like Dostoevsky said,

"An advanced society is known by the way in which it shows mercy to its prisoners."

In closing, people in the community — those capable — are called to help both the victim and the law-breaker. They are all a part of the same community and must live together. But as long as man controls the laws on earth, it is God who is still in control for the believer, who must accept the will of God no matter the outcome of the parole board and all that a minister can or has done for the I/M in living life no matter the place or situation. Any assistance a minister can do for a "least one" is still a step in the right direction. However "hitting it out of the park" to an I/M is showing you are willing to get involved with them and do something more of a sacrifice that is both positive and meaningful, not just words with no meat, or of a surplus or pitiful amount or effort. End.

Sample parole Board Packet.

Every inmate going up for parole needs this. As a minimum, this is like a "portfolio" or e-portfolio one would take to a job interview or utilize for a business plan.

APPLICATION

FOR

PAROLE

TO

BOARD OF PAROLE

For

Miss I ma Winner
DOC# 123456

INDEX

Copy of Packet to Board for Parole   I
- Parole Hearing Checklist

Statement from the Applicant   II

Letters of Recommendation   Sample
III
(Church, Prison, Military, Colleges, Vocational, Prison supervisors, etc.)

Major Certificates of Achievement   IV
(Church, Prison, Military, Colleges, Vocational, etc.)

Institutional Record   V
- Inmate Jobs and Program History
- Disciplinary Record

Military and Community Service
VI
- DD-214

Sample

Home and Job Plans   VII
- Application to Halfway house
- Letter of Guaranteed Employment

MICHAEL MARASCHIELLO

(Copy of the whole parole packet goes here) I

Sample Check list

SPONSOR'S 60-DAY
FINAL CHECKLIST BEFORE INMATES MEETS
THE PAROLE BOARD

NAME: _____ DOC I.D.# _____ AGE: ___

Prison Years: ____ to ____ Total Years: _____

PAROLE HEARING DATE: _____

**** These issues need to be completed at least *__60 days__* prior to hearing.

(Check if Ready/Done)

1. PAROLE PREP PACKET SENT TO BOARD
    Comments: (E-mail verification of receipt of Pkt) ☐

2. MAKE PHYSICAL CONTACT WITH INMATE'S FAMILY
    Comments: (Set-up possible meet-n-greet over a meal) ☐

3. Get permission to view Inmate's living quarters
    Comments: (Get E-mail confirmation from Chaplain) ☐

4. MAKE ADDITIONAL TIME TO MENTOR INMATE PRIOR
   TO HEARING TO FINALIZE SPONSORSHIP OBJECTIVES
    Comments: (Schedule or have more "1 on 1" phone time to go ☐
    Go over issues to speak about at the board)

5. Make contact with Parole Board to ensure everything has
   been done on Inmate's end and by Sponsor ☐
    Comments: (E-mail for time to talk or see Parole Board chair)

6. Submit (e-mail) any last minute Letters of Support and/or
   Vital documents to the board ☐

end

Prison Ministry In Covid America

Sample of Inmate's Letter to the Parole Board II

MIS. IMA WINNER, #1234567

Dear members of the board and all present,

December 7, 2000 was the worst day of my life having stolen a truck from the ACME Shipping Company, in what I thought was just going to be to sell it for money to buy drugs. I regrettably made a big mistake causing loss to the owner, harm to my family, and hurt society as well as other victims.

But before I continue, I want this board to know that I am personally responsible for my actions, failing God, my parents, and everyone else by not following common sense, the law, and being drug-free to avoid making wrong choices.

Make no mistake, I could have avoided doing what I did by seeking help for my addiction and choosing to be responsible. I chose wrongly, and was selfish believing I could just steal that truck to avoid my responsibility working honestly. There's not a day that goes by that I don't regret what I did.

Please know that over these past four years in prison, I have let the consequences of my actions sink in deeply, causing me to never again want to turn to crime as a solution to my problems. I had to make a choice in prison to go in another direction, one which would lead me on the right path and to a bright future my parents, society, this board, and others would approve of to be a benefit to society, not a liability. My disciplinary record shows I have done so by being "drug free" since my arrest so long ago, and I will continue to be law-abiding to solve my problems according to the law and through other normal means.

Members of the board, I believe, as do my sponsors Mr. and Mrs. Help, that I have merited a chance for this board to favorably look upon me as a viable candidate for parole based on the changes in my life I have made over these four plus years. My record is before you; I hide nothing. I've made mistakes; however, with the support group of my mentors, family, and church, and from the many victim-impact classes, anger management, and communication skills classes and drug rehabilitation programs I have completed, I now have the ability to follow the laws of life, and will do so successfully when released. I have finally "seen the light," and have transformed my character to be that of a productive citizen once again.

Lastly, to my victims, I ask that you look upon me as a person who has changed for the better. Please consider that I am a humbled man, and have greatly improved my life because I have listened to my mentors and sponsors who have guided me and uplifted me to see I can be a good person and live my life for the good of others, not just for myself.

So, I ask the members of this board to have mercy upon me, and vote favorably for my release. Even if you decide to not grant my parole at this time, I will accept your decision, and thank you for the opportunity to be considered for release.

Sincerely,
    I AM WINNER

    Date: _____

List of Letters of Recommendation III

SIGNIFICANT FREE-WORLD SUPPORT / SPONSORS

YEAR	NAME	RELATIONSHIP
1998 – Present	DR. JAMES DEAN, PH. D	SPONSOR
	DEACON MARTHA WHITE	SPONSOR
	REV. BRUCE SPRINGSTEIN	MT. BAP. CH.
	DR. MATT DILLON	BUSINESSMAN
	MRS. FRANKIE LANE	CHRISTIAN
FRIEND	MRS. MARILYN MONROE	TEACHER
	** MR. JIM MORRISON	MUSICIAN/FRIEND
	** Wheelchair	

SIGNIFICANT PRISON WORK SUPERVISORS

YEAR	NAME	JOB	INSTITUTION
2016 – Present	CCO SANDY HOOK	MAINTENACE SUPV	FCCD
2009 -	CPT WATER GATE	SHIFT CDR	RLSI
2008 -	CORONA VIRUS	FOOD SVC. MANAGER	RLSI
2007 -	CORONA VIRUS	FOOD SVC. MANAGER	RLSI
2006 -	CORONA VIRUS	FOOD SVC. MANAGER	GHSI
2000 -	IRAN CONTRA	G.E.D. TEACHER	HDCF
1998 -	IRAN CONTRA	G.E.D. TEACHER	HDCF

Major Certificates of Achievement IV
(Church, Prison, Military, Colleges, Vocational, etc.)

YEAR	QTY	COURSE	DATE	PRISON
1995	1-	STUDIES IN THE BIBLE	10/31/1995	JAIL
1996	3-	STUDIES IN THE BIBLE	10/10/1996	JAIL
1997	2-	GUIDE TO THE BIBLE	04/14/1997	JAIL

COURSES / PROGRAMS WHILE IN PRISON

1997 – 2000 EMPLOYED as: Teacher's Aide & Inmate Advisor		
2000-	**CORE** SAFETY COURSE	08/17/2000	
2004 -	**HIV / AIDS EDUCATION**	10/05/2004	
2004 -	**ANGER MANAGEMENT**	12/03/2004	
2004 -	**SUBSTANCE ABUSE**	12/03/2004	
2004 -	**DYNAMICS DOMESTIC VIOLENCE**	11/24/2004	
2008 -	**HEATING, VENTILATION & AIR**	10/03/2008	
018 -	**EMPLOYMENT READINESS**	02/08/2018	GECX
2018 -	**PARENTING SKILLS (TPOM)**	04/05/2018*	GECX

2018 -	CAREER MNGT SERVICES (CMS)	2019	GECX
2003 -	LIFE SKILLS	2003	GECX
2004 -	GOOD CONDUCT CERTIFICATE	08/20/2004	GECX
2004 -	OCCUPATIONAL EXCELLENCE CERT.	08/20/2004	GECX
2010 -	PRELIMINARY TRAINING	07/01/2010	GECX
2010 -	ORIENTATION CLASS	08/26/2010	GECX
2011 -	CERTIFICATE OF SERVICE AWARD	07/26/2011	GECX

Major Certificates of Achievement
IV
(Church, Prison, Military, Colleges, Vocational, etc.)

MILITARY CERTIFICATES & AWARDS
(Iraq War Veteran)
    RANK: Staff Sergeant (Active Duty)   **Position: Platoon Sergeant**
Discharge: Honorable (2007)   **UNITS: 101st Airborne, 3rd Infantry Division**
    ☑ **BRONZE STAR**   ☑ Commendation Medals   ☑ Achievement Medal
    ☑ Army Service Ribbon   ☑ Overseas Medals   ☑ 2007 (Afghan Freedom Medal)
Number of Tours in Warzone: **2**   **BADGES:**   Parachutist Badge; Combat Medical Badge

(*SEE* DD-214 and more in packet)

COLLEGE EDUCATION & OTHER
    •**ACADEMIC COLLEGES:** (Highest Level) **Bachelors Degree**
AA- HORTICULTURE (OBAMA COMMUNITY COLLEGE) **2000;**
 BA -PSYCHOLOGY (STATE UNIVERSITY OF TRUMP) **2002**

    • **Vocational & Trade Schools:** *SEE* Complete Parole Packet

Institutional Record   V

    • **Inmate Jobs and Program History**
1) LEGAL ADVISOR
2) MAINTENANCE (ELECTRICAL REPAIRER, HVAC, ETC.)
3) FOOD SERVICE COOK
4) INMATE SUICIDE PREVENTION TEAM

    • **Disciplinary Record**
1) ALCOHOL & DRUG-<u>FREE</u> ENTIRE TIME IN PRISON!

2) ONE (1) Disciplinary Write-up ---- in <u>**4 Years**</u>!

Military and Community Service
VI
- Provided Medical Support in wartime to Local Nomadic Tribes
- Continues to be active in community affairs

CURRENT ORGANIZATION MEMBERSHIPS
- Veterans of Foreign Wars (VFW) ------------------------- Aspen, Colorado
- Disabled American Veterans (DAV) ---------------------"*Life*-Member"
- Islamic Mosque East   --------------------------------------- Aspen, Colorado
- PRISON SUICIDE PREVENTION TEAM
    - Counseling assistance to prisoners with outside support

Home and Job Plans   VII

- Application to Halfway house
- Letter of Guaranteed Employment

> **Tip:** Keep the parole packet ONLY to the essentials. Read over aids on how and what to say at the parole board magnifying your support of and the good character of your inmate, pointing to his or her accomplishments, and your time helping them to be successfully transitioned to the outside. STABILITY (job ability, support group, no threat, mental health plan, etc.) which are the <u>*key*</u> things the inmate must have and address for release. And number one -- demonstrate they have changed.

Prison Ministry In Covid America

LETTER OF ACCEPTANCE FOR HOME PLAN

FOR: <u>Inmate:</u> _____

TO: Parole Board

Date: _____

After review of applicant _____, who needs a home plan (residence), I, _____, will accept him into our temporary housing program or my residence located at: _____ _____ upon release or shortly thereafter.

☐   He must pay the fee / rent of $_____ before his release date.

☐   No fee is required for him to pay in advance of his stay at this residence.

☐   He does not have to pay any fee to stay at this residence.

_____
Authorized Signature of
Residence Head

Phone No. _____

LETTER OF ACCEPTANCE FOR JOB PLAN

FOR: <u>MICHAEL F. MARASCHIELLO, 274760</u>

To Parole Board

EMPLOYER: _____
Address: _____
Phone: _____

I, (supervisor/ owner) _____, agree to hire Inmate _____ upon release from prison to work for my company / business, above, starting at $_____ per hour for the first 30 days, then to $_____ per hour thereafter.

_____
Employer

Date: _____

CERTIFICATES

for 20____ Parole Board

APPLICATION FOR PAROLE

Submitted by:

"Success begins with yourself believing you can."

Sample Free-World Recommendation Petition

Send the message your organization supports your sponsoree -- and you.

FREE-WORLD SUPPORT PETITION FOR PAROLE

For: _____

We the undersigned, supporters, family, and or friends respectfully request that our collective recommendations for _____, #_____, **be considered for his parole.** We have had the opportunity to know and understand him and aspects of his case, his life, and the positive changes he has made while incarcerated. We have taken notice of improvements in his law-abiding attitude to follow rules, his taking responsibility for his actions, his educational gains, and of his general character to function successfully back in society as a positive contributing citizen. We strongly believe he is an excellent candidate, and humbly and respectfully request that you carefully consider him and his case as a whole to grant parole. Thank you.

Please don't hesitate to contact us if you have any questions.

NAME: _____ Occupation: _____

Relationship to Inmate _____ Years known: ____ Tel. No. and/or e-mail address: _____

NAME: _____ Occupation: _____

Relationship to Inmate _____ Years known: ____ Tel. No. and/or e-mail address: _____

NAME: _____ Occupation: _____

Relationship to Inmate _____ Years known: ____ Tel. No. and/or e-mail address: _____

Page 1 of _____
Continuation page for parole recommendations for: _____ #_____.

NAME: _____ Occupation: _____

Relationship to Inmate   **Years known:**   **Tel. No. and/or e-mail address:**

NAME: **Occupation:**

Relationship to Inmate   **Years known:**   **Tel. No. and/or e-mail address:**

NAME: **Occupation:**

Relationship to Inmate   **Years known:**   **Tel. No. and/or e-mail address:**

NAME: **Occupation:**

Relationship to Inmate   **Years known:**   **Tel. No. and/or e-mail address:**

NAME: **Occupation:**

Relationship to Inmate   **Years known:**   **Tel. No. and/or e-mail address:**

NAME: **Occupation:**

Relationship to Inmate   **Years known:**   **Tel. No. and/or e-mail address:**

Appendix 4
Sample Letters People can send the Parole Board in Support of Inmate's Release

Recommendation Letters to the Parole Board

Typical letters for the parole board should reflect the parole candidate's readiness and transitional attributes to include observational patterns of conduct reflecting the candidate's character. For the Christian, no greater emphasis can be stated than that of God's *forgiveness* of the parolee regardless of the crime(s) they committed.

The parole board centers their attention on the following:

- The circumstances of the crime
- A candidate's remorsefulness
- Victim impact
- Does offender show he/ she changed?
- Risk or threat of offender to others
- Courses/ programs taken while in prison
- Offender's disciplinary record
- Offender's support group and/or family situation
- Education and job history
- Home and job plans
- Military and/or community service in the past
- Health condition (Mental & Physical)

Statements should be: short, referencing your time that you spent with or have known the candidate, the relationship, whether you have forgiven them (for religious reasons), if you have made contact with offender's family, housing arrangements (e.g. half-way house), whether you mentor them or are their sponsor for *re-entry*, how they worked and communicate with others through your observations, and, most importantly, whether you *trust* them to work for you, be around children, in the community, and any other qualities that distinguish the candidate from the pitfalls of stereotypes most offenders are labeled.

NOTE: The inmate is relying on <u>you</u> to tell the parole board the truth supported by facts. Too much "schmooze" and you will be helping the candidate lose. Mail a copy of your letter and e-mail your letter to the board because it matters the day of the hearing.

DO'S and DON'TS

First, any ambiguous statements, open-ended facts, or questionable phrases should be <u>avoided</u>. By claiming something that is open to interpretation, this can have an adverse effect causing the board to believe there is conflicting evidence about the candidate. Secondly, don't over do it by "puffing up" the candidate. Honesty and reporting what you know is the *simplest* and *best* way to help the board "see" who you are writing about. Less is best, and bullet comments get noticed.

Your support letter is a "snapshot" the board will read, so make it count with maximum effect showing the offender -- your "friend," "worker," "church member," "mentoree," etc. is ready for release and you have their back!

Bottom line: Does your letter state clearly the facts the parole board should know?

Prison Ministry In Covid America

Example of Actual Letter of Support (Names changed)
RICHARD DULLIS
Musician & Driver

Subject: MR. MARK C. CLARK, CHRISTIAN MENTOR
Date: February 19, 2018
To Whom it may Concern:

My name is Richard Dullis, and it is with immense pride that I share my story with you to confirm to all the true character of a great servant of Christ, Mr. Mark C. Clark, who I believe embodies what it means to be an *effective* Prison Minister and Mentor.

This is my story.

Thanks to Mark's help and personal involvement, I was able to survive and leave prison better than most prisoners. I was sent to prison for Second Degree Murder in the early 1990's when the prison "system" was very violent and corrupt. I struggled with the horrors of *prison life* badly, trusted few people, and my faith in God was dying. I needed a change.

Then, in 2006, I was sent to the Martian Colony Prison on Mars, where I met this man playing bass guitar in a church service. His name was Mark Clark, a former Navy Captain and jet pilot. (I didn't know at the time, but he was also a college graduate and was a trained counselor.) As a former musician, we connected immediately and even formed a prison Blues band and ended up working together in the prison kitchen.

Let me tell you that there is no finer and more loyal a friend than Mark. He would bend over backwards to help you, and his ability to accomplish things from behind bars is uncanny. I've watched him settle gang disputes, show compassion to inmates who were mentally, emotionally, or spiritually ill, and assist people with their parole, family, medical, and legal needs with amazing results. As a Christian myself, not only had Mark built up my character and attitude, but helped prepare me with encouragement and advice for life *after* prison.

FACT: With tears in my eyes, let me tell you that Mark – from prison – was the **only one** for a time providing me *financial* and moral support. (We had few sponsors in those days.) Upon release, Mark raised money for a cell phone for me and a post office box on Mars so I could find a job. When I was living in my car, he raised money for a partial car payment and even got a junk yard to donate a FREE tire to me when I had no spare. I was humbled to be restored with the help of Mark's mercy and kindness.

A Soul Winner.

Every prison ministry and church leader should honor this servant who has clearly "walked the walk" and still assists dozens of men – and women -- in and out of prison. Mark gave me hope, raised me up when I was down, and sacrificed much for me -- a poor sinner -- who was once fighting for my life when I was released from prison. Frankly, this letter doesn't cover one tenth of what Mark is doing while in prison and has accomplished for Christ. He is truly a *soul winner* and my hero whom I recommend for anything he needs because he makes a difference in saving people's lives.

Today, I am happily married, live in a house, and have a stable job; I owe much to Mark. I am proud to call him my brother and a true friend, and will always do so with love in my heart, especially in the phone calls and letters between us.

Please do not hesitate to call me anytime. I would be more than happy to share with you more works Mark has done in my life and for others.

Sincerely,

Richard Dullis
Mark's *Brother* for Life

Appendix 5
Re-Entry Tips, Ideas, and Facts (Note: Seeing your facility's Pre-Release Coordinator is a must for up-to-date policies, procedures, and tips for a Successful Release.)

Sample of a Board's Criteria for Release

COMMON SENSE PAROLE (Goal): "The fog of hatred causes the Victims and those that are Ignorant to reject the truth And not do what is right."

The following are factors that can be considered as mitigating or aggravating considerations which *may* be utilized in case decision-making by the board:

Mitigating Factors?	FACTORS THAT MAY BE CONSIDERED	Aggravating Factors?
	CIRCUMSTANCES SURROUNDING THE OFFENSE Role in crime (Leader, minor role) Bodily injury Use of deadly weapon Victim injury Multiple victims Vulnerability/ Cruelty to victims	
	AGE At time of crime Current age	
	PHYSICAL / MENTAL CAPACITY	
	VICTIM AND COMMUNITY INPUT	
	GOOD FAITH ATTEMPT TO COMPENSATE	
	ASSISTED THE AUTHORITIES	
	FEDERAL DETAINER	
	INSTITUTIONAL BEHAVIOR Either meritorious or disciplinary behaviors beyond those Identified in Section III: Institutional Behavior	
	VICTIM / COMMUNITY Support/ Opposition	
	OTHER, specify:	

Copied from a 208 Parole Board Guidelines   February 2018

From *The Maximum Times* 2019

Prison Ministry In Covid America

RE-ENTRY MYTH DE-BUNKED:
"YOU *CAN* LIVE ON $200 DOLLARS IN FOOD STAMPS"
By M. F. Maraschiello (2019)

Several people have said that they *can't* live on $200 worth of food stamps per month when they get out of prison. Baloney!

If you look at the cost of a fast food place like Burger King, McDonalds, or Wendy's you will see the average cost of a breakfast (egg muffin, coffee, hash browns), lunch (burger, fries, coke), and dinner (chicken sandwich, fries, coke) is $5.00 for each meal. That's $15.00 dollars per day or $450.00 a month and does not include salads, fruits, or large amounts of vegetables and other vitamin and mineral rich foods with fiber you need.

Now let's compare the food stamp purchase for $200.00 dollars and see what you can buy as of the September 1st, 2019 Labor Day Sale assuming you do your shopping on sale day with no coupons.

Below, are items randomly selected from the shopping section of the Labor Day sale at *Foodland, TN*:

Item	Price	Item	Price	Item	Price
Ketchup	1.50	Pineapple, 4 cans	5.00	Peas, 4 cans	3.50
Mustard	1.00	Peaches, 4 cans	5.00	Green Beans, 4 cans	3.50
Cereal, bag	6.00	Coffee	5.00	Ice Cream, gal	4.00
Tub Butter	3.50	Milk	7.00	P-nut Butter	2.00
Pickles	2.00	Orange Juice	4.00	Crackers	2.00
Onions	2.00	Lettuce	2.00	Soups, 5 cans	5.00
Salt/Pepper	2.00	Mayo	3.00	Ramen Noodles	6.00
Sugar	2.00	BBQ Sauce	1.00	Beef, ground	10.00
Cheese slices	4.00	Eggs	2.00	Kool-aid 12-pk	6.00
Potatoes	4.00	Sausage	4.00	Turkey meat	6.00
Hot Dogs	1.50	Jello, 2 boxes	2.00	Yams	2.00
Bread	4.00	Corn, 4 cans	3.50	Kidney Beans, 4 cans	3.50
Chicken	10.00	Chocolate	6.00	Apples	3.50
Rice	6.00	Bananas	2.00	Nuts	6.00
Pasta	6.00	Green Peppers	2.00	Frozen Veggies	8.00
Pie	6.00	Beans, 10 cans	9.00	Bacon	5.00

Total: $ 200.00 dollars (no taxes added)

No Comparison – you come out *better* with the $200.00 dollars spent at the supermarket. The Bottom Line is the smarter you shop will save you money and give your body the nutrition it needs. Today's prices are not like they used to be, and the way food is packaged and sold has changed with varying reasons for market prices to fluctuate, especially in different parts of the country where shipping to the market costs the greatest. Remember items like medications, cigarettes, liquor and others your food stamps can't be used.

Tips for the newly-released person going grocery shopping:
1. Make your purchases on sale days (you can save more money)
2. Know the manager, butcher, deli person who can give you news of upcoming sales
3. Go to the food pantry or food bank and get your <u>canned goods</u> **free** each month
4. Shop with a friend and split the larger "economy size" to save.
5. Buy foods you can make meals with and freeze to make meals for later eating
6. Go to the "discount stores" where damaged goods are or items missing labels.
7. If a can is dented, or the date has expired, ask the manager for a discount
8. Look for stores going out of business who liquidate their items quickly
9. Look for free deli samples. Sometimes leftovers are sold cheap or given away
10. Use Coupons or collected credits

ARTICLE ON INMATE'S JOB INTERVIEW ON RE-ENTRY

THE *REAL* JOB INTERVIEW and Thank You Letter

by M.F. Maraschiello (Legal Aide and former Commerical & Military Pilot)

What do I know about job interviews? Easy, **experience** – I hired over a *hundred* people, both men and women – and ex-offenders -- in my line of business with the military. And the bottom line is – **attitude and qualifications.** I hired people who could get the job done – period! My focus was on: Primary Experince and Trainability. I could feel and "test out" the prospect hire's character by the way they carried themselves before, during, and after the interview. Believe me, I even went so far as called their current job supervisors to find out what their co-workers thought of them. And in my line of work, *Aviation,* safety was the number one thing because you can't pull an aircraft over like a car, and hiring *competent* people was paramount.

THE INTERVIEW. Your interview is a reflection of you – your character, attitude, and ability to project confidence and capability. When you step out your home or apartment, you are who you are by your posture, speech, knowledge, and spirit. ALWAYS prepare for the interview starting at home. Know that everything from the people in the parking lot to the person standing at the reception desk could be your future boss or supervisor. From the minute you step out of your car you are under the microscope. EVERYONE is a potential source of information about you, especially what you do on camera, and say on the *internet.* Remember, **"K.I.S.S." Keep it simple stupid.** Don't complicate the simple, and don't simplify the complicated. Be prepared to justify what you did and said in your life because you "OWN" your past. Sometimes you may to be tested to see if you will <u>cave</u> to pressure, like being asked a situational question. Many "interviewees" fail these tests when told they don't have the *right* qualifications, so they just give up during the interview. Most employers want to hear what you "bring to the table," and want to see how you react and fight for the job by stating your strengths. Doing so could mean all the difference to an employer who is looking for someone who is assertive, confident, able to lead, trainable, and not fixated on self [pride] trying to be someone they are not. HONESTY is most important, and can make all the difference especially if the job will place you in charge of money and/or valuable equipment or lives.

Lastly, make sure before you leave the interview you have checked off in your mind all you wanted to get the interviewer to know, primarily what they will benefit by if they hired you. That is what they want to know, **bottom line.**

Before and After The Interview.
It pays to be Professional all the time.

Timing is everything, they say. Being on time, dressing right, posture, confident hand shake – and most of all to have EYE CONTACT which tells the job interviewer whether or not you are a responsible confident mature person they want to consider hiring or sending to the next level of the interview. Always give 100% whether you are told that the position is filled or not. You may be the one they really are looking for, and move the other person they hired before you to another job more suited for them.

Case in Point. This actually happened to me. I drove 60 miles for an interview to a job that was already filled for over two weeks. The position was a supervisory one for a job that had me manage over 150 people. I waited before the interview in the secretary's office, went in, then gave a 10-minute *desk-side* briefing with a 11x12 tablet portfolio of photos and documentation, and presented my brief relevant "sales pitch" based on actual experience he could see from the tablet. I walked him through each page where he could *visualize* his benefits and results to be the same **if** he hired me. Even though he told me the job was filled, I presented my facts so he could see that I was *more* qualified than the guy he hired 2 weeks previously, and that I needed no training. He saw me out to see his secretary, and I politely left my business card and resume' with her. I then moved out of her office to the waiting room. To my astonishment, while sitting there, I overheard the boss tell the secretary, "Hire this man (me), and call (name withheld) and tell him to call me." The next day, I received a call from the secretary who told me I got the job.

Lesson Learned: Standing out from the pack gets an employer's attention.

Post-Interview thank-you note. This is another "extra mile" that may pay dividends. It is always good to send a thank-you letter following a job interview. Today, that can be done via e-mail. The key is to follow-up, as some *start-up* companies are just collecting hiring and you may still be in the written, the thank-you letter – like interview using a tablet -- instantly candidates, many of whom don't zeal to want the job. Just a little stand out. Everyone you up letter. And make each one  pools of prospective candidates for running for one of those jobs. Well- the pitch with the desk-side sets you apart from other take the time to show initiative and extra effort on your part makes you interview with should get a follow- unique with questions because it shows the depth of your candidness and commitment to detail employers want to know.

What constitutes a well-written thank-you letter? Again, KISS. It should be short and to the point, use bullets, no more than one page. It is your opportunity to reiterate key points, reinforce your skill set, and remind them what you can do to benefit their company.

COMPOSITION. Three distinct sections: *the opening* (gratitude for the interview), *the middle* (your main points), and *the closing* (your follow-up action). Remember, the letter is another means to **share <u>additional</u> information and/or elaborate** on the best things discussed during the interview such as your skills, qualifications, achievements, awards, etc. which bolster the reason why they should select you out of the pack. Use the letter also to turn around anything that you perceived as negative out of the interview or incorrectly projected. Doing that could change the employer's mind knowing you are not afraid to admit mistakes and also fix them.

In the end, employers of businesses and companies with lots of employees want to hire people who have the right skills and experience, especially those enthusiastic about working for them. Writing a thank-you letter communicates to them that they were important enough for you to thank them for the chance to be hired. If you can do that, you sent them the message you are not an average person just looking for a job, but rather someone who is exceptional, professional, and eager to be hired above the pack.

For job resume' assistance, there are examples on-line or from a re-entry office.

Article from The Maximum Times 2018 on Job Interviewing
THE DREADED INTERVIEW QUESTION FOR *FELON* AT THE JOB INTERVIEW

Q. I see, here, you are an <u>*ex-felon*</u>. Can you tell me a little about it?

Yes. Regrettably (pause), I made a mistake ___ years ago. Since then, I transformed myself into a better and more humble man. I took classes such as Victim Impact, completed another college degree, and attend church regularly. Most of all, I've earned the respect of my sponsors and family who like the responsible man I am today.

Q. What was the *nature* of your crime?

Sadly (pause), I regretfully (took a man's / my wife's) life ___ years ago.

Q. What are your major strengths you can bring to our company?

I am noted by all my previous employers as trustworthy, on time, etc.

Q. If you were an animal, which one would you be?

An beaver. I am hardworking, I stay on the job at hand, etc.

Q. Tell me a little bit about your education?

I graduated from Deshaun High School with a 3.7 grade point, etc.

Q. Can you give me three good reasons why our company should take a chance on you being an ex-felon?

Absolutely. I have experience and you don't have to pay for training, I live close by, so in emergencies, you can call me off-hours, and my good letters of recommendation and past job history show that had it not been for my error, I was a reliable steady dependable producing worker.

HONESTY, INTEGRITY – CAN YOU DO THE JOB RESPONSIBLY – THAT'S WHAT THEY WANT TO KNOW. DO YOU WANT TO WORK GIVEN A SECOND CHANCE? SHOW THEM WHAT YOU CAN DO TO PROFIT THEM AND **WHY YOU SHOULD BE HIRED OVER EVERYONE ELSE. STAND OUT. LET THE INTERVIEWER KNOW "YOU ARE THE PERSON TO HIRE. THEY WANT TO HEAR YOU, SO SPEAK UP AND "SELL" YOURSELF.**

Sample Needs List for an Inmate leaving Jail/ Prison that could be circulated on-line, at your ministry, or organization

NEEDS LIST FOR RELEASED PRISONER

Inmate: Rick E. Ready (Age 42)   Date: _____
Former Gardner and construction worker.
City living in: Greenville, OK

Note: Please know that Rick has lost everything while in prison, and we hope to have people help him as he has humbled himself before God and turned his life around and now seeks to avoid homelessness.

RICK NEEDS HELP WITH THESE ITEMS

1. Money for Driver's License
2. Money to register & insure vehicle
3. 2 months rent + deposit ($2,200)
4. 60-days Health insurance
5. Gas and Food Debit Card
6. Sleeping bag, cot, thermos
7. Linen, towels, blanket
8. Eating items: Pots-n-pans, stove, etc.
9. Tools (cordless drill, box, etc.)
10. Clothes, shoes, etc. (work, casual, etc.)
11. Set-up "GOFUNDME" page for CAR)

NOTE: Rick will work for these items/ needs or make some type of financial plan, if necessary.

Rick's Goal: Find a good job, place to stay, and a good church and support group to continue being a law-abiding citizen.

Rick's JOB PLAN NO. 1: (Nashville, Tennessee) **HVAC Technician**
EMPLOYER: *AIRWORX*, 1925 Singalong Ave., Nashville, TN 37123, (615) 455-2222;
Supervisor/ Owner: Ready Freday

Rick's JOB PLAN NO. 2:   (Kentucky)   **Property Manager & Sales**

Michael Maraschiello

EMPLOYER: *INTERNATIONAL HOG CO.*, **(PIGLET FARM)**, P.O. BOX 316, Fair pRICE, NY 52010 (502)947-6666: **Supervisor/ Owner**: Farmer John Stone   e: Stone5@aol.com

WHY SUPPORT RICK?

1. He deserves a Second chance. (Rick is a 1st time offender)   6. **Honorably Discharged Veteran**
2. He has humbled himself and is remorseful
3. He has done a long time in prison
4. He has "life experiences: and a message to help vulnerable youth
5. Rick's Prison record: EXCELLENT – NON-VIOLENT

About Rick *"I have learned my lesson these past 12 years and made the changes to my character to be a productive law-abiding citizen once again. Please give me the chance to live in society and to positively contribute again, especially to those who need help – the vulnerable."*

So, please, let's help Rick reach his goal. Anything you contribute helps. Thank you.
TO HELP, CONTACT: **Dr. Do Wright** at: Dowright.do@org

An article on Preparing your Inmate for the Parole Board

R.M.S.I. LEGAL NEWS:
PREPARING FOR THE PAROLE HEARING:
Part I: "YOUR PAROLE FILE(S)"

By M. F. Maraschiello, RMSI Legal

THE BOARD PROCESS

The criteria for granting or denying parole is clearly spelled out in Chapter 1100-01-01 **Conduct of Board of Paroles Proceedings.** (SEE Tenn.Comp. R & Regs. 1100-01-01.07) The *process* of the board hearing is covered in 1100-01-01-.08. Simply put, the board is going to look at whatever information is on TOMIS, sent to them (e.g. electronically, hand-written, or verbal), and what's in the board's parole file on you.

ADDRESSING PREJUDICE, INACCURATE, AND *FALSE* INFORMATION

At least **SIX (6) MONTHS** before your parole hearing, you should have made a "Parole Packet," or obtained some parole preparation from your law library to put together your parole packet. Your home plan, job plan, mental health plan, etc. should all have been completed and available before you go to the board. Making a checklist of the things you need is critical to be ready for the board with a Parole Presentation Book in your arms to respond appropriately at the board.

Misleading and false information? You can begin by filling out a *Request to See Institutional File* and get with the IPO (Institutional Parole Officer) or Unit counselor to check it. You can request to see your parole file too. Both files should contain both FAVORABLE and unfavorable information about you that is correct. ** It is your responsibility to point out any discrepancies and try to get them corrected. Some of the necessary corrections are easy, such as making copies of missing educational and Victim Impact certificates and other documents showing that you completed courses and have obtained or have skills for rehabilitation and success for re-entry. Other problems might be more difficult, such as changing the P.S.I. (Pre-Sentence Investigation Report), which *may* take a court order. An example would be the PSI stating you committed rapes in other states; however, you didn't, and no state ever convicted or accused you. This error just suddenly appeared in your PSI and is now part of your TOMIS record. Such a problem would take something from the courts mailed to the TDOC CENTRAL RECORDS in order to change your TOMIS record. A lawyer may even have to be retained. Some changes, like record of missing GED certificates or DD-214 forms can be easily entered by your Education Department or your Unit Counselor with a certified copy from sources such as State Vital Records, Branches of the U.S. Military, or other certified recording agencies.

As for the surprises at the parole hearing, such as the hearing officer showing you something on TOMIS that you say is contrary to the truth, if you have a document or witness there, **_don't hesitate to show it_**. That's why planning ahead and making a Parole Presentation Book that you can carry to the board and even mail to the board prior to the hearing is a good idea.

Prison Ministry In Covid America

Just remember, no one from the State is paid to prepare you. That is why making certain that accurate information is provided to the board prior to the hearing. By doing so, you will be ready to address issues that come up. If the board knowingly is using FALSE or misleading data, that *may* be a ground for appeal.

Therefore, if you are "dressed for success" (ready for release), the board is going to see that _before_ the hearing. The pertinent and accurate information will be on TOMIS and the correct information and answers will be available for the hearing officer at your hearing. "Gee, I don't know," or "I don't have that plan ready," are the wrong responses at the hearing. If you think going to the board requires no effort on your part, just ask those who were denied parole and found out later that their institutional file was filled with prejudicial information and missing the correct data. **Facts are facts until new "facts" replace them.** And until the board sees something different, they are going to believe what they have in front of them about you.

SEE: Part II: "THE FACTS AND THE VICTIMS" in the next issue of the Maximum Times.

| Fall 2017 | 28 | *THE MAXIMUM TIMES* |

R.M.S.I. LEGAL NEWS:
PREPARING FOR THE PAROLE HEARING:
Part II: "THE FACTS AND THE VICTIM(S)"
By M. F. Maraschiello, RMSI Legal
THE BOARD PROCESS

As discussed in **Part I: "YOUR PAROLE FILE(S),"** the criteria for granting or denying parole is contained in Chapter 1100-01-01 **Conduct of Board of Paroles Proceedings.** (SEE Tenn.Comp. R & Regs. 1100-01-01.07) The *process* of the hearing is covered in 1100-01-01-.08. Simply put, the board is going to look at TOMIS information, what has been sent to them (e.g. electronically, hand-written, or verbal), and what the victim(s) and others say.

VICTIMS HAVE RIGHTS – AND HAVE YOU CHANGED?

First, anytime there is a victim involved (i.e. rape, murder, assault, etc.) the victim – or victim's advocate(s) -- have a *right* to speak; it's the law. (TN Const.Art. I, § 35; The Crime Victims' Rights Act of 2010) After all, they sustained an injury – a fact in your case the board wants to know about and its aftermath. Therefore, the way in which your *attitude* is presented at the board will either reflect that you are a changed person and remorseful, or the opposite. It is only to be expected that a victim who suffered pain and/or injury may be embittered by whatever an offender did to them or their loved one. Hopefully by the time you meet the parole board they have become *survivors*, and any hatred of you has decreased or gone away. (Some victims even forgive their offender(s) and become supporters.) Consider, now, some victims who don't support your release who are legitimately protestors. They can be expected to show-up at your board, send protest letters and DVD videos, and/or have representatives speak on their behalf. In this document, we will address **extreme** protestor actions from *other* sources (e.g. newspapers, TV, strangers, vigilante victim rights groups, hearsay testimony, etc.) which *can* negatively affect your parole, especially if they are exaggerating or spreading *false* information.

The following are just a few sources that may contain information that may prejudice you if not addressed or *corrected* prior to or at the hearing:

1. Paper or electronic recordings (i.e. E-MAILS) containing *FALSE* and/or *MISLEADING* questionable information about you such as: Court Opinions, transcripts of testimony, confessions, psychological records, law enforcement officer's note books or statements, etc.
2. Your **P.S.I. (Pre or Post-Sentence Investigation Report)** by the Probation Department which contains the State's "version" of who you are, your history, potential for rehabilitation, how the crime "went down," manner of death, your education, etc. which all then goes onto TOMIS and for the board to consider.
3. "Confidential" letters from the DA, the judge, the sheriff or police chief, the victim(s) (i.e. Victim Impact Statement), the Victim Coordinator, victim rights groups, and others which – most of the time – you never get to see.
4. Anything else negative entered onto TOMIS, such as Disciplinary write-ups or TOMIS "contact" notes.
5. Any other questionable sources brought to the attention of or looked at by the board.

IS JUSTICE FAIR RE-JUDGING YOU?

NOTE: YOU are being looked at electronically – and on paper -- before and at the hearing. And if the board is seeing **_FALSE_** information about you (For *Example:* Your P.S.I. says you had "2 prior felonies for rape") and all you are *really* in prison for is one (1) count of Burglary, the board is going to look at you MORE **negatively** and most likely – due to the prejudicial false information – deny you parole because you appear to be not only a burglar, but also a rapist, even if you have NO conviction and never raped anyone. And if a victim is there who says things that are false, you may be in even worse shape. Calling the victim a "liar" or becoming hostile is not the approach to take. If you did your homework and prepared your *Parole Presentation Book*, respond appropriately and humbly disagree – nicely. If you have a *rebuttal* document or witness there, offer them to the board. **DO NOT** argue with the victim! Your parole hinges on many aspects including your empathy and attitude towards the victim. Some victim's memories fade over time. Regardless, they still deserve and should be given respect. After all, you caused them to be victims.

So, remember, **parole is a privilege, not a right**. And the parole board has a *duty* to protect the public, consider the needs of the prisoner – by due process, and look at the overall changes, rehabilitation, and merits of the prisoner and their prison record. Bias and prejudice are not supposed to be a part of any hearing, and the board can consider anything to help it decide.

An article on the Parole Board and Parole Procedure

PAROLE "THE PLAIN TRUTH"
(In a Nutshell)
By M. F. Maraschiello (2018)

Disclaimer: This information compiled at the time of writing this guide is subject to change based on new rules, policies, procedures, cultural, moral, and legal shifts in attitudes and manner towards parole. This is a general and basic look at parole based on the time this material was collectively assembled, and may or may not contain and/or answer all categories of questions or subject matter pertaining to the entire scope of parole and the affected disciplines of penology, criminology, sociology, psychology, theology, and any other field of study related thereof.

CONTENTS and CREDITS

- **Introduction**
- **Articles:** "**Preparing for the Parole Hearing**" Part I: Your Parole File(s) and Part II: The Facts and the Victim(s), M. F. Maraschiello (*Maximum Times*, 2018); "**How Parole Boards Keep Prisoners in the Dark and Behind Bars**", Beth Schwartzapfel, (The Marshall Project, March 2017); "**Pardon Me**": How Executive Clemency Works in Tennessee (and How It Doesn't), Benjamin K. Raybin, (Tennessee Bar Journal, Vol. 52, August 2016); "**Wrongfully Imprisoned Man Awarded $1M**" by Andy Humbles (Tennessean March 27, 2018); "**Nashville Judge Strikes Down Law That Has Revoked Thousands of Tennessee Driver's Licenses**" (NPR Radio, July 2018); "Power of Parole," The intricacies Behind the American Presidency's most Imperial Perquisite, by Joseph Connor (April 2018); and "**One Case Reveals Flaws in Parole System**" by Stacey Barchenger (The Tennessean, September 26, 2017)

    - Policies Affecting Prisons and Parole
    - Procedures Affecting Prisons and Parole
    - Rules Affecting Prisons and Parole
        This section also includes:
        - Common Sense Parole: Parole Board Guidelines List (February 2018)
        - Form to Request Audio CD of I/M's Parole Board Hearing
        - Form to Appeal a Parole Board's Decision
        - Address to Send all information and packets to Board of Parole Operations

Note: For more information about parole and how to help an inmate, you can search the internet or go to other sources for additional materials.

INTRODUCTION

This section comprises several different perspectives and attitudes towards the concept of and administration and application of parole, especially for the Tennessee prisoner, of whom this guidebook generally will be the focus group as applied to church prison ministry sponsors, mentors, and volunteers. To avoid the perception of bias or prejudice in the making of this guidebook, the authors decided not to delve into many of the specific case legal *precedence* because the objective of the guidebook is to assist the prison minister to have an *understanding* of parole as it relates to their theological duties, attitude, and responsibilities they assume rather than the guidebook taking on the appearance of "recruiting" the prison minister to be a purely **pro-parole** supporter or *advocate* for parole.

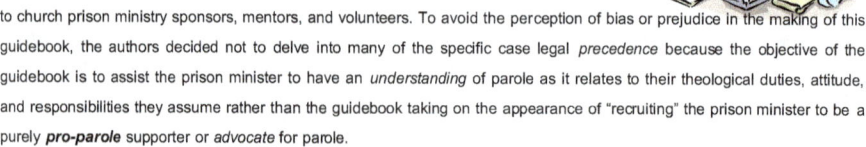

Cont.

Cont.

Wherefore, these policies, procedures, and laws in this section are not the focus of attention, but rather just the "plain truth" for the informed church minister to know what the prisoner, his family, the victim, and the process of the board encompass, and, perhaps, for the church minister, sponsor, or mentor to be of assistance in the process. After all, these laws, policies, and rules are – have been – *officially* approved and written to be implemented and utilized for parole. And the **way** they are used or "interpreted," even a theologian who studied Biblical exegesis can tell you, it is the way they were written and by whom and for what purpose which can be a source of public contention. Laws, policies, procedures, and rules can also be interpreted *differently* and applied as such into un-just or un-intended "practices", especially if they are *void* of specifics and *vague* leaving the subject matter for parole open to interpretation and liberal application or *usurpation* of the law which could be different than the original legislators on Capitol Hill had intended parole was and is to be administered.

Ergo, the parole board -- an *administrative* body – which has been given the authority to administer by the legislature – *legislative* body, could, theoretically, interpret the law and create its own "style" of parole, not as the legislature voted into law. In all states, on many issues, laws enacted by legislatures begin with good intentions, until some time down the road, attitudes of the administrators governing the law with the authority to carry them out, pervert the law into something else, not exactly as the lawmakers intended the law to be. And the law that has been perverted -- if not brought to the legislature for correction – stays on the books, it could have monumental and fatal prejudice denying rights to persons or injustices affecting life and or liberty, as in the case of parole.

So, in conclusion, it is incumbent on the religious church sponsors, mentors, ministers, and religious leaders to be aware of what may or may not be affecting or at stake with the prisoner(s) they encounter and encourage to seek God for guidance in life. Without a doubt, heavily on a prisoner's mind is his or her freedom, which is either the first or second-most important thing they ponder. A prisoner with many years in prison who is in need of help for parole consideration takes on a greater need for understanding and what needs have to be met for the prisoner to maintain the hope, than a prisoner leaving prison in just a few months or years. For many Godly volunteers, it is crucial to show prisoners that they are not forgotten, that they have a God that loves them and will not forsake them, and that it is the involved volunteer sponsor or mentor that fills the prisoner's heart with that hope that God has for them. Prisoners can SEE God in the level of care their church ministry provides them.

CAVEAT. Simply put, the prisoner *knows* his shepherd by the **way** he is cared for. Giving a Bible, Koran, or Torah to a prisoner with no love behind it, is like giving a *toothbrush* to a prisoner who needs a pair of shoes. Parole -- probably **the single most** important *earthly* concern for a prisoner, second to faith in God, must be familiar to serious church volunteers whose audience or influence parole will affect. EVERY church has a spiritual and civic duty to assist in the community those marginalized (i.e. prisoners, homeless, the sick, the poor, etc.). Christ didn't put labels on the *least ones*, nor did he tell people to quit and give up or do nothing for criminals. In fact, it was a criminal on the cross who Jesus last ministered to that was the focus before HE died. Not pleading to kings, but to the lowest. And for the redeemed criminal, his reward was paradise. The message was clear, then: People can change. Jesus knew it, and so should we. That is why PAROLE is such a controversial aspect of life in societies. The way our God wants our people treated – and protected – is different from mans approach. Restorative justice seeks release as early as possible over retributive justice that seeks mass incarceration and no mercy -- no release. However it seems, it is always the prisoner who gets the scraps after the dogs have eaten.

Benjamin Franklin said of prisons, "A man not behind the plow takes away from the community." Franklin – one of the first American penal system architects – advocated SHORT sentences and get the errant back to his farm, quickly, so it would not fall into ruin nor his family fall into social poverty. This made the community healthy, and kept families in tact so, primarily, the children did not fall victim to illiteracy and the wives to divorce and/or social vice to survive after losing the farm and having no place to stay. (That idea, however, is lost in America today. That is why lawmakers, community leaders and church leaders have to be involved, for the community welfare.)

end

List of Federal & State recognized parole/ clemency points

Note: This list is not all inclusive, and may have updates not available at the time of this publication.

SOME CLEMENCY / PAROLE/ PARDON POINTS

1. Deserve 2nd Chance? (Have family and community support for release?)
    a. Rehabilitated? (Drug, AA, Anger Management)
    b. Took Self-improvement Course(s)? (CMS, GED, College, Barber, PNB, etc.)
    c. Low or No Disciplinary Record?
    d. Victim Impact? (Remorseful – show responsibility for your actions)
2. 1st Time Offender?
3. Public Service (or Military) *before* Incarceration? (Fireman, EMT, Social Worker, Teacher, etc.)
4. Spent a lot of time in prison already? (Over *10 years*)
5. You were *less* culpable than others with the same offense? (Didn't commit crime for "gain" or without "passion". (e.g. accident, youth led astray by adult, etc.)
6. Humanitarian Service? (e.g. Founded a Charity, donate time/ resources to mentally-ill, teach people how to read, etc.)
7. Victimless Crime (i.e. D.U.I., Possession of Drugs, Trespassing, etc.)

NOTE: These, above, are not only what you should limit yourself to.
The *"merits"* of what your have accomplished are your focus.
Everything *"good"* counts. The fact you *"changed"* is key.

> You are *not* the same person you were years ago; be proud.

"When the legend becomes fact.... print the legend." --- Editor's Motto

(Meaning, if you want the "perception" of WHO people believe you are to change, you are going to have to change to show people you've "changed". Then, "the legend" (perception) of who you *were* will change because the FACTS have changed. "Change" does not come unless you go into action. You must change those facts to convince others you are no-longer that person "of the past" who was arrested, as your judgment sheet or State's Opinion" says (describes) you as.)

Continued.

Continued.

Taken from News: July 26, 2018

NASHVILLE – GOV. HASLAM GRANTS CLEMENCY TO FOUR TENNESSEANS

"These individuals have distinguished themselves in both their rehabilitation and their contributions to the community," Gov. Bill Haslam said. "After thoughtfully considering the circumstances of each of their cases, I believe exercising the executive clemency power will help further these individuals' positive influence on their communities and the lives of their fellow Tennesseans."

BELOW ARE SOME TIPS FROM THE ABOVE REDACTED ARTICLE

Positive "Phrases" described for granting of clemency / commutation were:

10. distinguished themselves through rehabilitation
11. distinguished themselves through contributions to society
12. distinguished themselves through contributions to the community
13. distinguished themselves through personal growth programs

Meritorious acts and achievements for granting of clemency / commutation were:

1. distinguished themselves through obtaining higher education of a college degree
2. distinguished themselves through mentorship of others (i.e. inmates, youth, etc.)
3. Served as a mentor and leader to other inmates
4. Earned the respect and support of both prison officials and numerous community leaders and organizations
5. Personifies Model Inmate

Other information or acts for granting of clemency / commutation were:

12. Served large (extended) number of years in prison
13. Less culpable than others for the same crime
14. Over age 70 (Federal criteria)

15. Held jobs that attested to clemency candidate's character and community/ society contributions
16. Military Service – Honorable
17. Accepted responsibility for the crime, speaking out about *reforming* one's self
18. Awards, certificates, etc. for distinction
19. Letters of character
20. Transformed – "changed" -- self into a new person
21. Medical Condition (e.g. terminal illness, blind, amputee, etc.)
22. "Release will help further these individuals' positive influence on their communities and the lives of their fellow Tennesseans." – Gov. Bill Haslam

NOTE: Clemency is at the grace and mercy of the governor. The governor, as recommended by the parole board, can perform either a Full Pardon, commutation or exoneration in some form. Further, these reasons, above, are not limited, as there are other reasons for recommending clemency be granted.

A list of items needed upon re-entry from prison (male)

These are items your group, church, family, or volunteers can resource and have ready upon release. The goal is to outfit people re-entering society with the basics so they can enter the work force quickly. Money they make has to go for transportation, registration of driver licenses, and other costs including telecom phone and other money to function in today's electronic society.

TOP ITEMS NEEDED UPON RELEASE FROM PRISON CHECKLIST

Release Date: _____
NAME: _____ DOC# _____
AGE: ____ Height: _____ Weight _____ Waist: _____ Length _____
Shirts: <u>L-M-S</u>   Jackets: <u>L-M-S</u>   Shoes: _____

(Check if received)

1. Two (2) pair of casual slacks, Khaki
2. Two (2) knit casual shirts, short sleeve (Any color)
3. One pair casual/ dress shoes, Brown
4. One jacket, Wind Breaker
5. One jacket, Medium, Fall-Type
6. One pair gloves, winter
7. One Umbrella
8. One Rain Coat
9. One flashlight
10 One LEATHERMAN TOOL
11 One DUFFLE BAG/ COLLAPSIBLE SUITCASE
12 One TOOL BAG OR BOX
13 One SET POTS-N-PANS
14 One Laundry Basket/ Bag
15 One Sleeping Bag
16 One Coffee Thermos

17 One Alarm clock
18 One Pillow
19 Two Sets: Bed sheets and one (1) blanket
20 One cot
21 _____
22 _____
23 _____
24 _____
25 _____

                                                                                                   End

Note: This is just a basic list and not an all-inclusive one.

A list of items needed upon re-entry from prison (female)

These are items your group, church, family, or volunteers can resource and have ready upon release. The goal is to outfit people re-entering society with the basics so they can enter the work force quickly. Money they make has to go for transportation, registration of driver licenses, and other costs including telecom phone and other money to function in today's electronic society.

TOP ITEMS NEEDED UPON RELEASE FROM PRISON CHECKLIST

Release Date: _____
NAME: _____ DOC# _____
AGE: ____ Height: _____ Weight _____ Waist: _____ Length _____
Shirts: <u>L-M-S</u>   Jackets: <u>L-M-S</u>   Shoes: _____

                                                                                         (Check if received)

10. Two (2) pair of casual slacks, Khaki
11. Two (2) knit casual shirts, short sleeve (Any color)
12. One pair casual/ dress shoes, Brown
13. One jacket, Wind Breaker
14. One jacket, Medium, Fall-Type
15. One pair gloves, winter
16. One Umbrella
17. One Rain Coat
18. One flashlight
10 One LEATHERMAN TOOL
11 One DUFFLE BAG/ COLLAPSIBLE SUITCASE
12 One curling iron
13 One SET POTS-N-PANS
14 One Laundry Basket/ Bag
15 One Sleeping Bag
16 One Coffee Thermos
17 One Alarm clock

18 One Pillow
19 Two Sets: Bed sheets and one (1) blanket
20 One cot
21 One purse
22 cosmetic bag
23 feminine personal container
24 make-up kit
25 _____

                                                                   End

Note: This is just a basic list and not an all-inclusive one.

Article on Address Prejudice at Parole Hearings

HOW TO ADDRESS *PREJUDICIAL* PROTEST SOURCES BEFORE AND AT THE PAROLE HEARING
By M. F. Maraschiello, RMSI Legal Aide (2017)

First, anytime there is a victim involved (i.e. rape, murder, assault, etc.) the victim has a **right** to protest because of the injury sustained to them. The way in which your *attitude* is presented at the board will either reflect that you are a changed person and remorseful, or the opposite. It is only to be expected that a victim who suffered pain and/or injury may be embittered by whatever an offender did to them or their loved one. Hopefully by the time you meet the board they have become "survivors," and any hatred of you has dwindled or gone away. (Some victims even forgive the offender.)

Those victims in the category, above, are legitimately protestors, and can be expected to show-up, send letters, or have representatives speak on their behalf. In this document, we will address protestor actions from other sources (e.g. newspapers, TV, strangers, vindictive victim rights groups, hearsay testimony, etc.) which *can* negatively affect your parole.

The following are just a few sources that may contain information that may prejudice you if not addressed or *corrected* prior to your parole hearing:

6. Paper or electronic recordings (i.e. E-MAILS) containing *FALSE* and/or *MISLEADING* information about you such as: Court Opinions, transcripts of testimony, confessions, psychological records, law enforcement officer's note books or statements, etc.
7. Your **P.S.I. (Pre or Post-Sentence Investigation Report)** by the Probation Department which contains the state's "version" of who you are, your history, potential for rehabilitation, how the crime "went down," manner of death, your education, etc. which all then goes onto TOMIS and for the board to potentially look at.
8. "Confidential" letters from the DA, the judge, the sheriff or police chief, the victim(s) (i.e. Victim Impact Statement), and the Victim Coordinator, victim rights groups, and others.
9. Anything entered onto TOMIS, such as Disciplinary write-ups or TOMIS "contact" notes.
10. Any other sources brought to the attention of or looked at by the board.

NOTE that YOU are being looked at electronically and/or on paper before you go to the hearing. And if the board is seeing **_FALSE_** information about you (For *Example:* Your P.S.I. says you had "2 prior felonies for rape") and all you are *really* in prison for is one (1) count of Burglary, the board is going to look at you MORE negatively and most likely – due to the prejudicial false information – deny you parole because you appear to be not only a burglar, but a rapist, even if you have NO conviction and never raped anyone.

Continued.

SO, HOW DO I MAKE SURE THE BOARD HAS THE RIGHT FACTS? AND HOW DO I RESPOND TO ANY FALSEHOODS OR PROTESTS AT THE BOARD?

Continued.

   You can begin by making sure **before** your board (6 months out) that you get with the IPO (Institutional Parole Officer) and ask to see your *Parole File*. Your file should contain both FAVORABLE and unfavorable information about you that is CORRECT. ** It is YOUR RESPONSIBILITY to point out any discrepancies and try to get them corrected. Some of the corrections are easy, like making copies of missing educational and Victim Impact certificates and other documents showing you completed courses and have obtained or have skills for rehabilitation and success for re-entry. Other problems might be more difficult, such as changing the P.S.I., which *may* take a court order, such as the example, above, to remove the 2 rape counts from the P.S.I. which would them go to TDOC RECORDS downtown to be changed on the TOMIS computer system. Some changes, like H.S. diploma, can be entered by your Education Department or your Unit Counselor who would have to have a certified copy from a source like State Vital Records or military DD-214 Service Certificate.

   As for surprises at the parole hearing, such as the hearing officer showing you something on TOMIS that you say is contrary to the truth, if you have a document or witness there, don't hesitate to show it. That's why planning ahead with a Parole Presentation Book that you can carry to the board and even mail to the board prior to the hearing is a good idea.

   Just remember, the state pays for a Victim Coordinator to assist the victim; that's there job. No one is paid to prepare you. That is why making sure ACCURATE information is provided to the board, so that you are ready to address issues that come up. Your attitude is key. If you are "dressed for success" (are ready for release), the board is going to see that **_before_** the hearing because the information is on TOMIS. But if you think going to the board requires no effort on your part, just ask those – and we've all talked to them – who were denied parole, and found out later that their parole file was filled with prejudicial stuff and missing all good stuff about you. Facts are facts. And until the board sees something different on the TOMIS screen or in your file, they are going to believe what they have about you.

> The "bottom line" is you must be humble – period. YOU – the offender – "did it," and there is no one in the room else to blame. YOU are it, so be careful what you say. Even if you were attacked, or the person you hurt started it – they are the victim to the board, **not you**. You can only talk about your transformation into a person that is law-abiding and ready for return to society. That is what counts most – you, and your apology for what you did. Stick to that and you are doing what they and society expect you to do – OWN UP to your crime – period, by taking responsibility.
>
> End.

Here are some examples of actual Supporters and Inmate's statements and notes for Speaking at the Parole Hearing:

Sample 3 X 5 Card for Parole Candidate to take to the board

PAROLE BOARD NOTES — "Focus on the prize" (K.I.S.S.)
<u>Keep It Simple Stupid</u> – **Show You Changed – No Threat**
<u>No#1 Best Approach</u>: Have a *POSITIVE* ATTITUDE.
1) I'm not just changed; I am transformed. (I am Humble.)
2) I've learned what anger is. It's insidious nature.
3) I understand how communication heals – THRU FORGIVENESS
4) I've surrounded myself with people who care about me: <u>Victim Impact</u>
5) I'm sorry for what I have done; I follow the rules.
6) If you see fit to give me your vote, I assure you I won't let you down.
NOT KILLED FOR PROFIT. Not intentionally abused, etc.
- PAUSE PAUSE PAUSE! Between answers and questions.
- SNAPPED? – SAFETY Issue? PASSION Crime? Provoked?
- Job related responsibilities?
- (If kids) A FATHER'S JOB: TAKE CARE OF HIS CHILDREN
- A HUSBAND'S JOB IS TO TAKE CARE OF HIS WIFE & FAMILY

OTHER

<u>On Reverse, Inmate can make a specific note(s) about their crime.</u>

(On The Crime of Passion (Explanation, Spousal)

"Motherhood and fatherhood are gifts. However, she blew it and I blew it as parents with our disabilities and didn't think of what is best for the children -- let the courts decide. I chose the "lesser of 2 evils" to do something rather than nothing to protect my daughters. In war, we destroy so others could live, and to protect others who couldn't defend themselves."

NOTES ON PAROLE BOARD
AUGUST 2018

An Actual Typical Hearing that was "Squared Away." Result: *Granted* Parole

Board. Asked canned background questions, then made comments board looks at staff & free-world letters

Character Witnesses for inmate going up for parole: Family, Mentor, Church, Law Enforcement

SOME CHARACTER WITNESS STATEMENTS MADE AT THE BOARD:

"He's my spiritual father, consistently showing me the right example of how to live."

"He's not an inmate. He lives like a confident and successful *free person*, serving others while in prison."

"He's more than ready to be discharged, having completed every course or classes while in prison."

"He is going to make a great impact on society at our church, and has a great story to tell."

"He is consistent, never angry. He accepted his circumstances & I admire him for the changes he's made."

"I can vouch for his good character and friendship he builds; he's surely proved his remorse to me."

"I'm his mentor since 2009. We play music at church services where he sings and plays guitar."

"We are ready to see him out, and he has a job waiting with us. That's the power of God."

"He is the "real deal" of a mature man who admits his faults, fixed his life, and is ready to continue to do good things when released."

"I represent a church of over 12,000. There is an ARMY of people around him to hold him up."

I'm an ex-police officer and I dealt with numerous men and women who broke the law. I recognized change when I see it in people who made mistakes and recover their lives."

"He is a leader and servant for Jesus Christ, now, who helps others, and will help many more to make our communities better."

NOTE: Not one witness spoke about *victim rights* or the *offense* in this particular case. The board member did, and the statement made by the inmate was less than 2 minutes long – right to the point about being remorseful, learning a lesson, transforming himself, and that release is a privilege not a right, concluding by thanking the board for the opportunity to be considered. (The inmate plead guilty to the crime of attempted murder, shooting a man who raped his daughter.)

NOTES ON PAROLE BOARD
AUGUST 2018

An Actual Typical Hearing that was
"Squared Away." Result: *Granted* Parole

Board. Asked canned background questions, then made comments board looks at staff & free-world letters

Character Witnesses for inmate going up for parole: Family, Mentor, Church, Law Enforcement

<u>SOME CHARACTER WITNESS STATEMENTS MADE AT THE BOARD:</u>

"He's my spiritual father, consistently showing me the right example of how to live."

"He's not an inmate. He lives like a confident and successful *free person*, serving others while in prison."

"He's more than ready to be discharged, having completed every course or classes while in prison."

"He is going to make a great impact on society at our church, and has a great story to tell."

"He is consistent, never angry. He accepted his circumstances & I admire him for the changes he's made."

"I can vouch for his good character and friendship he builds; he's surely proved his remorse to me."

"I'm his mentor since 2009. We play music at church services where he sings and plays guitar."

"We are ready to see him out, and he has a job waiting with us. That's the power of God."

"He is the "real deal" of a mature man who admits his faults, fixed his life, and is ready to continue to do good things when released."

"I represent a church of over 12,000. There is an ARMY of people around him to hold him up."

I'm an ex-police officer and I dealt with numerous men and women who broke the law. I recognized change when I see it in people who made mistakes and recover their lives."

"He is a leader and servant for Jesus Christ, now, who helps others, and will help many more to make our communities better."

NOTE: Not one witness spoke about *victim rights* or the *offense* in this particular case. The board member did, and the statement made by the inmate was less than 2 minutes long – right to the point about being remorseful, learning a lesson, transforming himself, and that release is a privilege not a right, concluding by thanking the board for the opportunity to be considered. (The inmate plead guilty to the crime of attempted murder, shooting a man who raped his daughter.)

Prison Ministry In Covid America

SOME CLEMENCY / PAROLE/ PARDON POINTS

1. **Deserve 2nd Chance?** (Have family and community support for release?)
    a. Rehabilitated? (Drug, AA, Anger Management)
    b. Took Self-improvement Course(s)? (CMS, GED, College, Barber, PNB, etc.)
    c. Low or No Disciplinary Record?
    d. Victim Impact? (Remorseful – show responsibility for your actions)

2. **1st Time Offender?**

3. **Public Service (or Military) *before* Incarceration?** (Fireman, EMT, Social Worker, Teacher, etc.)

4. **Spent a lot of time in prison already?** (Over *10 years*)

5. **You were *less* culpable than others with the same offense?** (Didn't commit crime for "gain" or without "passion". (e.g. accident, youth led astray by adult, etc.)

6. **Humanitarian Service?** (e.g. Founded a Charity, donate time/ resources to mentally-ill, teach people how to read, etc.)

7. **Victimless Crime** (i.e. D.U.I., Possession of Drugs, Trespassing, etc.)

NOTE: These, above, are not only what you should limit yourself to. The *"merits"* of what your have accomplished are your focus. Everything *"good"* counts. The fact you *"changed"* is key. You are *not* the same person you were years ago; be proud.

"When the legend becomes fact.... print the legend."   --- Editor's Motto
(Meaning, if you want the "perception" of WHO people believe you are to change, you are going to have to change to show people you've "changed". Then, "the legend" (perception) of who you *were* will change because the *FACTS* have changed. "Change" does not come unless you go into action. You must change those facts to convince others you are no-longer that person "of the past" who was arrested, as your judgment sheet or State's Opinion" says (describes) you as.)

Michael Maraschiello

"HIGHLIGHTS" of
ACTUAL PAROLE HEARING DECISION:
Immediate Release – "Granted"

Facts:

Offense: 1ˢᵗ Degree Felony Murder
Not "1ˢᵗ time offender"
Was not the "trigger man"
Had 11 write-ups on Disciplinary Record (No Class "A" offenses)
Only had a G.E.D. education but 3 college courses
** Hearing board member was a woman

Pled Guilty. Did 24+ years in prison.
Was on probation at the time.
Had *no* "CMS" class or "Psych" eval
Had mental illness history
Not a military veteran

- No victim's family, victim's rights group, DA, or sheriff showed up at hearing
- No letters of protest from DA or sheriff, only 4 letters from victim's family
- Had three (3) __seasoned__ advocate "supporters" speak on inmate's (I/M) behalf say all the right stuff and NOT talking about the victim
- I/M's sister (speaker No. 4) spoke on "family" wanting I/M him out as soon as possible
- I/M turned in Parole packet (completed courses, support letters, etc.) which were "scanned in" by IPO and sent to the board
- Board member made very good eye contact with all supporters and I/M showing listening and asked them all questions.
- ALL supporters stood when speaking; I/M never got out of the chair
- Supporters focused on I/M "changes" he made in his life
- I/M was asked, **"Did you plead guilty, or were you convicted?"** I/M stated that the board member felt I/M was less culpable than others in the crime to include stating the member "felt" that the I/M was not represented by a good lawyer.
- I/M's opening statement was he understood parole was not a right, but that he didn't kill the victim, but rather he was "guilty" because of his "part."
- Supporters nor I/M talked about the aspect of the crime.
- I/M focused his statement further on the changes he made in his life and to help others when out
- I/M felt most worried at the hearing when the board member asked about his past criminal history and prison disciplinary record.
- NO MENTION OR QUESTIONS WERE MADE AT THE BOARD AT ALL ABOUT "MENTAL HEALTH"
- NO MENTION OR QUESTIONS WERE MADE AT THE BOARD AT ALL ABOUT "PHYSICAL HEALTH"
- I/M WAS ASKED the question, "**DID YOU TRY TO REACH OUT TO THE VICTIMS?**" I/M responded, "I tried to reach out, but I was scared and didn't know how." One of the supporters then stood up and stated the I/M contacted her years ago, and that it was "ADVISED" he wait for the victims to contact him which was a recommended procedure some victim impact studies had shown." The board then responded positively that at least the I/M __DID__ try to reach out.

TAKEAWAY: Make sure your supporters cover IN-DEPTH all the "major" topics: Victim Impact, you are changed and on a new path in life, supporters want you out, job plan, home plan, etc., and don't bring up the aspects of the crime unless the board asks. __DO NOT__ "VOLUNTEER" INFORMATION – PERIOD!

Prison Ministry In Covid America

AUDIO TRANSCRIPT OF 2019
FIRST DEGREE MURDER PAROLE HEARING
(4-Member Votes needed for Parole)

Hearing officer read the ARREST REPORT, and read the REVIEW FILE before coming and will add things to the file, if necessary.

SOME SIGNIFICANT QUESTIONS TO PAROLE CANDIDATE:
WHO WAS THE VIC? HOW DID YOU KNOW THE VIC? WHY DID YOU _____ (DO WHAT YOU DID)?
"I WAS HORRIFIED WITH WHAT I READ... IMAGINE THE VICTIM ....."
BECAUSE YOU THOUGHT LIKE THAT, YOU MURDERED?
DID YOU KNOW _____ HAD A KNIFE?
SO, WAS IT A RANDOM KILLING?
THE VICTIM WAS AN ONLY CHILD. DID YOU KNOW HIS MOTHER WAS NOTIFIED ON "MOTHER'S DAY?"
WERE YOU A MEMBER OF A GANG?
LOOKING AT YOUR HISTORY, YOU WERE A JUVENILE OFFENDER?
THIS WAS NOT THE FIRST TIME YOU COMMITTED CRIMES, RIGHT?
WHY DID YOU DO THESE OTHERS CRIMES?
YOU DROPPED OUT OF HIGH SCHOOL, WHY?
YOUR EMPLOYMENT BEFORE COMING TO PRISON WAS WHAT?
ARE YOU A GANG MEMBER?
CAN YOU DESCRIBE YOUR JOB IN THE TDOC?
HOW DO YOU LIKE....IN THE TDOC? (RUNNING THROUGH YOUR LIST OF COURSES ON TOMIS.)
YOU HAD NO WRITE UPS SINCE....., IS THAT CORRECT?
**HAVE YOU HAD ANY CONTACT WITH THE VICTIM SINCE THIS OCCURRED?
DID YOU WRITE THEM AND TELL THEM YOU WERE SORRY?**
(READING FROM A *CONTACT* NOTE): WHY WERE YOU FIRED FROM YOUR JOB AT TRICOR?
YOU HAVE FOUR (4) LETTERS OF OPPOSITION; LOTS OF SUPPORT LETTERS.

PAROLE SUPPORTERS
BOARD MEMBER: "PLEASE DON'T ALL OF YOU SPEAK OR REPEAT ABOUT THE SAME THINGS."

SUPPORTER 1. (TPOM MENTOR)
"Good morning. My name is _____, and I have only known _____ for nine (9) years. I can only speak for myself and can't speak for his past, but from that of a friend and a brother in Christ. Can I begin? I was in high school when _____ was born. I graduated in 1973. That being said, I feel as though am an older brother almost like a dad when we set down and discuss things. I call _____ a "gentle giant." I was pretty intimidated when the first time that I met him because of his physical size. During that short period of time that his (unreadable) and love for god supersedes that body, that size. Again, I'm a college football fan; I follow the University of Tennessee that right away I found out we had in common. I found that _____ is an insatiable reader. Any materials, history, religion, whatever if might be, I don't know, I've sent archaeological magazines – he loves to study as with continual Scriptures. He loves God, he loves Jesus Christ, he loves his family, his sister _____, and his mother. He wears his mother's picture around his neck; I noticed that right away. In the time that I have mentored _____, he's always been eager to study God's word, and that's our primary focus with Tennessee Prison Outreach Ministry that's been associated with the churches of Christ... to study God's word and see how we can encourage while we're here. He's very familiar with God's word, the Scriptures, he can easily find references that we study together. Each time we study, he sees a new application for his life and what it means to him moving forward. I always heard, in my life, that a person is known by the ones that he associates with, whether it be family or friends that, that is what his character is about. And his cellmate, know as "Fish," speaks very highly of _____. As a matter of fact, he says he has many words of adoration for him, as do many others. In the future, if _____ is granted parole, he wishes to help others in the health care industry he has shown he is willing to do any task, here, in the prison. I know he works at times cleaning tiles, the grout and tiles in the showers. _____ is willing to do anything to serve. His kindness was shown to me, personally, and to my grandchildren this last Christmas; he's very creative and likes to make bears. And likes to sew bears, out of socks. He made three of those for my small grandchildren which I watched him make. In closing, if paroled, I think _____ being a feeling caring person that is willing to serve others in any capacity if elected. Thank you."

SUPPORTER 2. (LAWYER/ FORMER CHAPLAIN)
"Good morning". My name is _____, and I was David's chaplain, here, for about five (5) years. I have know him for a total, now, of nine (9) years at this point. Your accounting of _____'s past, what I'm hearing being recounted are so many stories that I've known from here, being on the inside, and that's the story of really dumb young kids getting into trouble doing things that are destructive and harmful. And that was _____'s past. But, there's also a person who never planned a murder, never once killed anybody.
Well, one of the things that I learned being on the inside, here, working with people and talking with people is how quickly things (unaudible) out. That story didn't have a plan. And that's the situation he's now found himself in.
All I can tell you about is the David that I know. His nickname here is presumed is "Fluffy." He's a big guy and he's a big fluffy *soft* guy. One of the things that struck me about immediately about him is how incredibly sensitive he is, emotionally sensitive ... caring. I was just picturing right now about the story about him sewing teddy bears for the grandchildren. He used to sew "angel dolls" for my office. The stole I still wear today is one that he made; it was hand-made. He came up often, probably weekly, for pastoral counseling and I can't tell you how many times we sat on the bench in front of the chapel where _____ talked about how devastated he was and the choices he had made. You know when he was thinking of reaching out I can tell you that SEVEN years ago, _____ was talking about being on the right path if only he could talk to

Michael Maraschiello

the VICTIMS in this instance. He was terrified to even try to do that. There are programs for that, but victims have to initiate that. That's not something that he could do. So what he tried to do is live the best life he could since being here.

(Dramatically stated) And I want to tell a very quick story that I think exemplifies the _____ that I know.

Several years back, I guess this was probably about six years ago, there was this prisoner here by the name of Jerry Honey. And Jerry was dying from Hepatitis C. Now when that's happening, normally, someone would get sent to Special Needs. But the reality is that most people don't know except from inside of here is that that's the last place a person wants to go when they are dying because people have "community" here. They develop community – they develop *positive* community, they develop healthy relationships, and Jerry was terrified of dying alone. And so the (un-audible) called, it wasn't his job, no one made him do it. David "stepped up" and started taking care of Jerry. He would help him get to the chow hall and (un-audible) taking him to chow hall because he didn't want him to die alone. Day in, day out, despite his job, despite all his programs, he made sure that he was Jerry's primary caregiver and was there with him. And the night that Jerry Honey died, _____ and I were in his cell – with him – so he didn't die alone.

I watched this big guy's heart break over so many things in prison; over feral cats, are they going to kill the cats? The person before you is not a kid any more who makes bad decisions and hangs out with the wrong persons. The person in front of me is someone who has been struggling for his own redemption for a quarter of a century. And he is somebody who is dearly loved and respected and looked up to by insiders. And I think that he is far more valuable to our community, now, after a quarter of a century, to come back to us, in our beauty, to reach out (in-audible) if you continue to lock him up, here. He is not a threat to anyone, his family needs him, his sister needs him, his aunt needs him, and we need him.

So, thank you for your time and consideration.

SUPPORTER 3. (SISTER)

"Good morning. I 'm _____, I'm _____'s sister, and I 'm here to speak on his behalf. Yes, there's a lot of things that David did as a young man. He was a very troubled young man, but he has grew, he has matured, and he is focused on his family. We lost our mom in 2009, and I know she waited and waited for this day to come. His job, or Aunt Rosey, or David (unreadable) waited for this day to come for him to serve in his next chapter of his life, he will have a lot of love and support. And he is a good man, and he is not the person that he was. And he does the best he can in here. He follows the instructions, orders of his supervisors, peers … reverend also knows what he does in here. When he enters society he'll be a good man. And he'll help other people, with maybe even help younger people with telling his story. And that's all I have to say. Thank you."

PAROLE BOARD MEMBER: "Now, you're the one that he wants to live with when he get's parole?"

SISTER: "Yes. Yes. He will live with me and my husband; we talked about that. And I talked to him, and said to him that we'll be there to love him when he get's out, we'll support him, and eventually, I'll have enough saved up to where he can get his own place to where he can get on with the next chapter of his life."

SUPPORTER 4. (TPOM REP)

"Good morning. My name is _____, and I am with Tennessee Prison Outreach Ministries and have known _____ for the past (9) years, and I've been a volunteer with TDOC for the last 20 years. I've been with (un-audible) and have know _____ for 9 years, he's been a part of our church service when I first started here. He has also taken several classes, here, of which you talked about this morning: Anger Management, Parenting, and all kinds of life skills. In fact his teacher, James Kelly, is in support here today, too. The course he takes are called New Life Behavior. And one of the main reasons I wanted to speak is to let you know that the Tennessee Prison Outreach Ministries, here, will help him with employment, if he lives here. We have a new re-entry center that's been open for 4 years. We have put through there probably about 400 to 700 former inmates who are very successful in what they do. When he comes in, he will receive a case manager, a counselor, he will receive training in *resume*' and get raining in job readiness, and ethics – all the things he needs to become employed. He comes in on a Monday and with an interview. We support him with some 300 companies here in Nashville are willing to hire former felons. Typically, 90% of the people that we take into our system are employed within 10 days at a wage *better* than *minimum* wage. And they do very well in the work force. And again, typically, although we know that the State is that a person leaving prison is 46% they return within 3 years, in the four (4) years we've been open, our recidivism rate is 80%. We feel very good about those people that wee have accepted into the program. _____ has been accepted for that program should he be granted parole. We're happy to help him and to get him his first job. Thank you very much."

"TAKING THE WIND OUT OF THE SAILS OF THE HORRIBLENESS OF THE CRIME."

OTHER FACTS OR STORIES WORTH MENTIONING

How he is with kids, how he handles problems, anger, where to go for help. Self-sufficient – people go to him for advice.

"People believe in him; he inspires others, write articles, TEACHES younger people "life lessons, ' readies others for parole ready to re-enter society; helps them with job interviews, resume writing, other employment and health care issues to help them overcome the fears of transition back into society, etc."

Lawyer: What exemplifies _____ is that he: spent enough time in prison, is less culpable trhan others who did the same crime, is old, has done humanitarian service before and during prison, assisted the police, is remorseful, took responsibility, etc. gave his entire estate over to benefit his children, and personally insisted that he not call his oldest daughter to the stand to re-live the horrors of child abuse and give her present marriage a life more pain do deal with having to raise two minors herself, a teenager, a deployed husband – her 3rd, and alcoholism from an abusive 1st marriage herself. ALL out of love and taking responsibility. That was a loving, intelligent, wise, and caring decision on his part myself and others are proud of for not thinking of himself but his daughters whom suffered the most and now need his help. Mike has a MASTERS DEGREED. The 2017 study on recidivism rates for persons in prison obtaining their Masters Degrees is zero."

PAROLE SAMPLE PRACTICE QUESTIONS (Oct. 2019)
(NOTE: Questions by the board member may be paraphrased in part. ALL are actual questions by past boards.)

A. Phase I. Initial TOMIS Data Verification.
Q. "My name is _____, and today is _____. I will be evaluating you at this, an initial hearing, for consideration for parole. After we are done, I will make a recommendation which will then be passed onto successor board members. If you receive four (4) votes for release you will be granted that release in accordance with any specifications they make. If you are denied, you will have 45 days to make an appeal. Do you understand this?"
A.
Q. Please state your name, TDOC number, and date of birth for the record.
A.
Q. How a many years have you been incarcerated?
A.
Q. I show you committed the following offenses, X, Y, and Z. Is that correct?
A.
Q. Is it true the offense of _____ was dropped? Can you explain that?
A.
Q. And you were sentenced to _____, is that correct?
A.
Q. Why did you plead guilty?
A.
Q. Which offenses were Class D felonies? Misdemeanors?
A.
Q. Were you on drugs at the time of these/ the offense(s)?
A.
Q. I see you were put off at the last board for *Seriousness of Offense* and a drug program. Is that true?
A.
Q. Did you complete the drug program since the last board?
A.
Q. Were you aware that you were having a hearing today?
A.
Q. Have you completed any classes or courses since the last time you met the board?
A.
Q. Do you have a job at the prison? What do you do?
A.
Q. Any "disciplinaries" (since last hearing/ in the last 10 years/ Class B or A)?
A.
Q. Any detainers or new charges?
A.

B. Phase II. Questions Specific to Charges.
Q. On what day was your crime(s)?
A.
Q. How did you get this charge ... what led up to your arrest?
A.
Q. Were you on probation or community corrections at the time?
A.
Q. Explain how you got arrested?
A.
Q. Explain why you (used a gun, a knife, went with a weapon, etc.)
A.
Q. Who was with you, your "charge partner?"
A.
Q. So, you sold drugs but did not use them. Is that correct?
A.
Q. Did you know people buying your drugs were *addicts* – victims of addiction, harmful to them?
A.
Q. Did you know that _____ was against the law, yet you did it anyway?
A.
Q. When did you know there were people in the house you were robbing?
A.
Q. Are you receiving any kind of *mental health* treatment here?

Michael Maraschiello

A.
Q. Were you receiving any kind of mental health treatment before you came here?
A.
Q. Did someone sit down with you and do a *Strong R* Assessment with you?
A.
Q. Were you ever affiliated with any kind of STG OR GANG AFFILIATED and whom with?
A.
Q. Are you now?
A.
Q. Were you ever on parole/ probation, and did you successfully complete that parole?
A.
Q. Did you violate parole/ probation, and what for?
A.
Q. I'm showing something different on the TOMIS: You did not tell me all you charges, is that correct?
A.
Q. Who was/ were the victim(s) in Charge 1, charge 2, and charge 3?
A.
Q. Were you ever in the military?
A.
Q. Did you receive an Honorable Discharge?
A.
Q. What was your job in the military and did you receive wounds like PTSD from a war?
A.
Q. What was your job(s) at the time of arrest, and did you have a family?
A.
Q. Is this your first time in prison?
A.
Q. Have you tried to contact the victims for reparations or to make amends?
A.
Q. If you didn't contact the victims, why not?
A.
Q. Are you currently on any medications? What's your *mental health* plan?
A.
Q. Where do you intend to live if released and how will you live there?
A.
Q. Where do you intend to work if released and will that support you financially?
A.

C. Phase III. Protesters Speak and Supporters (4 each).
Q. I would ask all those speaking to clearly state your name and relationship clearly for the record.

D. Phase IV. Final Inmate Questions.
Q. Do you have any other documents you want to turn in for the board to consider why you should get parole?
A.
Q. DO YOU HAVE ANY FINAL COMMENTS THAT YOU WOULD LIKE TO MAKE?
A.
Q. Anything else, sir?
A. .   END OF EVIDENCE AND TESTIMONY.

BOARD'S RECOMMENDATION (50/50 Shot. Merit is no "trump card" nor is your prison record.)
"Give me just a moment to look over everything and I'll give you my recommendation. The board is considering the following: (1) Reviewed of your charges (2) Completed classes since last board (3) Your prison job (4) No disciplinaries, detainers, or pending charges (5) 30+ support letters which we read (6) Victim's Impact (7) Your sustainability to live in society (8) Your remorse (9) Made amends to victim(s) (10) Ability to follow directions/ rules on parole (11) Role in the crime (i.e. did not pull the trigger but sat in car outside house) (12) Mental state – under duress (i.e. Crime of passion - shot man raping a child) (13) other." **Examples Decisions:**
 • Recommend Parole release at RED with half-way house.
 • Declined for Seriousness of the offense... come back up for parole in October of 2023.
BOARD CAN ASK YOU *ANY* QUESTION. SO ANSWER INTELLIGENTLY and NO LIES. The board can smell out a "con job" and if you don't care or are arrogant. This is your most important "JOB INTERVIEW" – don't blow it!

"Plans to prosper you and give you hope." – *Jer. 29:11*

Stewardship – Showing others You Care

How you speak and act reflects your character, establishes your reputation, and either attracts or pushes away people. Jesus was lied on and falsely labeled many things; they didn't know him and LEARN about what he was talking about. Have you been misunderstood? God knows what is in your heart. And if your heart is like Jesus', show it, because that is the way to salvation. (Rom. 10: 9-10) Like Jesus, he met haters too, but he dealt with them HIS way, not the world's. Jesus showed love of life, respected the person, and had love of neighbor in mind.

So, "Do not be selfish nor breakdown the team" (Paraphrasing) (Phil 2:3-4). Christ is counting on mentors, sponsors, church leaders, and regular Christians to make the right choices and stand up for social justice and faith decisions that mimic Christ's "team" of disciples who engaged in conduct and character to change people's minds and hearts. Teachers must first "teach themselves' otherwise they are "hypocrites." (Rom. 10:21; Matt. 23)

Seven Tests for a Christian

1. Walk in the light
2. Admit you are a sinner
3. Obey God's will
4. Imitate Christ
5. Love others (The Supreme Test: 3 Attitudes towards others:
    a. Hatred (Murder)
    b. Indifference (No concerns)
    c. Love (Spiritual and Physical)
6. Relationship to the world – Lust of the eyes and flesh; Pride
7. Prove Christ is Righteous by Your Life (Be committed – Be Christian – "In the light.")

How do you know Heaven will be your final home?

1. **Realize there is no one good.**
   Rom 3:10
   As it is written, there is none righteous, no not one.
2. **See yourself as a sinner.**
   Rom 3:23
   For all have sinned and come short of the glory of God.
3. **Recognize where sin comes from.**
   Rom 5:12
   Wherefore, as by one man sin entered into the world. And death by sin, and so death passed upon all men. For that all have sinned.
4. **Understand God's price for sin.**
   Rom 6:23
   For the wages of sin is death. But the gift of God is eternal life through Jesus Christ.
5. **Realize that Christ died for you.**
   Rom 5:8
   But God commendeth his love toward us, in that while we were yet sinners, Christ died for us.
6. **Take God at his word.**
   Rom 10:13
   For whosoever shall call upon the name of the Lord shall be saved.
7. **Claim God's promise for your salvation.**
   Rom 10: 9-10
   If thou shall confess with thy mouth the Lord Jesus Christ, and shalt believe in thine heart that God hath raised him from the dead, thou shalt be saved, For with the heart man believith unto righteousness; and with the mouth confession is made unto salvation.

THE LORD'S PRAYER
(LA ORACION DEL SEÑOR)

Our Father which art in heaven, Hallowed be Thy name. . .
▪*Padre nuestro que estás in los cielos, santificado sea tu nombre.*

Father Thy kingdom come, Thy will be done, in earth as it is in heaven.
▪*Venga tu reino. Hágase tu voluntad, como en el cielo, asi también en la tierra.*

Give us this day our daily bread.
▪*El pan nuestro de cada dia, dánoslo hoy.*

And forgive us our debts, as we forgive our debtors.
▪*Y perdónanos nuestras deudas, como también nosotros perdonamos a nuestros deudores.*

And lead us not into temptation, but deliver us from evil;
▪*Y no nos metas en tentación, mas libranos del mal;*

For Thine is the kingdom, and the power, and the glory, forever, Amen.
▪*Porque tuyo es el reino, y el poder, y la gloria, por todos los siglos. Amen.*

HOW DO YOU KNOW YOU'VE BEEN SAVED?
(How do you know heaven will be your final home?)

Realize there is no one good.
Romans 3:10 As it is written, there is none righteous, not one."

See yourself as a sinner.
Romans 3:23 All have sinned and fall short of the glory of God

Recognize where sin came from.
Romans 5:12 Wherefore, as by one man sin entered into the world, and death by sin, and so death passed upon all men, for that all have sinned.

Understand God's price for sin.
Romans 6:23 For the wages of sin is death, but the gift of God Is eternal life through Jesus Christ our Lord

Realize that Christ died for you.
Romans 5:8 But God commendeth his love toward us, in that While we were yet sinners, Christ died for us.

Take God at His Word!
Romans 10:13 For whosoever shall call upon the name of the Lord shall be saved

Claim God's promise for your salvation.
Rom 10: 9-10 That if thou confess with thy mouth the Lord Jesus, and believe in thine heart that God hath raised him From the dead, thou shalt be saved. For with the heart man Believith unto righteousness; and with the mouth confession Is made unto salvation

In today's postmodern COVID world with Millennial needs clashing with traditional church ministry practices and paradigms, Maraschiello puts forth various new approaches for effective prison ministry involvement, and explains the need for meaningful mentorship and sponsorship of youthful and adult offenders in trouble with the law by taking an active part in becoming not just a friend but rather a modern-day pimpernel and "life coach" instead. Not just preaching the *Word of God* to the "least ones," but showing them Christ's love through witnessing true discipleship in action for today's incarcerated specifically uplifting their social and economic condition for their successful transformation and return to thrive – not just survive -- in society. Not only is this book insightful for Church ministries, but also for organizations and the criminal and social justice systems, centers of learning, and the offender's family who all have in common the goal of bringing the offender out of prison in a way that gives them hope with a future as an incentive to changes and stay on the right path for life as fostered by an effective ministry support group.

Rev. Willie A. Darrow, Jr. "This is a book with real life experiences of faith I have seen work --- first hand, having been going to prisons as a minister for over 20 years and understanding what inmates need to put their lives together and prepare themselves as Christians to go back into society as Men of God."

About the Author, Michael F. Maraschiello, Ph. D. He has degrees in Christian Education (*I.C.C.S.* College), Psychology, and Sociology. His social work began in the early 1980s with study at Attica Prison on the Erie County New York Probation and Parole Department before becoming a Special Needs Teacher. He has experience in Military Law (UCMJ), was a police officer, and spent over 25 years in prison as a *legal aide* helping other inmates with their cases, parole, clemency, and re-entry issues. He is a decorated Gulf War helicopter pilot, a grandfather, and loves to serve others.

Design by Terry Phillips

www.ingramcontent.com/pod-product-compliance
Lightning Source LLC
Chambersburg PA
CBHW071950070526
44583CB00015B/1142